A CHRISTIAN VIEW OF
Hospitality

The
Giving Project
Growing faithful stewards in the church

The Giving Project Series

A Christian View of Hospitality: Expecting Surprises by
Michele Hershberger
A Christian View of Money: Celebrating God's Generosity by
Mark Vincent
Teaching a Christian View of Money: Celebrating God's Generosity by Mark Vincent

Contact for The Giving Project:

Telephone 1-888-406-9773
E-mail: GivingProject@Prodigy.net

A CHRISTIAN VIEW OF
Hospitality

Expecting Surprises

Michele Hershberger

Herald
Press

Scottdale, Pennsylvania
Waterloo, Ontario

Library of Congress Cataloging-in-Publication Data
Hershberger, Michele, 1960-
   A Christian view of hospitality : expecting surprises / Michele
Hershberger.
      p.   cm. — (The Giving Project series)
    ISBN 0-8361-9109-9 (alk. paper)
    1. Hospitality—Religious aspects—Christianity.   I. Title.
II. Series.
    BV4647.H67H47   1999
    241'.671—dc21
                                                  99-22035
                                                          CIP

The paper used in this publication is recycled and meets the mini-
mum requirements of American National Standard for Information
Sciences—Permanence of Paper for Printed Library Materials, ANSI
Z39.48-1984.

Scripture quotations are from the *New Revised Standard Version Bible*
(NRSV), copyright © 1989, by the Division of Christian Education of
the National Council of the Churches of Christ in the USA. Used by
permission.

A CHRISTIAN VIEW OF HOSPITALITY: EXPECTING SURPRISES
Copyright © 1999 by Herald Press, Scottdale, Pa. 15683
   Published simultaneously in Canada by Herald Press,
   Waterloo, Ont. N2L 6H7 All rights reserved.
Library of Congress Catalog Number: 99-22035
International Standard Book Number: 0-8361-9109-9
Printed in the United States of America
Cover photo by Jim Whitmer
Book and Cover design by Merrill R. Miller

06 05 04 03 02 01 00 99 10 9 8 7 6 5 4 3 2

To order or request information, please call
1-800-759-4447 (individuals); 1-800-245-7894 (trade).
Website: www.mph.org

To my parents,
John Dale and Phyllis Schrock,
who welcome every stranger they meet.

Contents

Foreword

*A*lmost everyone has a story about hospitality. We recall the joy of finding gracious welcome in a foreign place or the vulnerability of needing hospitality but not finding it. We remember the unsettling experience of welcoming a stranger only to find that things are not as they first appeared. We cherish memories of times when we felt too weary to invite someone in but opened the door anyway and discovered that our guest brought us life and refreshment. We have stories of abundance and sacrifice, joy and disappointment, grace and gift.

In the practice of hospitality, we encounter unlikely but wonderful hosts and difficult but divine guests. There are days of miraculous provision of food and other resources, and days of misread recipes, burned dinners, and grudging welcome. Many of our stories contain elements of surprise—the wonder of having enough or of receiving more than we give. How could we not be surprised by hospitality when there is always the possibility of encountering angels or Jesus himself? As Michele Hershberger explains, hospitality connects us with the wonder of having "a sandwich with the Divine."

Although most of us have a treasured story or two, few of us think about hospitality in a systematic way or give it the place in our lives that it deserves. Hospitality should be central to Christian identity. It is a fundamental practice of the Christian life, though it is frequently crowded out by other responsibilities and priorities. Challenges to grow in hospitality can feel overwhelming when we imagine adding one more task to schedules that are already too full. But, while costly, hospitality is also life giving. It is worth a closer look.

In this book Michele Hershberger gives us a chance to look more closely at hospitality. Through a marvelous collection of biblical and contemporary stories about hospitality, she brings the practice to life. Her book is, in a sense, a report from the field. It has the vibrancy of an adventure story. It is filled with personal accounts and anecdotes that help us see what hospitality means and looks like today.

Practicing hospitality involves learning to see differently. In answering the questions, "What is biblical hospitality, and what does it mean to take up God's call to be hospitable in our present age?" Michele Hershberger offers us a new way of looking at the world. We come to view God, people, situations, ourselves, and our possessions in new ways. We gain a different angle of vision as biblical and contemporary stories are brought into conversation with each other.

This is a book about transformations—stories of guests and hosts who were changed by the practice of hospitality. In her exciting, almost breathless reports from the front lines, we meet people whose lives are different and richer as a result of their experiments with hospitality. We find ourselves in the middle of the action where nothing is entirely predictable, but very ordinary people experience life in some extraordinary ways.

Experienced practitioners of hospitality are usually quite honest about the difficulties of the practice and about their own failings. Michele Hershberger is winsomely straightforward about her own struggles and avoids painting romanticized pictures of the experiences and outcomes of hospitality. She makes room for the disappointments and the unexplainable. In recognizing the risks and the dangers, she helps us come to grips with the complexity of a practice that often surprises us.

Simple acts of hospitality sometimes involve us in unexpected transformations, encounters with angels, and startling role reversals. Through Michele Hershberger's work, we are invited to anticipate and experience the life-giving surprises of hospitality.

—*Christine D. Pohl*
  Professor of Social Ethics
  Asbury Theological Seminary
  Wilmore, Kentucky
  Author of Recovering Hospitality as a Christian
    Tradition

Author's Preface

*T*here was always one thing I wanted in life. I wanted . . . some adventure, not the typical adventure like climbing Mount Everest or sailing around the world, but a more personal adventure. I could never put my finger on it—it was a nebulous thing in my mind, something just hanging out there. Sometimes my adventure sounded like the idealist's dream—I wanted to change the world, make a difference. Sometimes that wasn't it at all.

Slowly, the adventure took shape. I knew what I wanted. I wanted to . . . meet God.

Perhaps you've heard the story. The one about the Christmas guest? A lonely, widowed shoemaker is told in a dream that he will host the Christ child on Christmas Day. The man, in great joy, prepares his home for this very special guest. He awakens before dawn to prepare a nourishing breakfast and warm fire. He glances out the window at each passerby. Every mundane activity takes on new meaning as he waits for his guest, who will arrive soon to bless the man's home with his presence.

He expects Jesus any minute.

But Jesus doesn't come, at least not right away. An old woman happens by, hungry and cold. The old shoemaker invites her in and gives her the breakfast, since Jesus has not yet arrived. Around noon, a small boy knocks on the door. It's not Jesus, just a neighborhood waif, in need of resoled shoes. Though it's Christmas and the child has no money to pay, the shoemaker sets the boy by the fire and tends to the shoes. He hurries; he expects a special guest to arrive at any minute.

But still Jesus does not come. A young mother comes, though, with her baby. They are exhausted from a long journey, so the shoemaker finds them a quiet place to rest. He holds the fussing child and speaks words of comfort to the weary mother. Once in a while, his eyes wander to the window, hoping to catch a glimpse of the Christ child coming up the path.

The late afternoon melts into evening. With a heavy heart, the shoemaker prepares for bed. He realizes his special guest will not be coming. It is all he can do to fight back tears. "Why, Lord?" he whispers. "Why did you not keep your promise?"

Then, in the stillness, the voice of the Master whispers back. "Don't be sad, dear friend. I did keep my promise. I came to your home three times today. I was the old woman, cold and hungry; the little boy in need of shoes; and the young woman and her baby, weary from their journey. Three times I came, and three times you welcomed me. I was honored to be your guest."

I heard that story many times as a child, but it was not until my grown-up years that I realized it held the key to my secret adventure. That's what I wanted. I wanted to meet God in the people who came my way. Even though I am an inexperienced host with no Martha Stewart instincts, even though hosting makes me irritable or frantic at times, I wanted it, the shoemaker's dream. I wanted my mundane activities to take on new meaning as I watched out the window for my *guest*.

So I made a plan. I decided to pray every morning for God to send me a hospitality opportunity, a person I could host, a person who would be Jesus to me. It was a fine plan. But what if no one came? What if too many came? It took several weeks to get up enough courage to actually do it.

Skydiving seemed easier than that first morning, kneeling by my bed. But no sooner had I said "Amen," than the phone rang. It was the parents of a friend of mine who had cancer. It had been a particularly tough week. Could they come over?

"Sure," I said, blinking in disbelief.

I hung up the phone, and the doorbell rang. A stranger stood in my doorway, a fiftyish woman with red-blond hair. "Come in," I said, my eyes big as saucers.

"Oh, no," she said. "I just have this odd request. Pardon me for asking, but I noticed your lovely roses and my mother loves roses. She lives in one of the apartments behind you, and she is so sick right now." She looked away and patted her mouth in an effort to hold back tears.

I didn't have lovely roses. I had about five scraggly pink things that insisted on living despite my neglect.

"I'll get my scissors," I said, trying not to look like I'd just seen an alien. I restrained myself from looking out the window to see if there were angels in the driveway.

And so went that day and many days thereafter. To be honest, when there are days when no one comes, I wonder if I'm missing signals. Is God telling me to visit so-and-so, or is this indigestion? On other days, my hospitality seems so ordinary. There seems to be no ministry. I can't see Jesus anywhere.

But Jesus is there. I go by faith that he's there. I know that Jesus is there in those ordinary times because at other times, when I least expect it, I am caught off guard by a sudden awareness of his presence. Surprise.

I formalized my plan into a strategy for others seeking a similar adventure. I called it the Forty-Day Experiment. I asked forty people to do three things:

First, pray every day that God would send them a hospitality opportunity,

Second, record their experiences in a journal, and

Third, send their journals to me.

This book is one result of that adventure, one of the less significant outcomes. Lives were saved, relationships were healed, and angels were entertained. I'm sure of it. Who was most dramatically changed by the Forty-Day Experiment? The adventurers themselves.

We met Jesus and continue to meet Jesus every day. It's not an adventure for the fainthearted.

And we live differently. We glance out the window, watching for the Christ child. We live—expecting surprises. And we're not disappointed.

I want to give a special thanks to those who participated in the Forty-Day Experiment. They are Von Hershberger, Karen Kropf, Betty Garen, Carrie Jo Vincent, Mike Malott, Sheri Williams, Barb Grady, David Carpenter, Lillian Bair, Marian Hostetler, Marilyn Dunn, Harry Scribner, Velma Yoder, Cathy Powers, Susan Gotwals Lehman, Janine Martin, Elaine Maust, Tim Atwood, and Judy Yoder. Others who contributed their stories are Larion Swartzendruber, Bob Baker, Rosella Wedel, and Ron Collins.

I also want to thank all those who read and critiqued the book, helping to shape it to its present form. My deep gratitude goes to my friend and co-worker Mark Vincent for his encouragement and critique.

Words are inadequate to express my love and gratitude for my family—my husband, Del, and children Tara Lyn, Erin Beth, and John David. Their support and encouragement in this effort is an invaluable treasure to me.

—*Michele Hershberger*
Goshen, Indiana

CHAPTER 1

The Stranger as Host

He came to what was his own, and his own
people did not accept him. —John 1:11

The last time I tried to practice hospitality in the traditional sense of the word, it was a disaster.

We had invited some old college friends over, and everything had to be perfect. As I watched over the sizzling hors d'oeuvres on the stove, I whisked the kitchen counter until it sparkled. Every little spot had to be wiped clean.

Then my three-year-old son walked into the kitchen. He was hungry, he said, and could I make him a hot dog? Irritated by his lack of sensitivity to my stress level, I begrudgingly said yes. Better that than a temper tantrum—the guests were due any minute. The microwave was already in use cooking important things, so I set a pan of water on the stove for his hot dog. Another spill caught my eye. Swish went the towel to the problem spot, and then—time was wasting—back over my shoulder. I sighed with pleasure. Everything was under control.

As I turned to the refrigerator for the Jell-O salad, my husband walked in. "Michele, you're on fire!" He grabbed a towel and started beating my back. Suddenly, I felt a warm sensation around my neck. I really was on fire!

Frantically I struggled out of my burning vest. The smoke alarm blared, while the gourmet munchies did their own slow burn. Dingdong! The guests arrived.

What a welcome! Burning food, screaming kids, and a wild-eyed hostess—all to the tune of a blaring smoke alarm. And for what? That towel I was whisking around so efficiently got too close to the flames of the gas stove as I boiled water for the hot dog. Too busy to see the flames, I flipped the flaming towel over my shoulder as I scurried to finish preparations. My overwhelming desire to present the perfect home and family resulted in near disaster. My guests did not feel so much welcomed as entertained!

I can laugh about it now, but the memory still "burns." What went wrong? It's apparent that I need to be more careful with towels next to the stove, but is there a deeper lesson to be learned? Is there something wrong with the kind of hospitality defined by my actions and assumptions? Obviously there is.

In our North American society at the turn of the century, where busyness is the curse of the hour, materialism threatens to destroy our families, and homes are sanctuaries instead of centers of community, there is great need to redefine and to revisit this notion of hospitality. What is biblical hospitality, and what does it mean to take up God's call to be hospitable in our present age? These are questions we must face before our lives burn up in our frantic pace.

Ancient Concepts of Hospitality

Before we can redefine the meaning of hospitality for ourselves, however, we must take a look at its original understandings. In ancient Near Eastern culture, hospitality was of paramount value and importance. It was more than oriental custom or simple good manners; it was a sacred duty that everyone was expected to observe. Only the depraved would violate this obligation.

In nomadic life where there were few public places to obtain lodging and food, the practice of hospitality was necessary for survival. The wandering traveler was at the mercy of his host. On the other hand, the host had little chance to hear from the larger world except through the tales of the guest. Thus the two parties, usually strangers to each other, formed a sort of partnership. The host was obligated to provide food, shelter, and protection in return for the guest's stories from the outside world. Protection was the bedrock principle supporting hospitality in Islam. Here guest and host alike (the Arabic word *dayf* means both) stood at the mercy of a hostile environment and had to adhere to specific rules of hospitality to insure their survival and to win the protection of divinity.[1]

Religious beliefs strengthened and legitimized this partnership. In Greek epic tradition, the gods themselves put on human disguises and visited the unsuspecting host. If they were welcomed, they responded with good news or extraordinary gifts. Hindu legends likewise included tales of gods who became beggars in order to test a devout householder. In the biblical account of Abraham hosting his three angelic visitors (Gen. 18:1-15), which laid the foundation for hospitality in Jewish and Christian traditions, the strangers were also divine. As they received Abraham's hospitality, they brought the gift of the news of a son for the aged Sarah and Abraham.

This ancient concept of hospitality is still prevalent in many cultures today. "I have experienced that kind of hospitality [as protection, loyalty] in the West Bank, from a Bedouin nomad family in Israel, in South America, in the international community of Montreal, in low-income neighborhoods in Ontario and in native Canadian communities," says Mark Diller Harder. "Hospitality is deeply valued in many parts of the world, but particularly where a lack of resources make hospitable provisions necessary."[2]

While traveling in Turkey, Christy Risser once found herself in the middle of a moderate earthquake. "We were astonished. Here were people who had escaped their crumbling homes with only the clothing on their backs inviting us into their new 'home,' which was a blanket spread out on the ground in the park. Despite this situation, depressing as it was, the irrepressible Turkish hospitality came shining through. Had we not insisted on leaving to visit others in the town, we would have burst from all the tea offered to us." Later she writes, "I was approached by five Turkish women, dressed in the typical peasant dress. They came to apologize. They wanted very much to invite us all to their home for food and *chai*, but their home had been leveled in the earthquake, and they did not even have a teapot to make tea for us. They apologized over and over for this apparent lack of hospitality. . . .These people had literally lost everything, and they were more concerned about our comfort and safety than their own situation."[3]

The word *hospitality* is a translation of the Latin noun *hospitium* (or the adjective *hospitalis*), which in turn derives from *hospes*, meaning both *guest* and *host*.[4] This concept was undoubtedly influenced by the Greek word *xenos*, which refers to the stranger who receives a welcome or acts as a welcomer of others. Thus the origins portray layers of meaning—the fluidity of the guest-host relationship, the concept of hospice and hospitals, the idea of blessing and healing through partnership exchanges.

But under those layers lies a deeper meaning. The direct translation of the Greek word for hospitality is composed of two parts—*love* and *stranger*. The word literally means "love of stranger." This love of stranger is what Peter described in 1 Peter 4:9: "Be hospitable to one another without complaining." The root verb of *stranger* also means "to be entertained" or "to be surprised." Our love of the stranger brings about our entertainment. The stranger brings to us a delightful surprise.[5]

The Stranger Today

Contrast the ancient notion of the stranger as a representative of God with our picture of the stranger today. Newspaper articles and the six o'clock news pound into our heads that strangers are not to be trusted. "Lock the doors," we tell our children. "Don't talk to strangers." I catch myself scolding my children for waving at the stranger in the car behind us. What weirdo would wave to a four-year-old boy? My four-year-old thinks lots of people would want to wave to him. Why would that make people weird? Ah, the lessons are learned so early!

Sometimes the lessons are not learned in vain. Some strangers do threaten us. Some of us have experienced rape, robbery, or other threats—at the hands of complete strangers. We have been hurt as we practiced hospitality. Though we know in our heads that most assaults come from acquaintances or even family members, sometimes our hearts tremble at the thought of entertaining strangers.

Observations from W. Paul Jones

This week I received a pamphlet entitled "Surviving in Today's World"—a condensation of "wisdom hard-gained" as a practical guide for staying alive in urban America. The disposition for survival, the pamphlet insists, is what must become second nature by rooting in us the habit of suspicion—assuming that other persons are either enemies or predators. The logic seems inevitable. In a society where individuals are the basic units, related competitively in the pursuit of limited possessions, it is to be expected that one will need to protect oneself and one's possessions with such devices as window bars, bullet-proof doors, peep holes, mace, alarms—even concealed weapons. One should train one's child, the pamphlet concludes, to make caution and suspicion second nature.[6]

The *American Heritage Dictionary* (1979) defines *stranger* as "one who is neither friend nor acquaintance," or as "a foreigner, newcomer, or outsider." The stranger, then, is not only a person we have never met before, but also a person we know but consider an outsider. Family members or fellow Christians in our local congregations can be strangers to us. This view of the familiar stranger need not be negative if we adhere to God's call to love the stranger and if we accept ancient concepts of the stranger as one who brings entertainment and a pleasant surprise. But many times we choose to treat anyone who is unknown or different as a threat, as a person to fear.

Often hospitality to the stranger has turned into hostility. Says Henri Nouwen, "Our society seems to be increasingly full of fearful, defensive, aggressive people anxiously clinging to their property and inclined to look at their surrounding world with suspicion, always expecting an enemy to suddenly appear, intrude, and do harm."[7]

How ironic—the hostility and ill intentions we believe every stranger to possess actually radiate out as our *own* behaviors and attitudes when we confront the stranger. Could it be that strangers act unfriendly to us because they so often meet hostility instead of hospitality when they encounter someone new? Do strangers act like enemies because we treat them like enemies? Could it be that our own alienation, our own sense of "strangeness" from God and others, contributes to the hostility with which we treat the strangers we meet?

The cycle of hostility must be broken. That cycle can be broken with hospitality.

But our present form of hospitality isn't doing the trick. The word *hospitality* evokes in us an image of soft, sweet kindness, polite conversations, tea parties, warm appetizers, and scented guest towels on the guest-room bed. We neither invite the true stranger in nor truly welcome those we do have over. We fret and fuss in such a way that they too feel no welcome, even though they are our friends. Truly a redefining of hospitality is needed.

Getting Priorities Straight

One such redefining story is Luke 10:38-42. Jesus was on a journey to Jerusalem when he and his disciples needed a place to stay and food to eat. Martha and Mary were glad to accommodate them.

It was clear that this was Martha's home. She *welcomed* him. Whether she was the eldest sibling of the three (Lazarus does not figure into this story) or whether she owned the house personally, we don't know. Perhaps she was a patron of Jesus. She, like other well-to-do women of her day, probably supported Jesus financially and sometimes traveled with him at the risk of her reputation. And she did understand the value of her hospitality. The itinerant disciples, and indeed the Master himself, depended on the welcoming that she and other patrons provided (Luke 10:7-8). These extensions of hospitality, especially the meal, were not only essential for survival, but were also major settings for the Master's preaching and teaching.

Martha thought she understood, not only the value, but also the concept of true hospitality. That concept included a tasty meal and having the house just right. So she scurried around to carry forth this vision. The Greek text does not point in the direction of an extravagant dinner or preparations; Luke portrays her state of being distracted as an objective fact and not as neurotic obsessiveness on her part. There were just too many things to do. It was as if she were being pulled apart. The food, the table, the drink all seemed to call for her attention at the same time.

Who could blame her? Someone had to cook the food.

Jesus and the disciples had real physical needs. It was necessary work, important work. To neglect any stranger, let alone Jesus, was to breach the moral code. Because it was Jesus, she reasoned, her meal for him should be her best. The more and the harder she worked, the more she demonstrated her love for him.

It wasn't that she wanted to put on some show for Jesus. She honestly loved him.

But things were not going as planned. The bread was not rising, the fire was smoldering, and the soup was burning. And where was sister Mary? She was sitting at the feet of Jesus, of all things! Mary knew better—their hospitality was of greatest importance. Martha seethed in anger—even at Jesus: "Lord, do you not care that my sister has left me to do all the work by myself?" (Luke 10:40). The question was really an accusation. How could the Master, knowing the significance of the task at hand, allow her sister to neglect her duty?

Martha felt betrayed. She was wronged. But the worst was yet to come. Ironically, when she expressed her anger, her complaint turned into self-indictment. Who would have guessed? Jesus turned to her and said, "Martha, Martha, you are worried and distracted by many things; there is need of only one thing. Mary has chosen the better part, which will not be taken away from her" (Luke 10:41-42). "Martha, Martha." His words carried no harshness, yet there was the sting of disappointment. Martha's head began to spin. Where had she gone wrong?

Martha was so concerned about the kind of hospitality she wanted to provide Jesus that she became inhospitable herself. In her grand moment of welcoming, she became a barrier to that very welcome. She was so anxious and troubled, so caught up with the entanglements of life, that she did the unthinkable thing. She forgot the guest.

She forgot the guest. She called him "Lord," but she

did not listen to his words. She wanted to be the best host for him, and in her fury to accomplish this, she broke the rules of hospitality by asking him to intervene in a family rivalry. She did everything she was supposed to do except the one necessary thing, that one and only thing that would create a truly hospitable space.

She forgot the guest.

Maybe it's too simple to say that Martha missed the forest for the trees. Her anxiety and concern are understandable enough, but somehow her sincere endeavors missed the mark. Her sincere desire was not adequate. That's a sobering thought for all of us. What could have been done differently? What should have been understood differently? "Mary has chosen the better part." What did Jesus mean and how do we go about making that same choice?

Starting Points

Mary and Martha's experience gives us starting points for our own definition and practice of biblical hospitality. The story illuminates four key principles of hospitality.

1. We must first experience God's hospitality.

Martha, I believe, had a good heart, a godly desire,

December 24—

I have just had it with my mother-in-law. I am trying so hard to really be hospitable, flexible, because of this Forty-Day Experiment. I'm supposed to be the hostess, and yet I am criticized for everything I attempt to do. Let it roll off your back, I tell myself, but it is getting increasingly harder. She wants to control everything. I'm losing my mind. This hospitality thing is so much more difficult than I thought.

December 26—

Oh, what an eye-opener. Now I know why things have been going so tough between my mother-in-law and me. She's grieving the loss of T. This is the first Christmas without him, the first Christmas she isn't hosting. That's what the controlling is all about. Wow, if I would have only listened more when she first got here. She just needs to be loved, and loving in this sense is letting her have some control. Now I know, but she leaves tomorrow.[8]

and the right motivation to please Jesus. But she was seduced from a trustful preoccupation with the kingdom of God by a preoccupation with the practical affairs of life. That's a bad sign for any disciple, even when these practical affairs concern hospitality. It's not enough to have the right motivation; biblical hospitality must be centered in God.

What does that mean? Isn't service important? Are we all supposed to give up our posts at the soup kitchens and pray every day at the abbey?

Many scholars have used this story as an illustration of the dichotomy between contemplation and the active life. Mary, sitting at Jesus' feet, represents the contemplative life; Martha, the doer, represents winning salvation by good works. But this is not a story placing those two priorities against each other. Writer Luke intentionally placed this journey story after the parable of the good Samaritan, where hearing the word of the Lord (Luke 10:24) meant following the example of the despised Samaritan. We are to "go and do likewise" (Luke 10:37).

For Luke, service is highly valued, but if it is grounded in anything other than a transformative experience with God, it is unacceptable. The lawyer in the parable of the good Samaritan heard the word, knew the Law, but had no action. Martha had plenty of action, but it was not rooted in transformation by an encounter with the Word. Both are needed.

Both are needed because the two are inseparable. True listening to God leads to acts of mercy, justice, and kindness—acts of hospitality. The inward, personal transformation that results from feasting on Jesus plays itself out in a joyous feeding of others, a task that draws one back to the feet of Jesus—over and over and over again.

"You are putting yourself in an uproar" is a close translation of the Greek words describing Martha's predicament. Trying to do the good works we are called to do, especially the works of hospitality, will also put us in an uproar if we are trying to do them by our own strength. Well intentioned as they may be, the tasks will lose their joy. Like dutiful Martha, we will lash out at the very ones we are trying to serve. Unless we are hospitable out of a vital relationship with God, obligation and busyness will take the place of joy and contentment.

More than anything else, Martha and Mary's story is about hospitality. The words Luke used—*journey, welcome*—point to the centrality of this issue. And together Mary and Martha represent the proper response of hospitality. Both the doing and the being, the food and the listening, are important. As they are balanced, the actions grounded in the listening, these make for the hospitable place and attitude.

2. Our hospitality must allow for the fluidity of the host and guest roles.

Mary understood something about hospitality that escaped Martha's mind. For Mary, hospitality was not so much offering a service as it was receiving a gift. Jesus came as a guest. Martha welcomed him. Yet he functioned more fully as the host. Bearing the gift of his word, Jesus provided true meat that Mary accepted. Martha missed the point. She failed to see that the real host was the one who came as a guest.

This motif of interchanging guest and host relationships is a major theme of the Bible. The three strange visitors become hosts to Abraham and Sarah as they reveal the news of Isaac's birth (Gen. 18:1-15). Paul the prisoner becomes Paul the host many times as he shares the gospel under house arrest (Acts 28:30-31) and on board a boat on the stormy seas (Acts 27:33-36). When Cleopas

and his friend invite in the stranger who had been traveling to Emmaus with them, the stranger takes the bread,
breaks it, and becomes the Host in the truest sense of the
word (Luke 24:30-32).

Jesus is the ultimate guest/host. "He came to what was
his own, and his own people did not accept him" (John
1:11). Here John graphically portrays the almost unbe-
lievable depth of our estrangement from God. The
Creator of the universe, the one through whom "all
things came into being," the King of kings whose propri-
etary claim on this world is without limitation, came to his
own dwelling, his own domain, and no one let him in.

There was no room in the inn.

The immensity of this inhospitality, in the context of
Greek and Roman society, is beyond belief. In a culture
where hospitality was so revered, where it was the mark of
civilization and religious practice, the denial of the most
minimal expression of hospitality to an earthly king was
incomprehensible. How much more unthinkable that the
One who created all life be left out in the cold![9]

The story did not end in the stable, though. Jesus
embraced our overwhelming inhospitality and transformed it with his divine love. Jesus, the homeless preacher, invited people to banquets, both physical and spiritual. He partied with people no one else would speak to. His
table of hospitality even included his enemies as he
shared bread with his betrayer. In a final effort to show his
great love, he offered himself on the cross in the ultimate
act of hospitality, setting the stage and the table for the
biggest banquet yet to come.

In true hospitality, the guest many times becomes the
host. The healing that transpires in the act of hospitality—remember the linguistic cousin, *hospital*—happens to
the host as well as the guest. The roles blend and merge,
gifts are exchanged, and the divine is present.

3. True hospitality changes the status quo.

Something revolutionary was happening in what appeared to be a tranquil scene at Martha's house. While she was in the kitchen cooking the food, Mary was sitting at the feet of Jesus, listening to his words. Pretty peaceful—except, what was that part about Mary listening to the words of Jesus?

In the language of discipleship, that special relationship between rabbi and student, the phrase "listening to his words" meant follower, disciple. It was the technical term for pupil. Rabbis did not allow women to sit at their feet, that is, to be disciples, let alone listen to the lesson. It was one thing for Mary to be at the feet of Jesus, which could simply signify an acknowledgment of his authority, but to be listening, to be drinking in his words, presented a major shift from the status quo. Jesus completed the cultural turnaround when he praised Mary's decision over Martha's. Martha was doing the expected thing, filling out the role designated to her by her society. Mary, on the other hand, was finding her identity in a role forbidden to her.

Jesus, functioning as host, offered Mary a wildly liberating option. In his hospitality, he opened the door for new possibilities—a new way of looking at the world. When we participate in true biblical hospitality, we too offer liberation. That shakes up the status quo.

That's the difference between real hospitality and our softened versions of it. Many people share their resources in ways that are not truly hospitable. They reinforce the status quo instead of challenging it. Their charitable gifts address short-term needs; that is admirable but it does not allow for a changing of roles. The gift is given in such a way that nothing really changes. The unjust structures are not threatened: the giver will always remain the giver, and the receiver will always have to be the receiver. This false hospitality provides ministry to the weaker party but does not expect or allow ministry to flow from the weaker party.

When we give food stamps, we provide food. We stave off hunger, but we don't change the unjust system that produced the problem in the first place.

When we practice true hospitality, our personal status quo gets changed too. That new way of looking at the world comes to the host as well as to the guest. When we see the stranger in a new way, when we think of ministry *with* someone instead of *to* someone, our values are questioned, our views are broadened, and our own evil is exposed. In the newly created hospitable place, both guest and host can try on new roles, think new thoughts, and find safe places to be their real selves. When that happens, it always changes the world—our own world.

4. True hospitality pays attention to the guest.

"There is need of only one thing." Jesus was not referring to the number of entrees to be served at the meal or, on the other extreme, to Mary's need for salvation. The one necessary thing that Mary had chosen was, first of all, the one needed quality for hospitality: those who desire to be truly hospitable must pay attention to the guest. Yes,

Julius Rosenwald, president of Sears, Roebuck and Co., had acquired a large fortune by 1910. He used his wealth to finance 5,295 schools for African-Americans in the South from 1911 to 1931. According to the *Wall Street Journal*, "He believed it was his obligation to use that fortune for the welfare of others. He later said that many of his ideas about philanthropy were learned from his synagogue and from his rabbi, Emil G. Hirsch. . . . The Jewish morning prayers emphasize giving needy people an opportunity to work to earn income rather than giving them money or food. They also emphasize loving-kindness, which is superior to charity and requires personal involvement by the giver. Both of these ideas were crucial for Rosenwald. . . . Just sending a check was not Rosenwald's method of operation. He went to the counties where the schools were to be built and worked with the local people, black and white."[10]

we can add spiritual meanings to the one necessary thing, but Jesus was also speaking clearly to the issue of welcoming in the appropriate way. This was a vital issue, not only for *his* needs, but also for the itinerant preachers to come who would be a major part of the early church.

Paying attention to the guest is essential. Jesus was teaching Martha, and us as well, that hospitality to the preacher could not be separated from hospitality to the message. Jesus came to this house as the Prophet. By her attentive listening to his words, Mary acknowledged who Jesus was. She accepted Jesus as he was. She received the person of the Prophet, for a prophet is known by his words. There is nothing more welcoming than being received just as you are.

The strangers who come to our door must first of all be accepted as they are, on their own terms—gifts, problems, and all. To receive our guests in any other way, with our own agendas, conditions the welcome. The hospitality that pays attention to the guest is the hospitality that receives the guest unconditionally, that listens to hear the word of the Master through the guest.

How different Martha's meal might have been had she followed these plans:

December 16—

I must include in these notes the preparation in prayer and the planning, baking, cooking, cleaning that has been going into preparation for all of our family to be home for Christmas. We want it to be a special time where Christ is honored and where those who don't call him Lord will open the gates at least a little further. How much to do, how much to say, how much to be? Lord, we give them all to you. What a blessing they have been to us.

December 27—

A beautiful Christmas. All the ahead-of-time preparations paid off, so that mealtime was relatively easy. Lots of visiting, playing games, playing in the church gym, putting the Christmas puzzle together (a tradition from years ago). There was lots of help getting meals on and cleaning up. Just all being together was so special. I did crash this afternoon—slept for three hours! There is always a cost to giving—if not, it would hardly be giving, now, would it?[11]

Toward a Concrete Definition

True hospitality is more than having people over for Sunday noon dinner. It does entail bringing people into our homes, and food is an important element; but as Martha's story so beautifully illustrates, there is much more to it than food and lodging or even a strong desire to be welcoming.

Hospitality is more than an action. It is more even than a state of mind that we generate now and then for our convenience. It is a particular way of looking at the world. In its simplest form, hospitality is seeing the stranger through the eyes of Jesus. It is choosing to look for Jesus in the eyes of each stranger. It is loving the stranger.

It is a choice. We choose to reject suspicion as the first reaction to a stranger. We choose to minister alongside others rather than ministering to them. We choose to let go of some of our own control when we meet strangers and when we interact with those we've known for years.

We choose to expect surprises from strangers—good surprises that come from God. I will not shrink from the fact that this is a scary way to be in our world today. But we choose to walk this way because the alternative is to walk in fear, and to lock ourselves away from any new person and hence from any new ideas. The alternative is to condemn ourselves to lives full of hostility and loneliness.

If we do not choose this new definition of hospitality, we will become like Martha, frustrated in our efforts. We will work so hard at hospitality that we will become inhospitable. We will bark at the people we love. Perhaps we won't even attempt hospitality because it's too scary or too much work. Maybe, like me, we will catch our clothes on fire trying to impress our friends.

This book is about a journey into hospitality. Like the stranger who comes to your door, some of these ideas will be new and different. Some of them will seem scary at first, maybe even hostile. Let them come in and sit awhile, as your guests.

Expect surprises.

Notes

1. "Guest-Host." *Encyclopedia of Religion* (Provo, Utah: Macmillan Publishing, 1995), 1:471.
2. Mark Diller Harder, written communication.
3. Christy Risser, from a journal account of her experiences with Reconciliation Walk, an inter-Christian effort to retrace the footsteps of the Crusades in apology for their deeds and in demonstration of the true meaning of the cross.
4. "Guest–Host," 1:471.
5. Mark Diller Harder, "Hospitality to the Stranger." Unpublished manuscript, Associated Mennonite Biblical Seminary, Elkhart, Ind., 1992, p. 4.
6. W. Paul Jones, "Hospitality Within and Without," in *Weavings* 9 (February 1994): 7.
7. Henri J. M. Nouwen, *Reaching Out: The Three Movements of the Spiritual Life* (Garden City, N.Y.: Doubleday, 1975), p. 46.
8. Excerpts from the Forty-Day Experiment journals.
9. John S. Mogabgab, "Editor's Introduction," *Weavings* 9 (February 1994): 2.
10. Herbert Stein, "Rosenwald," *Wall Street Journal*, 24 February 1998.
11. Excerpts from the Forty-Day Experiment journals.

CHAPTER 2

The Stranger Brings Gifts

*In my Father's house there are many
dwelling places. If it were not so, would I
have told you that I go to prepare a place for
you? And if I go and prepare a place for
you, I will come again and will take you to
myself, so that where I am, there you may be
also. —John 14:2-3*

Dropped off Rebecca around 5:30 p.m. and was pulling
out of their driveway when a woman walked right
down the middle of the road in front of us! We were
momentarily startled as it was pitch dark, pouring rain,
and we were out in the boonies. No other traffic or lights.
Really weird. However, it seemed right to pull up beside
her and ask if she needed a ride. She was not wearing a
coat, and I could see that her face was bloody and
bruised, rain streaming down her body. She was really,
really mad at something or perhaps someone. She said
she wanted a ride, and we helped her get in. I immediately noticed the strong smell of alcohol, but said nothing. She was barely coherent when I asked her if she needed medical help. "Just go!" she said. I persisted as I drove.

"Do you need a doctor?" She assured me that she didn't, but said she hurt here, while pointing to her heart. What's a mother to do?

I drove about a half-mile down the road when she said "Let me out here." There was NOTHING there, just more rain and darkness. I told her I needed to take her home or to some place of shelter and that I wouldn't feel right leaving her in the rain. She said, "Well, he's back there in the ditch, so just take me home." It was another quarter mile, and she was able to recognize her house, so I dropped her off. There was a Russian couple there, and they came out as soon as I pulled in. I told them that *he* was down the road in a ditch. They thanked me and said they would take care of it now. Whoa! What a way to live!

The ministry part is easy to follow—she needed a ride, and I drove her home. But I felt I should have done more. But what? We did pass the car in the ditch just past Paul's driveway. There was movement inside, and the lights were on, but I didn't stop. I didn't feel safe. The woman had obviously been hit in the mouth and eye, and it wasn't from hitting the dashboard either. I'm unclear how much risk to take for the sake of ministering with someone. Did I pass up another opportunity by driving by him and his car in the ditch? I don't know.[1]

Expecting surprises is always more difficult if you don't have a guarantee that it will be a good surprise. The surprises that come with being hospitable fall into that category. One never knows. More than being undesirable, the surprise might be downright threatening. Sometimes strangers rob, kill, or rape.

Sometimes strangers don't appreciate your help. They don't want to come in from the cold or be taken to the doctor or listen to advice about how to improve their lives. Even if you know better than to give that advice, even if you try to welcome them as they are, even if you do everything just right, they may walk out on you anyway, grumbling. They might ask you to do something you can't do or just leave you in a cloud of ambiguity, asking, "Did I do the right thing?"

In the midst of all this, God calls us to be hospitable. First Peter 4:9 says, "Be hospitable to one another without complaining." Paul calls forth the great virtue of hospitality in Romans 14 and 15: "Welcome one another, therefore, just as Christ has welcomed you, for the glory of God" (Rom. 15:7). The Israelites were instructed to care for the aliens who lived among them. "You shall not wrong or oppress a resident alien, for you were aliens in the land of Egypt" (Exod. 22:21). Love for the stranger echoes throughout the Old and New Testaments. Even though this love may seem difficult and downright dangerous, the call to be hospitable is clear.

A Single Mother's Plight

The call to hospitality was clear for the widow at Zarephath too (1 Kings 17:8-16). But this woman probably wondered if God was calling the right person. First of all, she was in a desperate situation herself. She lived as a widow in a famine-ravaged land. There wasn't a green leaf for miles. She had no family except for a son. They had practically no food in the house. It was almost impossible for those who had husbands to stave off starvation, especially in those times, but it was hopeless for the two of them—hopeless, and not a cloud in the sky. She felt like she needed hospitality more than she had a responsibility to give it.

Looking over her meager supplies, the extent of their desperation hit home. There was only enough flour and oil for one more meal. That was it. One more meal. In her mind, she could see her son eating each crumb, slowly, tenderly. Then they would wrap themselves tightly in their shawls, watch the fire fade out, and wait to die. She shook her head to dismiss those images. She dreamed of her late husband, the joy they felt when the baby was first born, and the smell of freshly harvested crops.

A knock at the door jolted her back into the present. A stranger stood in the doorway, ragged and dirty. Through the grime, though, she could tell he was a foreigner, possibly an Israelite. What was he doing out here in this forsaken land? What would he do to her? She was so defenseless, with no husband to protect her, no one to run to. He was a stranger, a threat to her already precarious position.

He said his name was Elijah.

The widow didn't look much better to Elijah. He was a victim of the famine too; in one sense, he had caused it. He had told King Ahab that it would not rain except at his word. This dry spell would be an object lesson for their apostasy. Having said those brave words, Elijah promptly went into hiding at the Lord's bidding. There at the river of Cherith, God had taken care of him. The water flowed, and ravens came each morning and night with food.

But it was too good to last. Even there the famine took its toll. The river dried up, and the ravens left for greener pastures. The miracle, so real in his hands, was gone. The word of the Lord came to him again and said, "Go now to Zarephath, which belongs to Sidon, and live there; for I have commanded a widow there to feed you" (1 Kings 17:9).

Elijah was astounded. Believing that ravens would bring you food was easier than this. Sidon was Jezebel's territory; he would be on enemy ground. And a widow would supply him with food? Widows were by far the most powerless, defenseless, and undervalued class of society. Widows depended on others, often as sponges, because they had no way to provide for themselves. To be a widow in these times was a fate worse than death, but he was sent to one for hospitality in these tough times! What could this mean?

Two Bags of Groceries

Strangers and strange situations don't look that good to me either. My culture has taught me well the dangers of the unknown stranger. But beyond that, strangers can just be a bother. It's harder to read them, to know what they are thinking. They're different. It takes a lot of time and effort to get to know them. Most people are nice enough, but there are weirdos out there. I've had brushes with some.

Vonda was one of those strange people. She brought her kids to my daycare. She was—different. Her face was always pocked and marked kind of funny, like she had really scratched herself. She smoked one cigarette after another, her kids were a pain, and worse, she was really slow paying the bills. I didn't want my kids playing with hers because they were so crude. She always seemed to have a chip on her shoulder.

But that was only the beginning. She left me, left the daycare, sticking me with an unpaid bill of $500. For a struggling, new daycare owner, it hurt me badly. I had a very small profit margin, and I needed every cent just to make payroll. I shook my head. I should have known.

About six weeks later, one day in prayer God said to me, "Go buy Vonda some groceries."

"What?" I said.

Now I didn't actually hear the voice of God saying this to me, yet I heard this in the deepest part of my being. Just as deeply, I resisted. There were a thousand reasons not to do it. She owed me money, after all. And what about her dignity if she found out? I knew she was struggling, but that was her business.

Bottom line, I knew she needed a lot of help, and I didn't have it to give. I wasn't down to my last meal like the widow, but I was down to my last shred of sanity. I couldn't do it. I was a lay person in the church. I wouldn't know what to say to her. I had small kids. I was already burned-out on church work.

For two weeks, God said, "Just two bags of groceries, Michele. Just two bags of groceries." For two weeks I hesitated.

Finally I caved in. I sent my husband to buy about $50.00 worth of groceries on a Thursday night. The next morning we waited until we were sure she had gone to work, and then he delivered them. And that was it. No fanfare. No angel coming down to say, "Oh, what a noble person you are." The act was so uneventful that my husband barely remembers doing it. We did it just to get it done.

Back in Sidon

I wonder if that's how the widow felt when Elijah asked her for a piece of bread. At first it was just a drink of water. That was not hard, for she only had to fetch the drink from the public well. But bread? She could see the bottom of the flour jar, and it would take every drop of the oil to make one cake. One cake that she and her son would cherish. They would break it carefully, in sacredness, and eat it slowly and then wait for the cold and hunger to drift in.

I wonder if that's why she did it—just to get Elijah off her back. The Lord said he commanded her to supply Elijah with food. But her reply to Elijah seemed to indicate that she was not fully aware of the command.

"As the Lord your God lives," she said. It was an oath, an oath not to be taken lightly. "I have nothing baked, only a handful of meal in a jar, and a little oil in a jug. I am now gathering a couple of sticks, so that I may go home and prepare it for myself and my son, that we may eat it, and die" (1 Kings 17:12).

Why did she do it? Why, in her desperate situation, did she say yes to Elijah? Why did she extend her hand in hospitality—in a way that would surely mean death?

Henri Nouwen says that poverty makes a good host. Those who have little materially have nothing to lose. Their own life situations have freed them from the illusion that one can have everything under control. Their only hope is that God will provide, and if that is true, why not share?2 The widow had a poverty, not only of money, but also of soul. She was not full of herself, assured of her own opinions, and needing things to be done her way. She did not carry the burdensome North American dream of a white-picket-fence perfect world, with bright, shiny-faced children, two dogs, and a cat. She was open to new thoughts, new ways that God would work, even in this ragged stranger.

She had nothing to lose.

Full of Myself

I needed more prodding to be poor in spirit to Vonda. I forgot about her, except to bemoan my lost money occasionally. But then, six months later, God spoke to me again. This time too, the message was clear. Go visit Vonda.

I was so full of myself that I thought this was foolishness. There were a thousand reasons not to go, chief of which was that she had moved to another town twenty miles away, and I didn't know her exact address. No way was I going to leave my husband and kids on a beautiful Sunday afternoon for some feeling I had.

Two hours later I was in my car. "This is so stupid," I said as I drove down the road.

When I got to her town, I stopped at a phone booth. Surely her address or at least her phone number would be there. But it wasn't. Now I really felt stupid. A voice inside me said, "Drive down the streets."

Well, I had come this far, so I drove on. But with every turn of the steering wheel, I was saying, "Stupid, stupid, stupid."

Don't Be Afraid

I was afraid. I wasn't afraid of Vonda or any other stranger who might be on the streets that afternoon. I wasn't worried about being in the car alone. I was afraid of failure. I feared that even though I thought I had heard God's voice, I really hadn't; afraid that I would drive down the streets and nothing would happen, no one would be there; afraid of being a fool.

It has happened before, and it will happen again— being a foolish host. Sometimes I get this feeling that I should go visit someone, minister to someone, so I drive over to their house and—they're not at home. Was it indigestion? I feel stupid. I worry that the gift I offer, the hospitality I offer, will be rejected or will be counterproductive. I fear failure.

I want so badly to hear God's voice in my ministry, but what if it's in my head? What if I can't hear God at all? What if God isn't speaking to me?

"Do not be afraid," said Elijah. "Go and do as you have said; but first make me a little cake of it and bring it to me, and afterwards make something for yourself and your son" (1 Kings 17:13).

"Do not be afraid." She was afraid. Rightfully so. She was facing death.

But Elijah continued to speak. "For thus says the LORD the God of Israel: The jar of meal will not be emptied and the jug of oil will not fail until the day that the LORD sends rain on the earth" (1 Kings 17:14).

The jar of flour will not be used up. The jug of oil will never run dry. When the widow looked into Elijah's eyes, I think she saw someone else. I think she saw God. She looked past the dirty face, the ragged clothes, the foreign shape of his features, and she saw hope. She knew, maybe before he even spoke, that he came bearing gifts.

The jar of flour will not be used up. The jug of oil will never run dry. The widow offered hospitality to Elijah because she saw that act as part of her salvation. Suddenly the very thing that was life-threatening became life giving, became the very hospitality she so desperately needed.

For you see, he did come bearing gifts.

In real hospitality, the host always brings gifts. In true hospitality, the roles of the host and the guest always blend in such a way that they become indistinguishable. The hostess receives far more than she ever gives.

Here's the good news. We don't have to be afraid. We don't have to fear the surprises of hospitality because the guest comes bearing gifts. We don't have to be afraid because in some mysterious way the guest provides for the host. I realize that we might not see them at first, the gifts they bring, yet they do. They do.

The Gift

I drove down those streets, feeling so silly, looking for Vonda. Suddenly, on the third street I took, I saw her children. I was excited to see them, and they seemed over-joyed. They led me to their home and ran up the steps to get their mom. There, for the first time, Vonda and I gave each other a hug. Something happened in that moment. We met as friends. Not daycare director and client. Not superior and inferior—or worse, landlord and debtor. We were equals.

Vonda took me into her home, which was clean but

bare. There was no heat in the house, and spring evenings in Missouri are chilly. The children asked for food.

I could have seen all this before, but I didn't. I didn't want to.

We sat down, and for the first time, she began to tell me her story. For the first time, I was ready to listen. She told me about times of incredible abuse and hardship that I found hard to believe. Yet I knew them to be true. The scratches on her faces came from times when her husband scraped her face against the concrete walls of the garage when he was angry with her.

I cried and cried, but Vonda didn't cry until she began to tell me about the time she was going to commit suicide. Her face softened in remembrance, and through her tears, she told me a story that would change my life forever.

It was a Friday, and she was facing another weekend without food. She had spent so many weekends like that, too many weekends with hungry children, and she knew that she couldn't do it again. She just couldn't.

She borrowed a gun from a friend. The plan was to shoot the children that night and then kill herself. On the way home, she prayed to God for the first time. "God," she said, "if you're up there, I need to know really soon, because I'm going to shoot the kids and kill myself. If I ever needed a miracle, it's now."

When she drove into her driveway, she saw two bags of groceries. Dogs were circling around them, but for some strange reason, they didn't go near the food. Hungry as the children were, she put the food in the house and drove to the nearest church she could find. Vonda talked to a pastor and began a relationship with God that day.

Two bags of groceries. "An angel sent them," Vonda told me. I never told her otherwise.

Vonda gave me a gift that day. Oh, her life and the lives of her children were spared that day, but so was mine. I saw God that day. If I never, ever, receive a gift like that again, it will be enough. It will be enough.

Reluctant Giving

When I was growing up, I was encouraged to be a cheerful giver. The idea behind things like hospitality, I was taught, was to have the right motivation for these acts of love. I believe that there is some merit to that. I want to be so full of God, so transformed by God's love, that hospitality and sharing my possessions just comes naturally.

Yet the most transforming experience of my life began with reluctant giving. I did not love Vonda. I gave two bags of groceries in what surely was more an act of begrudging hospitality than anything else. I gave to get God off my back. God was not on my back. God is not a tyrant or a bully, but a loving, gentle presence. But I didn't understand that yet. I gave reluctantly.

True hospitality? I didn't invite Vonda into the intimate place of my dwelling or my life, not in that act anyway. True hospitality? I wasn't trying to change the status quo, and I was only beginning to be grounded in God's transformative love.

But the gift came anyway. The transformation came anyway.

God's gift through Vonda found its way to me despite my reluctance. I hesitate to base my whole theology on just one happening, yet my life was changed by this giving. What began as giving with less than true motives turned into true hospitality. It was Vonda's hospitality to me as she invited me in, as she became vulnerable with her story, as she challenged my worldview, as she presented me with the gift of seeing God at work.

Facing the Barriers

Does it help to know that the stranger we welcome brings a gift? We have been taught that we are supposed to be hospitable, that we are supposed to love the stranger, but it is very hard to do that and to live that way. Would it balance the fear we feel when we encounter new persons or familiar persons who are strangers to us for different reasons? Would the expectation of a gift help renew our energy levels when we already feel swamped with other Christian duties? Sometimes we don't want to be hospitable because we fear the experience. Not only do we fear the unpredictable nature of the stranger, but also we fear our own behaviors. Because this is someone new, we feel like we have less control. What if we say the wrong thing or do the wrong thing? We fear rejection, embarrassment, and failure. We sense that in our hospitality, something greater is meant to happen. What if it doesn't happen? We fear the disappointment.

At other times we hesitate to be hospitable because the possible ministry seems overwhelming. If we take one stranger in, maybe more will come. Even just one stranger with needs could really stretch us. Every stranger, because we do not know him or her, represents the tasks of opening ourselves to new ideas, new ways of communication, and new ways of solving problems and conflicts. Strangers threaten our security, not so much because they might hurt us, but because they force us to see the world through a different pair of eyes—their eyes and, I believe, God's eyes.

Perhaps that is the very gift strangers most often bring. I don't expect to see candy and flowers in the hands of every new person I meet. But I can anticipate being stretched spiritually every time. "Welcoming the stranger is a medium of growth toward fullness of life," writes John S. Mogabgab. "In the experience of hospitality both guest and host receive something they need that can only be obtained through the unique ministration of hospitable relationships."[3] God is always bigger, more complex than we are. We cannot, therefore, meet God only in the familiar. There is always a part of God that is new to us, a surprise for us, and a stranger to us. We relate to a new side of God, then, as we relate to the strangers among us.

When the Gift Is Not Apparent

What kind of gift does the stranger bring when the encounter ends in tragedy? Does spiritual growth come at such a terrible price? When strangers fill your home with violence, where is God in all of that?

The stranger who came to the Miami First Church of the Brethren had no good intentions on his mind. He killed the pastor of the church, Bill Bosler, and stabbed his 24-year-old daughter, SueZann, leaving her for dead. SueZann survived, however, and was left with the awesome challenge of grappling with the murder of her father. How would she respond to the *gift* of horrible memories and overwhelming grief?

The offender was caught and arrested a few weeks after the incident. The small Church of the Brethren congregation, despite all risks, chose to keep its doors open to the neighborhood where the offender lived. The members wrote letters to the judges trying the offender's case, pleading against the death penalty that hung over his head. They spoke of a pastor who was an outspoken activist against capital punishment. They banded together as a church family to overcome this immense evil with good.

No one worked harder at this than one of the victims herself—SueZann. For over ten years she talked to people, wrote letters, and testified in court, which itself was a torturous experience of reliving every gruesome detail.

She had one goal in mind—to save her would-be murderer from death. Ten years, hundreds of dollars, and three trials later, after being warned by the judge not to voice her opinions about capital punishment in the courtroom, SueZann achieved this goal. The defendant was given four life sentences, but he was no longer on death row.

With tears in her eyes, SueZann addressed the jurors. "Thank you for giving life and not death to James Bernard Campbell. . . . I'm so overwhelmed. . . . This is the happiest moment of the past ten and a half years for me. . . . I can't thank you enough. . . . I have worked hard for his life to be spared. Now I can go on with my own life."4

James Bernard Campbell did not come to the church bearing gifts that day, nor did this tragedy happen just so that SueZann could grow spiritually. In an imperfect world, terrible things sometimes happen. Yet God was able to work through willing people to bring good out of something very evil. The gift, reverberating through the victim and the offender and countless others who hear SueZann's testimony, is still in the process of being given.

The Gift Is from God

If we accept the premise that the stranger we welcome bears gifts, then that belief changes our attitudes about hospitality. The fear that once surrounded us subsides as we contemplate God's hand in the life of the stranger. Not only do we see the new person with new eyes, but also we take ourselves a little less seriously. If biblical hospitality promises a gift from the stranger, then the burden of hosting falls off our shoulders a little bit. We don't have to do all the giving. We don't have to always be the strong one, the one who facilitates healing. God intends to bring healing to us as well.

It's a humbling thought. Like the widow of Zarephath, we too are down to a half-cup of flour and two teaspoons of oil. We may not realize our desperate state like she did, but it's true. We are in as much need of hospitality as the stranger at our doorstep. When we do provide hospitality, it must come from the strength we receive from God, for otherwise the task is too immense.

"The jar of meal will not be emptied and the jug of oil will not fail." God promises us that the resources needed to be hospitable in our scary, unpredictable world will be there.

Sometimes, the guests will bring the resources.

Notes
1. Excerpt from the Forty-Day Experiment journals.
2. Henri J. M. Nouwen, *Reaching Out: The Three Movements of the Spiritual Life* (Garden City, N.Y.: Doubleday, 1975), p. 73.
3. John S. Mogabgab, "Editor's Introduction," *Weavings* 9 (February 1994): 3.
4. Sue Wagner Fields, "SueZann Bosler: 'I Forgive,'" *Missionary Messenger* (November 1997): 12-17.

CHAPTER 3

The Stranger Within

*Come to me, all you that are weary and are
carrying heavy burdens, and I will give you
rest. —Matthew 11:28*

People use many excuses for neglecting hospitality to
the strangers they meet. They're too busy. They're
stressed out. Strangers seem threatening. The act of hospitality feels uncomfortable and unsettling.

"I can't do your Forty-Day Experiment," wrote one person, "because there is some internal work I must do.
Things aren't right between God and me right now."[1]
When I first read this note, scribbled on a Forty-Day
Experiment response card, I was tempted to call this person on the phone and give him some encouragement.
After all, wasn't I transformed by the reluctant giving of
two bags of groceries? Wouldn't the gifts of the guests
bring the renewal he seeks?

But I didn't call—couldn't call. As I prayed about my
friend, I realized that he needed space. The best way I
could show Christian love to him and be hospitable to
him was to let him alone. There was a missing piece somewhere. He knew it, and I knew it.

My friend is on a spiritual pilgrimage where hospitality, at least at this point, seems overwhelming or burdensome. He senses that something has to happen before he can welcome strangers. He senses another stranger—a stranger on the inside.

Some people can name other issues. One writer for the Forty-Day Experiment wrote about her hospitality in a nursing home. "Today I just couldn't do what I felt the Lord was asking me to do. I felt this urge to go see Agnes in the nursing home, but I didn't want to go. There were good reasons not to go. I had so much to do anyway. The kids needed some special Mom time, there was Bible school in the evening, and my house was a wreck. But deep inside, I knew the real reason. The nursing home gives me the creeps. I just have a hard time handling people in wheelchairs, all the moaning, and the smell. What's wrong with me? Agnes isn't like that. So I have to walk down a couple hallways to get to her. I should be able to do this. I wonder, as I pray about this, am I that uncomfortable with my own mortality? I thought I had worked through this stuff."[2]

Unclean Food, Unclean Guest

Perhaps the apostle Peter shared some of these uneasy feelings about hospitality. God knew that Peter had a lot of internal work to do before he could invite in certain strangers who were headed straight for his door.

Acts 10:1-23 tells of an opportunity for hospitality, a chance for Peter to entertain guests sent by God. At first glance, it all seemed innocent enough. Cornelius, a Roman centurion, was a devout, upright man. He and his family feared God. Cornelius was generous in giving alms to the Jews, and he prayed to God continually. He was even instructed by an angel to visit Peter. Who could ask for more from a guest?

But he wasn't a Jew. He lived a pious life, he prayed to

the God of the Jews, but he wasn't one of them. He was a Gentile. He was a stranger. Because of who he was, he could never be invited in.

On a deeper level, the story of Cornelius represents whole nations of strangers. His conversion sets off the most critical phase of the expansion of God's people. It was disconcerting but permissible for the Christians to allow in the detested Samaritans—but this? An uncircumcised Gentile? What would it mean for the church to allow this man, or any Gentile, in?

Everything was at stake. The very identity of the new movement hung in the balance. Would the Way establish itself as a universal religion or only an ethnic religion?

Peter should have known this moment would come when the Gentiles would become followers. Jesus would be a "light for revelation to the Gentiles" (Luke 2:32). "All flesh" would see the salvation of God (Luke 3:6). Forgiveness of sins would be preached to "all nations" (Luke 24:47). The disciples would be witnesses to "the ends of the earth" (Acts 1:8). Surely this was God's intention. So why the two visions, the repetition of the story, and the stress given to the conversion of Cornelius?

Because Peter was not ready yet. The very ones sent by God, the servants of Cornelius, were set to be rebuffed by God's spokesperson, Peter. The Jewish Christians, having heard the proclamation of Acts 1:8 and having heard the prophecies of old (like Isa. 40:5) were still not ready.

Cornelius needed a conversion experience, but so did Peter.

Unlike Peter, Cornelius had a straightforward vision. While in prayer, an angel appeared to him and addressed him by name. Though he was in great fear, Cornelius clearly understood the angel's words. He was to send servants to Joppa to find Peter. Though he did not yet understand how his prayers and almsgiving had been remembered, his quick obedience proved that he was ready for a deeper experience.

Peter was not so lucky. His vision was obscure. A sheet came down from heaven, and a voice asked him to eat from a variety of animals in the sheet. Some of those animals were forbidden food for Jews (Lev. 11:4-7, 13-19, 29-30). Peter had never eaten the meat of these animals. Never. God was asking him to do what he had never done before. This vision called him to disobey God in order to obey God. Peter was in agony!

It was the line—the line he had determined he would never cross. It was the boundary line that kept secure his identity as a messianic Jew. He was already staying in the house of an unclean man, Simon the tanner; he was already preaching to people on the fringes of acceptable Judaism; he was already on the edge of the line—but to eat this food?

"Never," said Peter. "Surely not. It is not possible."

Everything he had been taught about what was right and wrong was at stake. Everything he understood about God, everything he understood about himself, was now up for debate. Eating these unclean animals would make him unclean. It would make him disobey God in the very attempt to obey God.

It was too much. The vision was obscure.

In his telling of the story, Luke gives us clues to the extremity of Peter's confusion and the later dilemma of the Jewish Christians. Three times the voice commanded Peter to eat the animals. This repetition, not only signals the depth of Peter's resistance, but also foreshadows the resistance of the leaders in Jerusalem (Acts 11:1-18) and in Antioch (Acts 15:1-2). This was not just any voice. By his use of the word "Lord," Luke identifies this voice as Jesus himself. Peter was in so much turmoil that he said *no* to the Lord he loved most of all. So contrary was this command to his identity that he could not believe what his eyes saw and his ears heard. Poor Peter!

What, then, could possibly help Peter make such a leap of faith? The vision alone was not sufficient. If the repeated command and seeing and hearing Jesus did not do it, what would? Three things worked together to help bring about the earthshaking reversal Peter needed to be ready for his fast-approaching guests. First, Peter heard voices. He was shaken from his thoughts by voices on the path below, calling out his name. They were strangers, Gentiles. Their voices did not make Peter suddenly understand the full meaning of the vision. But their presence at this crucial time, their voices as real as the dream seemed unreal, formed one piece of the puzzle that was quickly coming together for Peter.

The Holy Spirit held another missing piece. Even with the voices ringing in his ears, Peter was still pondering. The Spirit told Peter what to do. "Look, three men are searching for you. Now get up, go down, and go with them without hesitation; for I have sent them" (Acts 10:19-20).

Peter's conversion was aided by the presence of strangers and the direct call of the Spirit, but his transformation needed a third element, the element of contemplation. Peter's waiting and pondering can be easily overlooked in the fast pace of the story, but Luke accentuates its importance by repetition. "Now while Peter was greatly puzzled about what to make of the vision that he had seen," says verse 17, and verse 19 finds Peter "still thinking about the vision." What can it mean in the middle of the incredible activity of the vision, the Spirit, and the guests, that Luke twice portrays Peter as in deep thought?

Peter was emptying himself. He was owning his own bewilderment. Faced with two impossible choices, he stood watching solid absolutes melt between his fingers. He was pondering. He was waiting. He was looking into the deep abyss of his own lostness.

Perhaps I am making too much of Peter's contemplation. But when I imagine everything Peter could have done instead, I begin to see the importance of this emptying out. Peter could have dismissed the dream. He could have rationalized that his hunger at the noon hour made his imagination go wild. He could have walked away from it and come down off the roof to attend to important ministry chores.

That's what I'm tempted to do when faced with an impossible vision, with a red that should be yellow. I want to keep myself busy rather than face the ambiguity within. I want to hide myself behind mountains of work rather than work on the real issues inside me. I want to avoid the stranger within.

June Alliman Yoder tells a beautiful story about avoiding strangers—and learning a new way of being with God. "I heard a knock on my office door. It was a new seminary student, wanting to know if I wanted to 'waste some time.' No, I didn't want to, I thought. I didn't even consider myself to be one who wasted time. I *spent* time, but I didn't *waste* time. I gave her an excuse and went on with my work. The next day, she came again. 'Want to waste some time together? Have some coffee?'

"After four days, it became clear to me that she was not going to take no for an answer. If I had coffee with her, I reasoned, then it would be done. So we had coffee together. I did my duty and assumed my duty was finished. But the next day, there was that knock on the door. Oh, brother.

"We kept at this wasting time together until it became a part of my day. Every day by midmorning, I would glance at my watch. It was time to waste time with my friend. For you see, by now we had become good friends. Our friendship was based on this concept of wasting time. We had no particular agenda. We just enjoyed each other's company.

"Wasting time became a metaphor for my relationship with God. I began to realize I needed to waste time with God too. I needed to just be with God, to spend time without an agenda. I have other times with God that do have agenda, such as prayer and devotions. But it is imperative for my relationship with God that sometime, every day, we just—waste time.'"[3]

Making a Space

Peter needed a conversion experience. Something needed to happen inside him before he could be hospitable to the strangers headed for his door. We also need a conversion. We can't be hospitable to the strangers out there until we get in touch with the stranger inside. True hospitality means, not only making a home for the strangers we meet, but also being at home with ourselves. Susan Magnum writes about her need for conversion in this way: "For me, to open the door is a real struggle. How hard it is to 'practice hospitality ungrudgingly' (1 Pet. 4:9). My struggle goes far deeper than cleaning, bed making, and food preparation; deeper than the shake-up of my daily routine. [Hospitality] is being open, being vulnerable. . . . Am I afraid of being exposed, of losing something? Yes."[4]

We are afraid. We cannot mask our fear for long with polite conversation and gourmet meals. We must look inside, ponder the incomprehensible, and befriend the stranger inside. It is a process—a process of providing a hospitable space for ourselves, facing the stranger inside ourselves, and embracing our true identity.

Being at Home with Yourself

It is impossible to love the stranger outside unless we truly love the stranger inside. Yet we resist loving ourselves for various reasons. For some of us, it doesn't quite fit our theology. "Shouldn't I be filled with self-loathing for all the sins I committed or the good I have not done?" we woefully wonder. "Doesn't self-love lead to pride and a self-sufficiency that pushes God out of the picture?" It is possible to have a heart attitude that cons you into believing that it is you, not God, who made you so wonderful. But to wallow in self-hatred is to fall off the road on the other side. If we do not love ourselves, we are rebuffing God's work of redemption. We are ignoring the fact that God did make us wonderful.

Others avoid self-love because the process of getting there is too scary. Making a hospitable space for ourselves comes when we dare to look at ourselves without any pretenses, to rid ourselves of any self-justification. It happens when we crawl out from under that fantasy world of wishful thinking. To do that is to stand naked before God. It's a scary thing to do. But to our surprise, we find in that awful moment of vulnerability that God doesn't smash us. There is no bolt of angry lightning. As a matter of fact, when we finally dare to glance up, we see God—smiling.

Making peace with the stranger inside is risky because it comes only as we face up to who we really are, not who we think we are or want to be. But we find that God knew all along who we really are. Knowing all of that, even the ugly parts, he is still in love with us. God does not condemn us but reaches out to us in the life and death of Jesus and in the gift of the Holy Spirit.

When we begin to grasp even the tiniest part of the reality of God's love, it transforms us. We are changed. If we don't need to put on a show for God, if we don't need to do things to impress the Almighty, then we don't have

From a sermon on generosity

Remember the parable of the pearl? You know the story. Here is this man who buys and sells things. He is called a merchant. He has absolutely everything. He has a fine fur coat, a five-story mansion, four frothing fountains, a fishpond full of fish, four freezers full of food, and three fridges full of fizzy drinks. He even has this floppy felt hat. It is his favorite. And money? Why, the merchant has more money under his mattress than you could count. Much more. Yes, the merchant has everything he wants until . . . One day, while passing by a shop window, he sees something. Something special. It is a wonderful white pearl.

"How much?" he asks the shopkeeper.

"Fourteen million dollars," says the shopkeeper. Oh. This is more money than the merchant has under his mattress. Much more.

But he has a plan. He hurries home. He sells his five-story mansion filled with furniture, the four frothing fountains, the fishpond full of fish, the four freezers full of food, the three fridges full of fizzy drinks. He even sells his fine, fur coat. But the floppy felt hat he keeps. It is his favorite.

He borrows a barrow to trundle in the bundle. Off to the shop he goes to buy the pearl.

"You're six dollars short," says the shopkeeper. "Hey, that's a nice hat you have there. I'll give you six bucks for it."

The merchant thinks. It is his favorite hat. "Why, yes," he says, "you may have it."

"Here you go," says the shopkeeper.

"Hurrah! The pearl is mine!"

We know the story, and we know how to interpret it. God is like the merchant's pearl, we say. It costs us everything to know God. But God is the only thing worth having.

That is a correct interpretation. This is a story about stewardship, we say, a story about discipleship and full commitment. We're right. But what if another interpretation can stand along beside it? What if the main character of this parable was the same person that Jesus uses as his main character many times? What if the rich merchant was—God?

Here is the God who buys and sells things. God has a fine, fur coat, the five-story mansion, the fountains, the freezers. The floppy felt hat. God has everything you could ever want until . . .

One day God looks through heaven's window and sees something. Something, someone special. God sells everything he has to get that pearl, absolutely everything. And even though it hurts, it hurts so much, God even gives the floppy, felt hat. And you know who that is—Jesus.

And you know who the pearl is too. We are the pearl. It cost God everything to have us, but in God's eyes, we are so worth it.[5]

to put on a mask of perfection for others either. We can relax about the way the house looks, we can confess our feelings of inadequacy, and we can be who we want to be. We are free from the need to get compliments from those we serve because we don't need their stamp of affirmation to validate our worth. God has already done that.

False Self

Refusing to make a home for the stranger inside leads to a false self. Without the self-love, says Susan Magnam, this is what happens. "Someone knocks at my door. If I am anxious or resentful, I may 'put on a good face,' offer a cup of tea, a meal, or a bed, but I offer no real hospitality. The person I really am at the center of my being is unavailable, blocked by worry or the wish to control."6 Martha, in Luke 10:38-42, provides another example. Filled with anxiety, she was unable to welcome Jesus. Though she loved him so much, her preoccupation with trying to impress and her own neediness prevented her from sharing the one necessary thing—love. She behaved in ways that were not her true self.

Putting on a good face is only one outgrowth of a false self. Sometimes the issue is not so much a lack of self-esteem as a battle with good old-fashioned evil. Sometimes the stranger inside is not a poor, unloved child, but a sneaky little tyrant filled with prejudice, jealousy, and malice. It's not that God has stopped loving us but that sin reigns supreme. We can hide this fact even from ourselves, but we cannot be hospitable for long without the truth popping out. Strangers bring about new perspectives and situations, and that throws us off balance. The sin sneaks out. We project onto these new people all the worst in us. When that doesn't work, suddenly our dirty laundry is out there for the entire world to see.

Strangers can bring out the worst in us. This is especially true in times of great stress. When strangers went to the French town of Le Chambon during World War II, they were in desperate need of hospitality. Those strangers were Jews, fleeing to escape Hitler's death camps. Many people of the small town worked together to hide the refugees and help them cross the border into Switzerland. They gave their hospitality at the risk of their lives. But some of the residents resisted the strangers and pleaded with their neighbors to refuse hospitality to them. Surprisingly, the resisters were themselves Jews. Rosemary Luling Haughton describes the scene. "When the second German Jewish refugee came to the presbytery, Magda Trocme went to the wife of a well-known French rabbi who was staying in Le Chambon, after having escaped from the Occupied Zone. Could not this Jewish connection help other Jews? Magda thought. The woman angrily refused— these refugees were *German* Jews! She said, 'It is because of the foreign Jews that our French Jews are persecuted. They are responsible for our worries and difficulties!'"[7] Sometimes strangers bring out the best in us and sometimes the worst. Strangers help uncover the evil in us that is so familiar that it ceases to seem evil.

True hospitality does not mean we shove all our sins, our interior mess, into a closet and shut the door, hoping no one will venture in. The real host acknowledges the reality of the falseness and works through the clutter. The closet doesn't have to be totally clean to have guests over, but the interior needs to be cleaned out enough so that there is room for the guest, not only in the physical house, but also in the home of the heart.

True Identity

Cleaning out our interior mess and basking in a new God-given self-love, we emerge as new creations. We cannot help but be changed. Healthy self-acceptance of the stranger within produces behaviors in us that at once astound and bewilder people. We act in ways that reflect who we truly want to be. We act as though we are loved unconditionally, as we know we are. We don't put on a show, because we don't need to. The anxiety, resentment, and bitterness are gone.

We are also freer with our possessions. Without transformation, we need things to help cover up our problems and to help cover up our nakedness. Possessions are used to help prop up a sagging self-esteem. These things can become so important that we defend them as if they were our very identity. This is why hospitality, which implies the sharing of our possessions, threatens us so much. We are not sharing resources so much as diminishing who we are. W. Paul Jones says, "When we feel of little worth, there is no way in which we can be hospitable, for whatever we have will always be insufficient. In contrast, Christian spirituality insists that in this process of being filled by society, one comes to yearn for that emptiness of which hospitality is the expression."[8]

Our things can never provide us with the self-acceptance we yearn for. They can never dissolve the evil tendencies that lurk inside us. Not understanding that, in a desperate search for meaning and joy, we fill ourselves up with things. But it is only in emptying ourselves that the joy is found.

Sharing resources is a part of hospitality. Sharing joyfully is an integral part of real hospitality. When we find our true identity in God, when we rely on God to help conquer our selfishness and give us our sense of worth, we don't need possessions in the way we used to. Sharing joyfully is easy.

Hospitality for Introverts

Sometimes it is not conversion but a redefinition of

hospitality that is needed. The issue at stake is not one of the heart but of personality. Such was the case for Bryan and his wife, Teresa. "I kept judging my wife," says Bryan. "I would keep inviting people into our home, and she would get upset about it. One time an unemployed man came to our house seeking work. Our house needed painting, and I had this deep sense that I was to let him paint the house. More than that, I also invited him in to eat with us and to walk in and out of the house at will to wash paint brushes or to get a drink.

"For me this was no big deal, but my wife felt very uneasy about it. It wasn't so much having him eat with us, but the idea of him walking in the house at times. We had been through this discussion before, and I had judged her based on her unwillingness to be hospitable. Then it suddenly hit me. This didn't have anything to do with her spiritual life. Teresa just needs more personal space than I do. She is an introvert, and I am an extrovert. Realizing that difference helped us both. Now I talk to her before just inviting someone in, and she tries to find a healthy balance between taking care of herself and ministering with others."[9]

Hospitality looks different to people who are introverts. They also love the stranger, but the actions of love they demonstrate may have more clearly defined boundaries and more intentional personal space. Introverts still work to break down barriers and to treat their guests with dignity. They still rely on the Grand Host to give them the strength they need to step out of their comfort zones. While they cannot use their personality traits as an excuse not to practice hospitality, the faith community, particularly extroverted members, must also be accepting of the different ways people live out their hospitality. We all need conversion, but conversion plays itself out in many creative ways.

Hospitality never means being a doormat. Letting people walk all over you in the name of Christ is not healthy for anyone. God does not expect us to practice hospitality to the extent that we neglect our children or spouse. Sometimes it is hard to know where to draw the line, when to care for self and family and say no to the stranger, and when to invite them in. Hospitality is hard work. But God did not intend for it to be life draining. God wants our hospitality to emerge from an ongoing relationship with the most generous Host of all. God wants us to experience a conversion to hospitality.

A Conversion to Hospitality

When we empty ourselves—accepting the stranger within, facing our sinful tendencies, and discovering a new identity—we experience conversion. Cornelius went through this process as he heard the story of Jesus. Peter spoke of his own conversion with these words: "You yourselves know that it is unlawful for a Jew to associate with or to visit a Gentile; but God has shown me that I should not call anyone profane or unclean. So when I was sent for, I came without objection" (Acts 10:28-29). For Peter, conversion meant a completely new way of thinking and being. In this new way of understanding the world, Peter had to accept a new identity. He suddenly found himself a brother to his former enemy.

True hospitality usually calls for this kind of conversion. As Dietrich Bonhoeffer says, "We must see things differently, see people differently. No longer does the Christian see persons nakedly, but through the eyes of Christ."[10] For the first time, Peter saw these Gentiles as persons for whom Jesus had died. This obviously changed his own identity and forced him to look at biases he had that were evil. This new awareness also affected his self-love. If God can love the unclean Gentiles, Peter thought, think how God must love me—me in all my unworthiness. As we see Jesus loving the gritty, homeless man, the nursing home resident, and the AIDS patient, we experience in a deeper way his love for us as well.

Not only do we see people differently, but also we are freer to enjoy their differences. Peter did not force all of his values on Cornelius or the other Gentile believers. He did not impose circumcision or other Jewish practices on them; he decided what was really important and left the rest to God. Later, the Jewish Christian leaders decided to follow the same guidelines. They admonished their Gentile sisters and brothers to "abstain from what has been sacrificed to idols and from blood and from what is strangled and from fornication" (Acts 15:29). Other Jewish practices, like circumcision, were not mandatory.

If we truly become at home with ourselves, hospitable to the stranger inside, then we won't impose all of our values on the guests who stay in our home. Being truly hospitable is more than giving up our bedroom and sharing the bathroom. It is making room for the different and new values that the guest might bring. We wouldn't dream of forcing a guest to brush his teeth only a certain way or to eat all her green vegetables. But many guests have felt the cold welcome of our spiritual and moral expectations with no wiggle room. This is done, many times, not out of love for the guest, but out of our insecurities and fears, because of the unwelcome stranger inside us. That doesn't mean that anything goes when we are the hosts. There must be boundaries for people to live together in community. True hospitality, however, allows people to "come in" as they are. Perhaps as they "stay" with us, our values will become theirs. But they must be welcomed and be loved on their own terms.

This is exactly what Peter did to the three guests who called him down from the roof. He invited them in and gave them lodging. They sat down at the same table. In those simple acts of hospitality, the most fundamental change in the early church was born. The way was paved for the spread of the gospel to the uttermost parts of the earth. As they sat around that table talking and eating, the world was changed.

Hospitality can change our world too. But for many of us, we need to become hospitable to the stranger within us before we can even begin to host the strangers among us. Yes, to a certain extent, our very partnership with strangers can bring about the transformation we need. Like the men who called to Peter on the roof, strangers call out to us in ways that shake us into new realities. Our transformation can also come by obeying the Holy Spirit, like Peter did, even when we don't quite understand what's going on.

True conversion calls for a deep look inside. Nothing can substitute for an honest self-evaluation, an honest seeking after God to find answers for unanswerable questions. Peter had to sit with the stranger inside himself to be ready to meet the strangers at his door. We too must embrace our own darkness and empty ourselves in order to be filled.

We must be at home in our own house. Esther de Waal says, "There is a knock at the door and I have to respond; as I lay four extra places for supper I know that soon four people will be sitting round the table sharing a meal. If I am actually afraid and defensive (or aggressive, which is much the same), anxious, and insecure about the impression that I shall be making, I may offer a glass of water or a bowl of soup but any real hospitality of the heart will be lacking. I shall merely have fulfilled the social expectation. I cannot become a good host until I am at home in my own house, so rooted in my center . . . that I no longer need to impose my terms on others but can instead afford to offer them a welcome that gives them a chance to be completely themselves. Here again is the paradox, that by emptying myself I am not only able to give but also to receive."[11]

A member of an inner-city congregation experienced the same conversion that Peter did. "It's a simple story really—nothing too dramatic. And the end result was not planned. It just happened. It is no secret that the south central part of the city is known as a tough neighborhood. I never had a bad experience there, but over the years, I got in the habit of driving around that area. I'd go out of my way, because the neighborhood felt a little uncomfortable. I even had friends who lived there, and kids I mentored or picked up for Bible school. I had been to their houses and had great times, but still. . . .

"Another part of my story is Tuesday night basketball. I love to play basketball, even though I'm not twenty-something anymore. I look forward to regular recreation with my friends. After we finished the new gym at church, there were just a few of us who came to play, but then the floodgates opened. There were a couple guys from church, and lots from the neighborhood and across the city. Eighty-five percent of the guys were African-American, and I'm Caucasian, and they had different ways of doing things. All of a sudden, instead of coming to a relaxing night of basketball, I was in charge, organizing the play. Somebody had to—there were over thirty-five men there! I started to dread coming. So many guys I didn't know, and everything was so different. They had their own system for choosing teams, which I never figured out. It just happened. Their style of play was different too, but pretty high level. I was also not prepared for the disagreements and yelling that happened at the games. I grew up believing that yelling meant fighting, but here it didn't. Whatever the problem, it got settled somehow, and we continued playing.

"As the evenings went on, and I played on a number of teams, a real camaraderie developed. I found myself in the middle of a lot of bantering and talking on the sidelines. Some of the same guys came every time. We were glad to see each other. Many of us became friends over the winter. Being in the minority, I began relating to people I had not related to much before.

"One day I stopped to pick up my mentee, Elliot. He wasn't home. I went to the neighbors, who said her son was at the neighborhood basketball courts and would know where Elliot was. When I got to the courts, her son recognized me. He ran to the fence and agreed to guide me to where Elliot was. As we drove down the street, talking and laughing, I realized I was also looking to see if any of my gym friends were playing basketball or walking on the sidewalks. Suddenly it hit me. I wasn't scared anymore. What a contrast to the feelings I had before when driving down these same streets. Before I watched for these same young adults, watched to make sure they weren't following me or trying to mug me. Now I'm trying to find my friends. I'm telling you, I will never drive down these streets the same. I will never be the same."[12]

Listen to the voices calling you down off the roof. Listen to the voice of the Holy Spirit calling your name. Dare to look inside and become familiar with the stranger named you. You will never be the same.

Additional Reading

Hallie, Philip. *Lest Innocent Blood Be Shed: The Story of the Village of Le Chambon and How Goodness Happened There.* New York: HarperPerennial, 1994.
Norris, Kathleen. *Dakota: A Spiritual Geography.* New York: Ticknor and Fields, 1993.

Notes

1. Excerpts from the Forty-Day Experiment journals.
2. Ibid.
3. From an interview with June Alliman Yoder, May 1998.
4. Susan Magnum, "Open the Door," *Weavings* 9 (February 1994): 26.
5. Nick Butterworth and Mick Inkpen, *The Precious Pearl* (Portland, Ore.: Multnomah Press, 1986). This story was the inspiration for the sketch written by Michele Hershberger.
6. Magnum, p. 27.
7. Rosemary Luling Haughton, *Images for Change* (New York: Paulist Press, 1997), pp. 176-180.
8. Paul W. Jones, "Hospitality Within and Without," *Weavings* 9 (February 1994): 9.
9. Excerpt from the Forty-Day Experiment journals.
10. Dietrich Bonhoeffer, *The Cost of Discipleship* (New York: Macmillan, 1963), p. 257.
11. Esther de Waal, *Seeking God: The Way of St. Benedict* (Collegeville, Minn.: Liturgical Press, 1984), p. 121.
12. From an interview with Larion Swartzendruber, May 1998.

CHAPTER 4

Better to Receive

Listen! I am standing at the door, knock-
ing; if you hear my voice and open the door,
I will come in to you and eat with you, and
you with me. —Revelation 3:20

Remember the story of Hansel and Gretel, that grue-some little fairy tale from our childhood? That story always scared me when I was a little girl—the mean step-mother, the dark woods, and the creepy old witch in a gin-gerbread house. I feared the witch the most. What child could resist candy? Could I? The house would be so beau-tiful, so tempting. The smell of the gingerbread, the warm cookie in my hand—how could I say no? But to accept a treat from this woman, this stranger, would mean ending up as the main course for her next meal!

The message is clear. Don't trust strangers. Don't receive anything from strangers. We ponder the wisdom in these stories as we hear tales of dealers passing out drug-laced candy to children. We have our children's trick-or-treat candy x-rayed at Halloween. Look, we say, there are some facts to support the fear. We take our chil-dren aside to give them this worldly wisdom—don't take things from strangers.

If we hesitate to be so blatantly anti-stranger, we might opt for a less offensive statement: "It's better to give than to receive." That sounds more Christian; surely it says that somewhere in the Bible (Acts 20:35). I do prefer giving to receiving because the giver is usually the one better off in the first place. Being in a position to give means your state of affairs is healthier, your abundance is greater, and your security is surer. It's something to be proud of. To receive something is to admit that you have needs. Receiving humbles us and puts us down a peg.

Is it true that it's better to give than to receive? Who is it true for? Is there any validity in seeking to receive something from the strangers we meet? Is that too dangerous, as in the story of Hansel and Gretel?

Just a Drink of Water

I don't think Jesus was thinking any of these thoughts as he and the disciples made their way to Galilee under the hot noonday sun. All he was thinking about was how thirsty he was. His dry mouth and tongue longed for a cool drop of water. They had walked a great deal that day already, moving out of the tension-packed area around Jerusalem. As John records the story in John 4:1-26, the Pharisees were applying some pressure so Jesus and the disciples set out for Galilee.

To get there, they had to go through Samaria. They could have taken the eastern desert road along the Samaritan border that many Israelites took; however, the quickest way led straight through Samaritan territory. Maybe Jesus did need to get to Galilee fast, but perhaps something else compelled him here. Writer John uses the Greek word *dei,* which means "must" but also implies urgency. It was a divine necessity that Jesus travel through Samaria. It was God's will, God's purpose that he take this unusual route.

There was a stranger there that he needed to meet.

Actually there was a whole group of strangers to meet. The Samaritans were as alienated from the Jews as the worst of their enemies. Even though they shared a common heritage, the two groups were truly strangers to each other, enemies to each other.

This common history went back a long way. So did the hostility. According to the Old Testament version of history, the Samaritans began as a mixed people. When the Assyrians took the Northern Kingdom/Samaria captive, they deported many people and replaced them with people from other parts of their empire (2 Kings 17:23-24). These new residents were pagans who brought their own gods with them (vv. 29-31). The Israelites who were left in the area intermarried with these pagans; worship of Yahweh intermingled with their other religious practices (vv. 25, 28, 32-33, 41). This mixture of peoples came to be known as the Samaritans. The Israelites looked upon them as half-breeds with a religion tainted by foreign gods.

The Samaritans, however, saw themselves and their history differently. They weren't pagans at all but direct descendants of the northern Israelite tribes of Ephraim and Manasseh who had survived the destruction of the Northern Kingdom of Israel by the Assyrians in 722 B.C. They faithfully followed Yahweh according to the Samaritan Pentateuch.[1]

Different versions of history and the presence of other gods among the Samaritans kept the two groups apart. In time the Samaritans stopped worshiping so many gods and focused on Yahweh alone. But fragments of differing beliefs lingered that offended Jewish people who played their own role in fostering this bitterness. When the Jews returned from exile in Babylon, the Samaritans offered to help them rebuild their temple in Jerusalem, but the offer was refused (Ezra 4:2-3). Instead of appreciating the fact that the Samaritans at least worshiped the same God they did, the Jews dismissed them as impure. The Samaritans' half-correct belief system, combined with their ancestral claim to Jacob and the patriarchs, was just too much to bear for the Jews.

The situation got worse. The Samaritans refused to worship in Jerusalem and instead built their own temple at Mount Gerizim. Under Hellenistic influence, they dedicated it to Zeus Xenios. The Jews retaliated by burning down the Samaritan temple in 128 B.C. By New Testament times the hostility ran deep, and friction between the two groups was widespread. The Samaritans considered the Jews misguided and elitist; the Jews considered Samaritans unclean half-breeds who were to be avoided at all costs.

But not in the mind of Jesus.

Jesus and his disciples entered a village called Sychar. Sending the disciples to find food, Jesus sat down at the well of his ancestor Jacob. He saw the cool water in the ground, but he could not reach it, for he had no water bucket (John 4:11). He was tired. It was noon, and he was hungry.

Then along came a Samaritan woman to draw water. Their eyes met, a surprise to the woman. The barriers to any kind of a relationship were obvious. First of all, she was a Samaritan and he was a Jew. His physical features gave him away. Second, she was a woman. Men did not talk to women in public. Teaching on this matter went something like this: "One should not talk with a woman on the street, not even with his own wife, and certainly not with somebody's else's wife, because of the gossip of men."[2]

Finally, it was the noon hour, and they both knew what the implications were for women who drew water at this time. The respectable women drew water in the cool of the evening. Then the well became a social gathering place, a place to exchange small talk and gossip. Everyone came at this hour in almost ritualized fashion. Everyone, that is, except those who wished to avoid the community. Something made this woman an outcast among her own people, one of the objects of village gossip!

The stage was set for a dramatic confrontation. She was worse than a nobody—not only a Samaritan but also a woman of questionable character. He was a Jewish man.

Jesus said, "Will you give me a drink?"

Given the circumstances, it is amazing that the woman didn't faint from surprise. Ready to be reviled, mocked, threatened, given lewd glances, or at very best ignored, instead she was asked to provide a drink.

A drink for a man who should never have spoken to her? A drink for a man whose religious background decreed that her drinking cup was ceremonially unclean? A drink for a man who would by drinking the water make himself impure? "How is it that you, a Jew, ask a drink of me, a woman of Samaria?" (John 4:9). Did she ask sarcastically, or was she just shaken to her sandals in sheer amazement?

Jesus knew all this. He knew about the insurmountable barriers between them and the impossibility of ever getting through to her. Yet Jesus loved this woman. How could he reach her and reach her people?

He did it by quietly asking for her help, her hospitality. In one simple request, he cut through centuries of suspicion and animosity. It's not that Jesus wasn't thirsty; he was. It was a genuine request. Jesus was not simply using his need as a device to start a conversation. But Jesus also knew the woman's deeper needs. She needed to be needed. She needed to be asked.

The Master's request for water cannot be underestimated. He did not ask for just anything. He asked for water. Water, a sustenance of life, held deep religious meaning for both of them. Water was the symbol of Torah. When the woman gave the water, though it was only a simple liquid, she opened the door for Jesus the Guest to become Jesus the Host. He would turn around and offer to her living water, the spiritual sustenance of life.

We can do the same, when we open ourselves to receive hospitality as well as give it. Brenda Hostetler Meyer realized this truth in a new way in Lesotho:

"During the first three years we lived in Lesotho, in southern Africa, we were disturbed by children who came to our door on Christmas Eve, chanting, 'Give me Christmas!' Since we lived and taught in a vocational school compound, we thought they were singling us out as white people who had a long-standing reputation of giving handouts.

"When we moved to a rural village, we found the entire community taking part in this activity. All had prepared extra food and were gladly sharing it with those who came to their door. 'Give me Christmas' was not an expression of begging but of identity with the clan. People who belonged to one another had the right and the confidence to ask for food and assistance. The children at our door had not singled us out as white people but had treated us as members of their community.

"Sometime later I was carrying water home from a spring when I met two women I had seen but never personally met. They stopped me, saying, as they would to any member of their community, 'Give us water.'

"I was elated. I felt like I belonged, as though I were in the Bible. All at once I knew how the Samaritan woman, rejected by her community, felt when Jesus asked her for water. You only ask for something of those to whom you belong. Jesus was telling the Samaritan woman she belonged to his group. These women didn't know me, but they were saying that I was part of them."3

Backstage Blues

I learned this lesson the hard way when I was a youth pastor in Oregon. My husband, Del, and I took thirty youth to a Mennonite Youth Convention in Wichita, Kansas. I also served as the playwright for the convention, which gave me the added responsibility of designing and building the set for the plays.

I was proud of my job. I tried not to wear the staff shirt that said "playwright" on the back too much, but the temptation was great. I waltzed through the backstage area, talked with the speakers, and sat in on meetings where mighty words such as *renewal, conversion,* and *faith development* were tossed around. I had an important role to play. My dramatic sketches would help bring youth into a relationship with God.

But during the week of the convention, this illustrious job wasn't going so well. The set wasn't coming together as fast as I had planned. Every night the crew and I stayed up working on the building projects as long as the convention people would let us stay. But on Wednesday night, after hours of hard labor, little sleep, some personnel skirmishes that happen when people work too closely to each other, and a mental error on my part, I faced an impossible situation. I had only two hours to work, and the set for Thursday morning worship was not anywhere close to being done.

In the privacy of a tiny backstage room, I cried. I was completely frustrated and broken by a situation that looked impossible. On top of this, I had to meet with my youth group in five minutes for a quick, small-group session. I at least had to tell my husband why I wouldn't make it.

As I stepped out into the crowd, I hung my head so no one could see my tear-streaked face. I moved as fast as possible, feeling the stares of others. I was almost at the door where I could retreat again, when Brian, a youth group member, caught me. "What's wrong?" he asked.

"Oh, just allergies. It's nothing."

Brian wasn't fooled. He asked again. I hesitated for a long moment, and then told him my plight. "Listen," I said, "just go on without me. Tell Del where I am. I've got to get back to work."

I didn't go straight back to the stage. I found a safe corner and collapsed for awhile. Meanwhile, the meeting never happened. Brian gathered the rest of the youth group, and they organized themselves backstage. Some began painting, while others finished the construction. They looked over my drawings and started to improvise.

I was astonished when I saw the scene backstage. There were the youth I was to care for, caring for me. And it wasn't just any night when there was nothing better to do. One of the big concerts of the convention was about to begin. There were hundreds of relationships just waiting to happen. My youth group had spent many hours raising money for this night, for the freedom this night represented. The gift of their time was as meaningful to me as their many hands working.

The last of my bravado melted as these teenagers ministered to me. I was no longer the proud convention playwright or the self-sufficient youth sponsor. I was my real self, Michele, a person who messes up sometimes and a person who needs to receive help sometimes.

I was not a gracious receiver of this ministry. I lied to Brian! I believed the lie that I could somehow do the job on my own, the lie that said my ministry was to the youth and not with the youth.

Yet in my receiving and in their giving, we were all

transformed. Something foundational about the way we lived together changed that night. The high-schoolers saw my brokenness, my vulnerability. Before they saw me as a strong, have-it-all-together person. I always had the answers when they faced their brokenness. I always viewed them as the ones who needed me, as persons who could only take from me and could never give to me. It was a heavy burden for both of us. I felt compelled to live up to the illusion of constant maturity. I was lonely in those times when I crashed and was burned-out from giving too much. The youth were disheartened when they measured themselves against my maturity. They saw my "together-ness" but didn't know how to achieve it themselves.

A Need to Be Needed

My need to receive their gift was real, just as real as Jesus' thirst. Unknowingly, I also ministered to them as I revealed my need and allowed them to be my ministers.

The request for water was the beginning point of transformation for the Samaritan woman as well. By ask-ing for her help, Jesus helped her in several ways. First, the question jolted her worldview. It challenged the status quo. "How is it that you, a Jew, ask a drink of me, a woman of Samaria?" (John 4:9). Because Jesus dared to ask her for a drink, that impossibility suddenly became possible.

The Samaritan woman opened herself to new under-standings. The simple giving of water from the well paved the way for an understanding of living water. This differ-ent reality intrigued her so much that when Jesus gave the really tough request, "Go, call your husband and come back" (John 4:16), she didn't run away. Jesus knew all along that this question would cut to the heart of the mat-ter, yet it would have been an intolerable question when they first met.

Her act of hospitality, not only prepared her for

change, but also acted as an agent of change itself. She was forced to see herself in a new light. She had to entertain the possibility that she was a minister, that she was needed, and that she had worth. She gave Jesus a drink of water, and when he took it, he gave her back her dignity. It was a subversive act, a life-giving act.

Receiving hospitality is a ministry. Byron Warkentin, a Mennonite Central Committee worker in Central America, reflected on the hospitality he received: "I was a guest in this mountain hut. Two small rooms, a dirt floor. Usually there is only one source of protein a day—the egg that the hen lays. I watched as they prepared this precious egg and handed it to me, while they ate other things. It was so humbling for me. It was hard to accept that egg. But they gave it with such overwhelming joy. They wanted to give it. What else could I do but graciously, humbly accept it."[4]

Mark Diller Harder worked as a community service worker at the Welcome Inn Community Centre in Hamilton, Ontario. The two years there changed his perception of service and the role of biblical hospitality. "While I know I contributed to the community in many ways, much of my learning was the experience of people enriching my life. I was first of all welcomed into the community and into many people's homes and lives. While I came to serve, I was more often the guest, privileged to be a part of people's hospitality. . . . One of the biggest challenges as a staff came when we would take control of a particular program or project without the partnership of people in the community. The community could feel when we were patronizing, and relationships became more hostile. Part of working toward partnership meant that a number of people on the staff and the boards were from the community. These were people who would have originally been part of my definition of the

From a youth sermon on friendship

What happened when Peter didn't want to receive hospitality from Jesus? Peter did not want Jesus to wash his feet. He did not want Jesus to touch his dirty feet. Now it may be that Peter felt so guilty for not offering to wash feet himself that he could not stand to have Jesus do it. Perhaps it was more than he could bear that Jesus was degrading himself at Peter's expense. It could be that Peter thought it was a test. Jesus was testing him to see if he would allow Jesus to be his servant, and of course he would not. All those reasons for Peter's objection have validity, but when it comes right down to it, I believe Peter could not stand to be needy. He was too proud to let anyone touch the dirty part of him, let alone Jesus.

But Jesus was the very one who had to touch the dirty areas of Peter's life. He was the only one who could truly clean those muddy feet.

How many of us are just like Peter? We don't want anyone to see or touch the dirty parts of our lives. We don't want anyone to know our feet smell or that our grades are lower than average or that our parents fight or that we take medication for depression. We want to be strong— we don't want anyone to see

we have needs, that we have dirty, soiled areas of our lives. We are too proud, or maybe too scared, to let people, our friends, see us for who we truly are.

Jesus was teaching an important lesson here. He was teaching about a spiritual cleansing that only he can do, but he was also teaching us the only way to have real relationships with each other.

Do you want real friends? Do you want to be a real friend? You've got to let that friend wash your feet. You let that friend hear about your needs, you let that friend know about your dreams and your fears, you let that friend on the inside of you, and you let that friend help you.

Take off the mask. I know it's risky. I know people might turn away and laugh. But if they're real friends, they won't. Chances are, they'll turn around and share with you. Chances are, they'll rise to the occasion and live up to the trust you placed in their hands.

We Christians are good at serving others. Oh, yes, someone needs a house built, and we're there. Someone needs groceries; I can go. But that's only half of servanthood. Can we receive help as well as give it?

When we do foot washing at our church, I'm just fine when

I'm washing someone else's feet. I don't mind it at all. It makes me feel good inside. But when it comes time for that person to wash my feet, I feel weird. It's more than just worrying about whether or not my feet smell. I feel unworthy of her love. Maybe that's how Peter felt. I realize in a new way that my friends love me, not because of all the great things I do, but just because I'm me, smelly feet and all.

I must confess to you right now that realizing that kind of love has been very difficult for me. I struggled to be a perfectionist in my youth and pushed myself in my career. Sometimes I still do that, all in a relentless quest to gain somebody's approval. "What will people think of me?" I always thought. Living that way is a slavery. It hinders intimacy. It's not the kind of life Jesus meant for us to live.

Receiving help is the other part of servanthood. You know how good it feels when you help someone. You're blessed when that happens. Now think of the blessing your friends miss out on when you're too proud to receive their hospitality and their help. We talk about humbly serving others, but the real humility comes when we allow others to serve us. We have to admit that we need each other.

marginalized, or people I came to serve. . . . Hospitality did not mean service from a position of power to the marginalized, but rather it meant that service was a part of all of our lives as each of us were part of a community that moved toward mutuality."5

This concept of mutuality is also on the cutting edge of social services. Brent Kaufman works with the inner-city community in Elkhart, Indiana. "We are beginning to rethink our attitudes, beginning to change the system. Before it was always us helping them. But now we see we have to hear their value judgments, their stories. So often as professionals, as white American males, we have been the ones to determine the values, diagnose the problem, and make the judgments. There still needs to be leadership coming from social services, but the attitude is different. In the past, we've done an awful lot to and for people but not nearly enough with people."6

To Receive Is to Give

Thus the fluid blending of hospitality roles continues. The guest becomes the host and, by receiving hospitality, actually gives a gift. How do we give the gift of receiving? We can't walk up to everyone we meet and ask for a glass of water. Here are a few suggestions:

1. Be vulnerable.

The first step in the ministry of receiving hospitality is being honest with others about your needs. Allow others to see you as you really are—as a person who sometimes has it all together but who sometimes has no idea what to do or be next. Take off that mask of perfection! Ironically, many attempts at hospitality are just the opposite. We set out the fine china and cloth napkins, which is all right if we are trying to honor our guests. But if we are only trying to impress our guests and con them into believing this is how we always live, then we do not honor our guests or provide true hospitality. We are merely putting on a show.

2. Accept hospitality graciously.

The next step in this ministry is obvious, but many times it is poorly done. With grace and humility, we must accept hospitality when it is offered to us. Many times I catch myself asking people if they are sure they want to help me. "Of course," they say, "or I wouldn't have offered." To resist offers of help is to tell our friends we really don't need them. To deny them the opportunity to offer us hospitality is to deny them the blessing that comes with hospitality, the blessing of being a minister.

3. Look at familiar strangers with new eyes.

Some people are strangers, though not in the sense that we don't know their names. They are family members or church acquaintances. We think we know them, but we don't. We are tempted to see our family and congregational family members primarily in relation to ourselves. In doing so, we take them for granted. What gifts would we bestow if we allowed them to be strangers to us— strangers to whom we owe hospitality and from whom we must receive hospitality? What changes would happen if I encouraged my children, spouse, siblings, and parents to be themselves and not extensions of me?

This hospitality is difficult for many families. We find comfort in set patterns and roles for each family member. Receiving hospitality from others in the family or church family can be a first big step. If we anticipate receiving a gift from them, then we grow in appreciation for their uniqueness. We become more sensitive to their needs as we wait for them to offer it in their way and time. Waiting for a delightful surprise from them will bring gifts—gifts that we squelched before with our preset expectations.

4. Relax in the love of your host.

Let's be honest. There is also great blessing in being ministered to. We all need it sometimes. Just like Jesus, we desperately need that cold drink of water, whether it comes in the form of prayer, good conversation, or an unburdening of our souls. Perhaps we don't need meals and lodging like the sojourners of earlier times, but we need safe places. We must allow ourselves to find those places and to be cared for by our friends and by the strangers we meet.

Being cared for by people we don't know very well can be scary. We must by faith believe that the stranger always bears gifts. Perhaps it is only the gift of building our character or widening our worldview, but what wonderful gifts those are! One story pulled from the Internet expresses this well:

"We were at McDonald's—my husband and I and our eight-month-old daughter. We were enjoying our food when a ragged looking man walked in. He looked like he slept in the streets and smelled worse. He sat at a table beside us.

"He also caught the attention of my small daughter. He would smile and make a funny face, and she would laugh out loud. She was drawn to this man like a magnet, and he to her. He asked me if he could hold her, just for a moment. A part of my brain and heart instantly said no. I didn't want his grimy hands to touch her clean, soft skin. Another part of me read his eyes. There was kindness in those eyes. Speechless, I nodded yes. He took her and cooed baby talk to her. She laughed and waved her arms. The two of them were in their own enchanting world. As I watched, I saw a tear trickle down the man's face, then more and more until his whole face was wet. Perhaps he was remembering another little girl, in another place and time somewhere. In surprise, I felt tears on my own face.

"He tenderly handed the baby back to me. 'Thank you,' I said.

"'No, thank *you*,' he said and walked out the door."

Nelson Kraybill, president of Associated Mennonite Biblical Seminary, Elkhart, Indiana, tells this beautiful story of the ministry of receiving hospitality:

"A couple in our church have foster children. At a church retreat weekend I had the opportunity to meet a six-year-old boy who had just come to their home. Little Steve came from a rough background. He had suffered abuse of various kinds. His new foster parents told me he at first ate his food fast and held it close to his face—apparently because he had been tormented by having food taken away.

"At breakfast I sat with Steve, just the two of us. I asked him questions, and he mumbled answers in monosyllables. After breakfast, the church group gathered for communion and foot washing. I washed feet with another adult, and returned to my seat. Then I noticed little Steve craning his neck to see beyond the circle to the foot-washing activity. 'Would you like to see what they are doing?' I whispered to him. He nodded. Together we slipped out of the circle of chairs, and sat cross-legged on the floor to watch the people with basins and towels.

"I asked Steve if he wanted me to wash his feet. Again, he nodded. He sat on a chair, with his feet barely reaching down to the basin. I washed his feet, and he giggled when the towel rubbed his toes. It is customary in our church for people who have washed feet to embrace afterwards. But I was still a stranger to Steve, and couldn't embrace a boy who had been abused. So I put both my hands on his shoulders, and said, 'I'm really glad that you are part of this church.'

"Just as I was heading back to my seat, Steve tugged at my sleeve. He was saying something I couldn't understand. I leaned down to hear his small voice: 'I want to wash your feet.' My feet already had been washed, and in our church nobody is 'done' twice! Yet some divine nudging told me to say yes. A little boy who had been abused, who scarcely knew me, *washed my feet.* I won't forget that moment of grace for the rest of my life."[7]

So many times we only see hospitality as an act of service—something we give. That is an important part of hospitality, but it's not the only part. In true hospitality, the roles always blend. Loving the stranger means allowing the stranger to minister to us, even though they are the guests. When we receive hospitality in the name of Christ, we minister to our guests by affirming them as ministers with us. The blessings of giving and receiving hospitality come to all parties.

Like Jesus at the well in Samaria, we must practice the gracious art of receiving hospitality. As a ministry to our guests. As a ministry to ourselves.

Notes

1. "Samaritans," *The Anchor Bible Dictionary;* David Noel Freedman, ed.(New York: Doubleday, 1992), 5:540-47.
2. George Beasley-Murray, *Word Biblical Commentary,* vol. 36 (Waco, Tex.: Word Books, 1987), p. 62.
3. Joetta Handrich Schlabach, *Extending the Table: A World Community Cookbook* (Scottdale, Pa.: Herald Press, 1991), p. 26.
4. From an interview with Byron Warkentin, February 1998.
5. Mark Diller Harder, "Hospitality to the Stranger." Unpublished paper, Associated Mennonite Biblical Seminary, Elkhart, Ind., 1992, pp. 9-10.
6. From an interview with Brent Kaufman, February 1998.
7. J. Nelson Kraybill in a lecture series on 1 Peter, Associated Mennonite Biblical Seminary, Elkhart, Ind., January 1998. Story copyright © 1998 by J. Nelson Kraybill. Used by permission.

CHAPTER 5

Meeting Jesus in the Stranger

*Do not neglect to show hospitality to
strangers, for by doing that some have entertained angels without knowing it.*
—Hebrews 13:2

*I*f we understand biblical hospitality properly, then we
live expecting surprises. We accept on faith that we are
called to be hospitable, even to strangers and enemies,
and that somehow we will be blessed by their presence.
The stranger brings a gift. The guest mysteriously
becomes the host. God sits at the table with us when we
extend the cup of cold water in God's name.

What if it doesn't happen that way? What if, in good
faith, we extend the hand of hospitality and it gets bitten?
At least that experience is a surprise. Worse yet, what if
nothing happens at all?

Over forty persons participated in the Forty-Day
Experiment, a discipline of prayer for hospitality opportunities. They prayed for these opportunities for forty
days and wrote journals about their encounters with
strangers and with God. One major theme that emerged
from this experiment was the lack of clarity about whom
to minister to, how to minister, and what blessing from

God came to them. On some days, God didn't seem to send anyone their way, or if God did, the call was ambiguous, as was the blessing. No one was physically hurt or even threatened during the Forty-Day Experiment, but the threat of the ordinary loomed large.

"I wonder how you know if you've ministered to someone, especially if they don't tell you? Do you just know?"[1]

"Just a regular Sunday afternoon. Church in the morning, pizza for lunch, friends over in the afternoon. Just normal stuff. When I have the normal days now, I wonder if I'm overlooking my chances. I can't think of anything special where I had a chance to minister to someone. Are there chances daily? Am I missing them?"[2]

"I don't really have any amazing or exciting stories to tell. I started out on the experiment with a lot of excitement, eager to see what would happen. That was followed by some disappointments. I felt rather helpless. I would be presented with opportunities to minister, but I had no idea how or what to do. I think I was relying on my own resources rather than God's. So I got discouraged because they weren't enough."[3]

The ancient concept that God is always present when hospitality occurs is a scary notion in many of our hospitable encounters as North Americans. What if we don't see God at the table? Is it because we don't believe enough in miracles or don't have enough faith? Is God not working now in the same way as he did in Bible times? Are we the problem? Is there something we are not doing or are doing wrong?

Sometimes I wish I had lived in Bible times. Maybe I would have been present when God turned back the waters of the Red Sea. Perhaps I could have witnessed Jesus healing the blind man or raising the widow's son. I would have especially enjoyed sitting at the table with Jesus. There I would have seen true hospitality at work;

there I would have experienced the surprise of God in the midst of strangers.

But I don't live in Bible times. I sit here in the present, with lots of questions about why things are the way they are. I'm here in the present, looking ahead to a future that will surely bring me some answers.

The Sheep and the Goats

Matthew paints a telling picture of the future in Matthew 25:31-46. Here the real but future event of the judgment is portrayed. The Son of man is the judge arrayed in all his glory, with all the angels surrounding the heavenly, awesome throne. Throughout Matthew, Jesus is portrayed as king, but many times his glory is unrecognized except by a few wise men and poor peasants. Here, however, there is no question. It is the end-times judgment, and Jesus reigns supreme as judge and king.

The masses of people are separated. The group called sheep goes to the right of the throne. The goats line up on the left. Mixed flocks are customary in Palestine. They are separated at night because the goats need warmth and the sheep prefer the open air. Sheep are considered more valuable than goats and so are called the righteous in the parable.

There is a greater distinction between the two groups of people than there ever was between sheep and goats. The people on the right, the righteous, performed deeds during their lifetimes that were not done by those on the left. Those acts were feeding the hungry, providing drink for the thirsty, inviting in the stranger, clothing the naked, caring for the sick, and visiting the prisoner. Although taking in the stranger is listed specifically, all of the acts are a part of true hospitality. Anyone who is hungry, sick, naked, or in prison becomes a stranger in the community.

For both those on the right and those on the left, those acts of hospitality become the criterion for reward or punishment. Nothing is mentioned of the horrendous deeds that the wicked (or the righteous) may have done—deeds of murder, hatred, stealing, or lying. In our day we seem to emphasize the sins of commission more than the sins of omission, but here merciful acts become the plumb line by which all of life is judged.

The most amazing thing about the acts of mercy is that Jesus says *he* was in such need. Jesus doesn't say, "For starving people were hungry, and you gave them something to eat." He says, "*I* was hungry, and you gave me something to eat." Jesus identifies himself so completely with the poor and the needy that their plight becomes his. He feels their pain, their cold, and their thirst and hunger. Jesus even emphasizes the point with the phrase "Truly I say to you," the mark of an especially weighty statement. Jesus makes it very clear that in showing love and hospitality to those needy ones, the righteous show that same love to him during their lives

This is news to the sheep, however. The righteous are astonished—so astonished that they ask questions of clarification three times: "Lord, when was it that we saw you hungry and gave you food, or thirsty and gave you something to drink? And when was it that we saw you a stranger and welcomed you, or naked and gave you clothing? And when was it that we saw you sick or in prison and visited you?" (Matt. 25:37-39). The righteous didn't know. God's presence was not apparent when they extended their hospitality. They didn't recognize Jesus there at the table with them. The gift of the stranger was unclear, the ministry uncertain.

It was just ordinary stuff. "What? Jesus, do you mean that time I gave that woman directions at the airport? That was you?" What the judge deems important, what becomes the deciding factor between life and death, are the mundane, daily-life actions of a humble disciple. Not the eloquent preacher, not the profound teacher, not even the risk-taking evangelist is named. The righteous are those average disciples who give hospitality to other average people.

The integrity of the righteous is intensified specifically because they did not know it was Jesus. They were thoroughly unaware of the good deeds they did, which is what makes the deeds so good. They did their acts of mercy for the right reasons—because they cared. Who wouldn't have shown hospitality to a king, had they known? But in showing hospitality to a least one, they demonstrated the true motive for honoring God—the motive of love, not recognition.

On the other hand, the unrighteous or the cursed can't believe they didn't minister to Jesus. "Lord, when was it that we saw you hungry or thirsty or a stranger or naked or sick or in prison, and did not take care of you?" (Matt. 25:44). Are they astonished that they didn't recognize Jesus or astonished that they saw Jesus in pain or suffering and didn't help? Had they known that the homeless beggar on the streets was Jesus, would they have extended a welcome? In either case, this group is faulted only for their sins of neglect, their lack of merciful deeds to the least ones. In neglecting the needy ones, they neglect Jesus.

For this neglect, they pay a heavy price. Just as the righteous are called blessed and asked to come into God's presence, the inhospitable are cursed and told to depart from the presence of Jesus. The kingdom and its inheritance has been prepared for the righteous, but the wicked share the eternal fire prepared for the devil and his angels. The righteous are granted eternal life; the wicked, eternal punishment.

Bob Baker on Meeting Jesus

Paul met Jesus on the road to Damascus. The Ethiopian eunuch met Jesus on the road that leads from Jerusalem to Gaza. The two disciples met Jesus on the road to Emmaus. Matthew the tax collector met Jesus on a street in Capernaum. Peter, James, and John met Jesus by the seashore; John the Baptist, by the river. I have not surveyed the Bible, but I wonder if more people might have truly met Jesus outside the synagogues rather than inside.

I usually meet Jesus on Tuesday. And on that day I meet him at least ten times. I do not meet him on the road to Damascus, the road to Gaza, or the road to Emmaus. Instead I meet him on Portage Lane, on Burr Oak Place, on Bontrager Drive, and at the low-cost housing on Pleasant Plain. I see him also on Turner Street—in fact, I see him twice on Turner Street. And, of course, always I meet him on Hiawatha Drive. In fact, during the summer, I often meet Jesus twice a week on Hiawatha, always at the same place, 310 Hiawatha. If you ring the bell, you will not recognize it as Jesus who answers. But it is. Of course, we old people often see things younger people do not. Too bad; you miss a lot.

Recently I met Jesus at 2612 DeCamp Court. Such a lovely Jesus! Did you know that Jesus is black at 2612? But I have no trouble recognizing him. It's the only place I go on Tuesday where Jesus is not only black, but I see him in double form. It is remarkable what you can see when you are older, but the Jesus I see at 2612 is a she. Not only that but Mrs. Jesus is in a wheelchair. But that does not stop her from smiling. She always smiles and thanks me and so does Mr. Jesus who lives with her. Sometimes when I meet Mrs. Jesus in her wheelchair, I gently touch her hand and say a word or two.

Sometimes when I meet Jesus on Tuesdays as I do my Mobile Meal route, Jesus is crying. Sometimes I have knelt beside Jesus' chair where he is crying, and I pray for Jesus.

Did you know that you can pray for Jesus? Or did you think that Jesus only prays for you? You can. When I pray for Jesus, I pray that his home nursing care will not stop, that he will not have to go to the nursing home, that his daughter will visit him. I feel very close to Jesus. I wish I could stay, but I have to hurry because Jesus is waiting down the road, down the street for his hot Mobile Meal that I deliver each week on Route 1.

Did you say that is not really Jesus? The Salvation Army only delivers meals to people, people like me, like you? Did you say I am mixed up, that I should get some help, see a psychiatrist? Sorry, I may need to see a psychiatrist, but I don't believe he can convince me that I do not see Jesus each Tuesday.

You see, Jesus himself told me, "Inasmuch as you do it unto one of these, my brothers, my sisters, you do it unto me." So doesn't that prove I meet Jesus, see him each Tuesday? I think so. I figure those people on my Mobile Meal route who look like Tonya, Sylvia, Cora, Margaret, and all the others are really Jesus in disguise. But they don't fool me because behind their mask is Jesus.

Sometimes in the winter, instead of carrying a hot meal to Jesus, I carry a snow shovel, a small snowblower. And then Jesus has other names, lives other places. Then his name is Ruby, Gene and

Back at the Sheep Pen

There are several lessons we can take from this story in Matthew, lessons about our own hospitality and how we find God in the least ones.

1. We can prepare for the end times by living generously with others.

The story in Matthew 25:31-46 is preceded by parables and exhortations that carry the same message: "Be prepared." The preparation, be it for the bridegroom (Matt. 25:1-13) or for the master, (Matt. 25:14-30), is for the return of Jesus in the end times. Our story of the sheep and the goats follows the same theme. The call to hospitality is one way for the virgins to buy oil ahead of time (v. 4) and for the servants to invest their talents (vv. 14-15). It is our call as Christians to be good stewards of the household of God. Part of that stewardship is hospitality, the stewardship of ourselves.

We prepare for Christ's coming by practicing biblical hospitality. It should come as no surprise that this is true. Every important advent in the Bible narrative culminates in the arrival of a stranger—a stranger whom some

Erma, Anita, or Helen. Then Jesus lives on Sterling or Indiana or Huron. In the winter when I meet Jesus at such places, he comes to the door and says, "Thank you." Once he said, "I don't know what I would do without you." Think of that! And I don't know what I would do without Jesus! But whether Jesus comes to the door or not to thank me, we still talk to one another while I shovel the snow. Did you know that the Jesus who lives on Huron has a dog? I hear him barking. I think the Jesus who lives on Huron uses oxygen and has trouble coming to the door, so he has the dog bark to thank me. Yes, as strange as it seems, we still talk through the walls of the little house at 1602 Huron.

One of the nicest things about being retired is that you have more time to meet Jesus. It's better than Social Security or Teacher Pension checks.

Sometimes we are so busy that we do not even recognize Jesus when we see him. Then, like Mary, we ask, "Where is Jesus? Tell me so I can go to him." And all the time Jesus is standing right there beside us, sitting in a wheelchair, or lying in a sickbed. And we don't see him. We don't see him.[4]

received and some rejected. Jesus the Messiah was born in a stable, but only shepherds and wise men gave him welcome. The risen Christ walked unrecognized by his disciples as they journeyed toward Emmaus. It was only when they invited him in and sat at table with him that they saw their Lord. In great mystery, with tongues of fire and a mighty wind, the Holy Spirit came on Pentecost as the divine Stranger. The issue of welcome for Emmanuel, God with us (as Guest) will resurface at the second coming. We prepare for this arrival by showing hospitality to those who bear God's name.

We prepare for Christ's coming by practicing biblical hospitality. It should come as no surprise that this is true. Every important advent in the Bible narrative culminates in the arrival of a stranger—a stranger whom some received and some rejected. Jesus the Messiah was born in a stable, but only shepherds and wise men gave him welcome. The risen Christ walked unrecognized by his disciples as they journeyed toward Emmaus. It was only when they invited him in and sat at table with him that they saw their Lord. In great mystery, with tongues of fire and a mighty wind, the Holy Spirit came on Pentecost as the divine Stranger. The issue of welcome for Emmanuel, God with us (as Guest) will resurface at the second coming. We prepare for this arrival by showing hospitality to those who bear God's name.

Is our hospitality tainted if our only motivation for such action is to escape judgment? What about all those times when we didn't extend a hand of welcome to those in need? Sometimes I'm a sheep, and sometimes I'm a goat. Will Jesus have a third category for people like me?

These are difficult questions, questions that may not be answered completely until the judgment time comes. There are some truths we can count on, however. Jesus is a loving judge. Jesus the judge is also Jesus the crucified one, the resurrected one. Jesus came into the world to save it, not to condemn it (John 3:17). He came offering us transforming hospitality. It is from that transforming relationship that our own hospitality finds its meaning and strength. As we grow in our understanding and love of a God who is love, then we want to feed and clothe and invite in the strangers we meet.

2. Our ministry will be ambiguous.

Like the righteous in the story, we too will sometimes not recognize Jesus in the people we serve. The strangers we welcome may be boring, obnoxious, smelly, and rude. It may seem almost impossible to treat them as we would Jesus or to even think about them being Jesus to us. This does not excuse their behavior if they cross the line of safety, but looking at them as representatives of Jesus can help us take a second look before we judge them or walk away from them without offering hospitality. It can help us see the possible reasons why they are rude or bossy or smelly. If we allow ourselves to see them as Jesus sees them, broken yet beautiful, we are empowered to be agents of God's healing to them and to love them as Jesus does.

Knowing that sometimes we won't recognize the significance of our hospitality helps take the pressure off. It's okay not to see any results; it's okay if our hospitality feels like no big deal. The sheep couldn't remember their acts of mercy and neither will we on that final day. But the little things, the cup of cold water, will make a huge difference—a difference for the ones we serve and a difference for us. Maybe we can't see the difference, but we go by faith that it's there.

My father once lent his old truck to a troubled young man. My dad didn't realize he was troubled, nor was that a criterion for getting the truck; he always loans his truck to everyone who needs it. Many people coming into his gas station can't drive away without waiting a long time for their car to be fixed. So he hands the keys over and says, "Just be sure to bring it back."

This young man had car problems and had an important meeting to attend. So Dad gave him the keys, and because it was noon, my parents invited him over for lunch as well. They had a friendly chat, and then the young man proceeded down the road for his meeting, leaving his own car at the station.

The truck did not come back. One day, two days passed, and no young man. Dad was frustrated because he used that vehicle for many things. The insurance company would not pay for a stolen car when it was practically given away.

The townspeople had a big laugh over it. My father is well known for his generosity, for which he is simultaneously admired and called a fool. Both he and the truck, "Old Green," are colorful characters in the community. To make light of the situation, his employees began wearing bows made of twine pinned on their lapels. "We won't take them off until Old Green returns," they said. Others added to the fun with signs and newspaper ads, calling for help in finding the lost car. But "beater" trucks are popular among young men in the area, and everyone assumed that Dad's beater was gone for good.

A week later, the sheriff pulled up to the gas station. "We found your truck," he said, but his eyes avoided Dad's. "The boy used it to kill himself. He fixed up a pipe from the exhaust. Died of carbon monoxide."

My parents wept with grief and shock. The gift they had given, the hospitality they had extended, was used in an unimaginably horrible way. The truck they loaned out in good faith became the vehicle of death for the young man. "Oh, if we would have only talked to him about Jesus," my mother said, thinking over every detail of the lunchtime conversation.

The town too was in shock. The twine lapel pins came off quickly, as did the funny signs all over town. Dad sent employees to retrieve the truck, some 80 miles away, while the young man's car sat in a lonely corner of the parking lot with a $500 repair bill attached to it. Dad went with the sheriff to tell the boy's mother the sad news.

The experience has been a puzzle for my parents. They don't blame themselves for what happened. The young man would have found another way to commit suicide if he was determined to do it. Yet their hospitality seemed to be wasted, even counterproductive. Why didn't God intervene in some way? How could this tragedy have been avoided?

Sometimes we just don't know. We just don't know. But we keep extending our hospitality, extending ourselves, with the assurance that somehow God is there.

3. Jesus identifies with us, especially when we feel like one of the least.

Depending on our current life situation, we identify more with the least ones than with the sheep or goats. Many times we are in need of support that is life-giving, not just charity handouts. We may never actually hunger for food, yet we hunger for other essentials like community and a sense of belonging. Jesus knows this pain and shares it with us.

There are many Christians today, however, for whom the hunger and thirst are physical realities. More people have been killed for their faith in Christ in the twentieth century than in the previous nineteen.[5] It's a sobering thought that sisters and brothers in Christ face persecution in Ethiopia and poverty wages in India. Where are the sheep whom God has called to feed and clothe them? Jesus both walks in their shoes and calls us to share our possessions, power, and privilege with the ones who share our name. We are family.

Persecution in the 1990s

According to Amnesty International, in 1990 some eighty countries held prisoners of conscience—jailed solely for the peaceful exercise of their basic human rights. AI reported torture or ill treatment of prisoners in over one hundred countries; disappearances or secret detention in more than twenty-five.

Children are not immune to the violence. The British group Jubilee Campaign reports that homeless children in Brazil are frequent targets of death squads who kill and, in some cases, mutilate beyond recognition. Street children in Guatemala are attacked, tortured, and killed by police.[6]

4. Hospitality to the strangers among us is a way of entertaining Jesus himself.

Many Christians today are bemoaning a lackluster faith, an overwhelming sense of mediocrity that hangs over their heads like a cloud. They want to meet God, they say. They want a real experience. They want their faith to have purpose and meaning.

The sheep-and-goats story has one answer for them. "You want to find Jesus? There he is, among the poor."

Suddenly our faith has to become more real because it's the only sure thing in a world where new ideas and new ways of being come crashing in on us.

When we sit at table with strangers, with the needy, with the marginalized—surprise! Our net worth doesn't drop. We don't lose a day of our life expectancy. We don't suddenly become less educated. On the contrary— Jesus sits at the table too. It's an opportunity to entertain God! Because our guests are strangers, because this kind of hospitality takes us out of our comfort zones, it's also an adventure in faith! *Mediocre* is hardly the word to be used when we share a sandwich with people who experience the world differently than we do.

Suddenly our faith has to become more real because it's the only sure thing in a world where new ideas and new ways of being come crashing in on us.

I am not talking about having Sunday dinner after church with friends. That's a fine practice, but it hardly constitutes ministering to the least ones. If our hospitality begins and ends with our best buddies who are just like us, then the opportunity to meet Jesus in a special way is gone. If we never step into the unpredictable world of the stranger, we never exercise the faith that we do have. Like an unused muscle, it atrophies until it is barely usable anymore.

Our hospitality muscles do not act in isolation, however. They got there in the first place by the spiritual nurture of prayer and contemplation, the Scriptures, the Holy Spirit, and a relationship with Jesus. The two parts work together—the contemplation and the action, the exercise of the muscles and the feeding of the muscles, the being and the doing. They support each other.

If our faith is not nudging us into acts of mercy, then we need to stop and evaluate our lives. We need to step out of our comfortable lives and invite the stranger in. If our good deeds are not bringing us back to prayer and waiting on God, then we had better get ready for a collapse. Our table ministry with others produces a longing for table time alone with the Host. We must not neglect that longing.

John Koenig, in *New Testament Hospitality,* states that "the stranger received will enlarge our total well-being rather than diminish it."[7] Many participants in the Forty-Day Experiment would agree. Reflecting on their experiences, many wrote of almost-conversion experiences. Through their encounters in hospitality, they entertained God. Their words say it better than I can.

"I have a guess that God did not lead you to ask me because it would have any bearing on your book—but because God wanted to confront me with some things. I think what this experiment is teaching me is not that momentous things like what happened the first day are always going to change someone else, but that I am slowly being changed. I am the one who has been ministered to."[8]

"About this time the pressures of school and life and everything were getting to me, and it was easy for me to fall into self-pity. I don't know how or when, but I began to go about my approach to this experiment differently. I guess I began to rely on God more, and he began to show me how to look beyond myself and my problems and how to use the gifts and skills he has given me. I don't know if

I made a huge impact on any of the people I ministered to, but I know that it helped me to focus less on my own problems and to form deeper relationships with the friends God has given me. I have always been shy and reserved and formed friendships slowly. This helped me learn how to be a more open friend to those around me."9

"I am also aware that I receive so much from God through others. For instance, the Mothers Club women give me so much. Many of them have come through horrendous life experiences where it seemed there was no one who believed in them or cared. I am overwhelmed that they can give me their trust. What a gift! The tears are coming to my eyes as I think about it. Today as I led their Bible study from John 2, they arrived with such eagerness—well, most of them did. One joyously reported that she would bring four new women with her to Mothers Club tomorrow. This was from a Japanese young woman whose weariness at concentrating so hard to understand English shows on her face at the end of the study. Lord, bless these dear ones."10

"Since we have moved here to a new church, I've struggled with some things. One hard issue for me has been how frugal people are. I was raised in an extremely frugal home and found that very difficult and something I wanted to get away from. I found it hard to again be faced with it and not know how to make it a pleasant part of my life. I also was thinking about how drained my work can make me feel and how I fit hospitality into a life that feels very full. Being a somewhat quiet person entered into the picture as I thought and prayed about how to reach beyond my own limits of comfort. I started the forty days with some hesitation, concerned that God would ask me to do something I didn't want to do at all or, on the other hand, not use me at all. . . . There is not any incident that stands out as dramatic. But as I prayed, the thing that I noticed most was my ability to move beyond what normally would be comfortable for me. I was more willing to talk with people at work about how they were doing and to take time to listen, even if that meant I was being delayed. I felt more concerned with how the other person was doing. I felt more at ease when entertaining and so more able to reach out to the people who were there. I continued to think a lot about frugality and my own lifestyle and felt more comfort in using some of the family heirlooms we have when entertaining. I was able to enjoy their beauty without feeling guilty or excessive or apologetic—a big step for me. I have always sensed this barrier in my own mind that told me I could reach out this much and no further. I never understood how to get beyond that. As I prayed, I really felt that resolve and knew how to reach beyond it. I was amazed as I watched that happen!"[11]

"Just another day in 'paradise!' Groceries, basketball game, Patricia's slumber party. Trish did tell me several times how much she appreciated my cleaning her room while she was at school. She kept saying, 'I just need to hug you again,' and 'I like having you around.' I think that was my ministry today, even though I didn't intend it to be. I'm thinking to myself, hmm, even in the ordinary and routine things—there he is."[12]

Yes, there God is. In the mundane, ordinary, small actions we do, in our simple hospitality around the table, God is there. God is at the table with us as we sit with someone new, someone different than we are. In that partnership with strangers, transformation happens. We are changed. Yes, the strangers get needed food, comfort, and shelter from the storm, but we—we get to meet Jesus. We have a sandwich with the Divine.

As we see Jesus in others, we begin to see Jesus in ourselves. If it's possible that the ordinary person before us represents the Christ, then despite our own ordinary lives, it is possible for us as well. Perhaps the legend of "The Hermit's Gift" illustrates the point best.

There was once an old monastery that had fallen upon hard times. Centuries earlier, it had been a thriving monastery where many dedicated monks lived and worked and had great influence on the realm. But now only five monks lived there, and they were all over seventy years old. This was clearly a dying order.

A few miles from the monastery lived an old hermit who many thought was a prophet. One day as the monks agonized over the impending demise of their order, they decided to visit the hermit to see if he might have some advice for them. Perhaps he would be able to see the future and show them what they could do to save the monastery.

The hermit welcomed the five monks to his hut, but when they explained the purpose of their visit, the hermit could only commiserate with them. "Yes, I understand how it is," said the hermit. "The spirit has gone out of the people. Hardly anyone cares much for the old things anymore."

"Is there anything you can tell us," the abbot inquired of the hermit, "that would help us save the monastery?"

"No, I'm sorry," said the hermit. "I don't know how your monastery can be saved. The only thing that I can tell you is that one of you is an apostle of God."

The monks were both disappointed and confused by the hermit's cryptic statement. They returned to the monastery, wondering what the hermit could have meant by the statement "One of you is an apostle of God." For months after their visit, the monks pondered the significance of the hermit's words.

"One of us is an apostle of God," they mused. "Did he actually mean one of us monks here at the monastery?

That's impossible. We are all too old. We are too insignif-
icant. On the other hand, what if it's true? And if it's true,
then which one of us is it? Do you suppose he meant the
abbot? Yes, if he meant anyone, he probably meant the
abbot. He has been our leader for more than a generation. On the other hand, he might have meant Brother
Thomas. Certainly Brother Thomas is a holy man—a man
of wisdom and light. He couldn't have meant Brother
Elred. Elred gets crotchety at times and is difficult to reason with. On the other hand, he is almost always right.
Maybe the hermit did mean Brother Elred. But surely he
could not have meant Brother Phillip. Phillip is so pas-
sive, so shy—a real nobody. Still, he's always there when
you need him. He's loyal and trustworthy. Yes, he could
have meant Phillip. Of course, the hermit didn't mean
me. He couldn't possibly have meant me. I'm just an ordinary person. Yet, suppose he did? Suppose I am an apostle of God? Oh God, not me. I couldn't be that much for
you. Or could I?"

As they contemplated in this manner, the old monks
began to treat each other with extraordinary respect on
the off chance that one of them might actually be an
apostle of God. And on the off, off chance that each
monk himself might be the apostle spoken of by the hermit, each monk began to treat himself with extraordinary
respect.

Because the monastery was situated in a beautiful forest, many people came there to picnic on its tiny lawn and
to walk on its paths, and even now and then to go into the
tiny chapel to meditate. As they did so, without even
being conscious of it, they sensed an aura of extraordinary respect that now began to surround the five old
monks and seemed to radiate out of them, permeating
the atmosphere of the place. There was something
strangely attractive, even compelling about it. Hardly

knowing why, people began to come back to the monastery more frequently to picnic, to play, to pray. They began to bring their friends to show them this special place. And their friends brought their friends.

As more and more visitors came, some of the younger men started to talk with the old monks. After a while one asked if he could join them. Then another. And another. Within a few years the monastery had once again become a thriving order and, thanks to the hermit's gift, a vibrant center of light and spirituality throughout the realm.[13]

Extraordinary respect for ordinary people. For ourselves. To that we are called. And when we answer that call, we find ourselves in the company of the Divine.

Notes

1. Excerpt from the Forty-Day Experiment journals.
2. Ibid.
3. Ibid.
4. Robert Baker in an address for Easter 1998.
5. Timothy K. Jones, "Freedoms Under Fire," *Christianity Today* 36 (20 July 1992): 29.
6. Ibid.
7. John Koenig, *New Testament Hospitality: Partnership with Strangers as Promise and Mission* (Philadelphia: Fortress Press, 1985), p. 5.
8. Excerpt from the Forty-Day Experiment journals.
9. Ibid.
10. Ibid.
11. Ibid.
12. Ibid.
13. "The Hermit's Gift" from *Hot Illustrations;* Wayne Rice, ed. (El Cajon, Calif.: Youth Specialities, 1994). Adapted from M. Scott Peck, *A Different Drummer* (Simon and Schuster, 1988).

CHAPTER 6

Hospitality as Worship

*On this mountain the Lord of hosts will
make for all peoples a feast of rich food, a
feast of well-aged wines, of rich food filled
with marrow, of well-aged wines strained
clear. And he will destroy on this mountain
the shroud that is cast over all peoples, the
sheet that is spread over all nations; he will
swallow up death forever. Then the Lord
God will wipe away the tears from all faces,
and the disgrace of his people he will take
away from all the earth, for the Lord has
spoken. —Isaiah 25:6-8*

*F*ood is an important part of hospitality. It's part of the package deal. In every culture, hardly ever is one invited in without the offer of at least something to drink. It's a standard thing at our house too. When my ten-year-old and twelve-year-old daughters bring friends home, they immediately go to the refrigerator. In their minds, it does not matter whether you just ate lunch at your friend's house—you walk in and you advance to the fridge.

Food and fellowship go together. You can be hospitable without offering food right away, but the guests who walk in our doors will eventually need nourishment. It doesn't just happen in our homes. Every major event in our lives involves food. Weddings and graduations have receptions, funerals have dinners, baby showers have party snacks, and birthdays have cakes.

Churches have potlucks.

But it's more than just the food itself. Shoving a bag full of peanut butter-and-jelly sandwiches out the door to your guest is not hospitality. Charity maybe but not hospitality. Eating at the same counter with people you don't know at Dan's Diner is not necessarily fellowship. It can be, if you acknowledge each other's presence and have a friendly conversation. But usually we pretend we're all alone in that crowded restaurant. Others could be sitting only inches away from us, but we keep our eyes on our food and eat fast, or we bring a newspaper as a companion.

It's more than food. It's how you eat the food. Cultures everywhere have set up rules to govern and direct this basic human function. In some cultures, you eat three times a day; you use a spoon, fork, and knife (unless it's McDonald's); you sit down at a table; and everyone eats at the same time. Dessert comes last. In other cultures, none of those rules apply. The elders eat first, you stand over the fire and eat with your hands, and dessert comes first. Even animal species have a social order for eating.

The taking in of food is a social practice with many implications. It's more than food. It's how you eat the food, and when, and with whom. Even these cultural mores change slightly depending on the social event. The rules partially serve to communicate whether you are in or out and just how *in* you are—whether you are welcomed at one level of intimacy or another. Take for example, the office party. There's food there, plenty of it. It is placed on some table where the office revelers go and help themselves. Everyone mills around, talking in small groups, switching groups, and going back to the food table. The food table serves more as something to do if you aren't part of a significant conversation than as a source of nutrition. These rules work splendidly for a group of people who don't know each other very well and aren't highly motivated to get to know each other better. Spouses and friends of the office workers can more easily blend into the background if they need to. It's fairly easy to excuse yourself from a boring conversation. You can even slip out and go home and not be noticed. There is food and some fellowship, but there are also rules that aid those who don't really want to share more than polite conversation and sandwiches.

The sit-down meal has different rules. Everyone is around one table. Movement is restricted, and eye contact is more important. If you want more food, you have to ask to have it passed to you. You become a part of the conversation of the persons at your end of the table, like it or not. If you leave, everyone notices. The rules seem more restrictive in this kind of food gathering, yet they fit the situation. People who sit down together to eat a meal tend to be more closely committed to each other than those at a buffet party. There's a greater level of intimacy. People are more engaged in each other's lives.

Does that mean that sit-down meals are good and party buffets are bad? No. Each set of rules has its place and serves an important function. We cannot be intimate with everyone we meet. Just thinking about that high standard wears us out. The North American myth of intimacy—that is, the idea that everyone should have a deep relationship with everyone else—is part of what hinders our hospitality. If you can't reach the goal of deep personal sharing with everyone you meet, so the logic in our heads goes, don't meet any more new people. But hospitality does not mean that we have to become best friends with everyone we meet. We can love strangers by providing for their needs, listening to them, accepting them for who they are, sharing our values with them, and working to see them as Jesus does. None of these tasks requires intimacy.

What an analysis of the different food rules does say to us, however, is just how important sharing food is. It is a cultural activity, with deep sociological implications. When we eat, we do much more than renew our bodies with food energy. We are playing out the drama of life. We are establishing boundaries, letting down our guard, sharing stories, welcoming strangers into a more intimate circle, and renewing our souls.

We can choose to eat our food in ways that renew our

Food stories from *Extending the Table*

"I thought we were teaching our children to eat responsibly. Our parents had survived famine in the Ukraine, and we, with our children, had seen hunger face to face on a previous service assignment in Africa. We all agreed that wasting food was unacceptable and overeating obscene.

"Then we went to Matabudukwane, a village in southern Botswana, and saw ourselves through the eyes of Rose and her seven children.

"As part of our orientation to the language and customs of Botswana, Rose graciously hosted us for a week. She made delicious meals with the basic foods we had brought along to supplement her supplies and served them on her best dishes.

"On the final day of our stay, Rose made a chicken dinner. Knowing we had not brought chicken, we realized she had sacrificed one of her few laying hens. She smiled at our expressions of thanks, telling us to enjoy the meal. The piles of gnawed bones on our plates testified that we had done that. Or so we thought.

"At dishwashing time I realized how vastly my ideas of eating responsibly differed from Rose's. Scattered about the kitchen floor were the bones from our plates. But these were shiny white, cleaned of every vestige of meat, skin, gristle, and juice. The waste from our table had become a banquet for Rose's little ones. Near the open door two of them played together, each still contentedly sucking a bone."[1]

bodies but not our souls. The fast-food phenomenon, supper in front of the TV, and soup-in-a-cup at the office desk all have ramifications for our lives. I'm not saying that the occasional drive-through meal is so terrible, but if we are spending every day grabbing lunch on the run, what does that say for us socially? Spiritually?

Food for Thought

Food is also an important concept in the Bible. It is usually not the food itself that is so weighty—"Food will not bring us close to God" (1 Cor. 8:8)—but what it represents. Jesus said, "I am the bread of life" (John 6:35). Doing God's will was so important to him that he called it his "food" (John 4:34). Paul likened spiritual maturity to solid food, and he spent many hours writing to the churches over the controversial issue of eating food placed before idols. While it is true that "life is more than food" (Luke 12:23), Jesus understood the importance of meeting physical needs, as demonstrated by the feeding of the 5000. The extreme importance of food for our physical lives parallels the necessity of spiritual food that comes from our relationship with God.

How we eat

In 1987-89, people in developed countries consumed nearly three times as much grain per capita as people in less-developed countries. In the developed countries, people ate 63 percent of the grain indirectly via meat, while people in less-developed countries ate 81 percent of the grain directly. On average, Canadians receive 129 percent of the calorie requirements in comparison to people in Ghana who, on average, receive only 76 percent of the calories they need."[2]

When God began his relationship with the family of Abraham and Sarah, food rituals were one way of explaining God's nature and establishing God's holiness. The Pentateuch, especially the book of Leviticus, spells out very precise rules about what to eat and what not to eat (Lev. 10:12-20; 11:1-47; 17:10-16). Orthodox Jews still follow these dietary guidelines today. While most Christians don't adhere to these rules, we can learn from them some important principles about God.

First, God was concerned about the health of the Israelites. These guidelines constituted healthier standards for diet and sanitation than in most of the ancient world.[3] Other religions had prohibitions against eating some of the same animals, but none came close to the precise Judaic instructions that promoted cleanliness and good health. A rationale for sanitation and health does not, however, thoroughly explain the many dietary laws.

Second, God was beginning to teach the people about holiness. God is God and deserves respect and obedience. God is holy. These things were hard for the Israelites to fully comprehend; they are hard for us to fully comprehend today. God is different from all other gods. Canaanite practices had their own food laws.[4] The Israelites were not to follow these laws, but they were to be holy, separated out. By choosing food as one of the ways to teach holiness, God struck a resounding chord with the people. Food was extremely important, and in the cultural setting, it already had religious significance. To eat was to live and worship your god. So God took a very significant element of life and with that began teaching what it meant to be "separate unto God."

Food and children constituted wealth in the Old Testament. Land, not currency, was the operative mode of wealth, and sons guaranteed that the land would be kept in the family name. The land, of course, was desirable because it produced crops and places for grazing livestock. Daughters-in-law brought dowry, usually in the form of livestock or flocks. The bigger the family, the greater potential for wealth—wealth that was most immediately accessible through some form of food.

Both food and children were also given from God. The Old Testament unequivocally ascribes the provision of these blessings to God. From the beginning, God gave humans all the vegetation of the earth to eat (Gen. 1:29).

After the Flood, God gave humans permission to eat animal flesh, but not the blood (Gen. 9:3-4). And as the Israelites traveled through the barren land of the Sinai Peninsula for forty years, God, through pure miracle, provided for their needs with manna and quail and water pouring from a rock (Exod. 16—17). Canaan, the Promised Land, is described over and over as the land of milk and honey (Exod. 3:8; Lev. 20:24; Deut. 11:9).

For these reasons, God asked for food offerings. With the exception of the incense offering, all of the offerings prescribed were some foodstuff. God asked for the first and the best of the harvest. No one ate of the new crop until the firstfruits offering was made (Lev. 23:14). There was also a firstfruits offering for all of the firstborn cattle and other livestock. Children, also a symbol of wealth, were also to be offered, but not in human sacrifice like the other nations did. The firstborn sons were redeemed, their lives bought back by the gift of a money purchase or the sacrifice of an animal (Exod. 34:20).

Food became the acceptable offering because food was the stuff of life. If the Israelites could trust God enough to give God the first and best of their food, even when this precious stuff was scarce, they were trusting God with their very lives. When God asked them to offer their food, God was really asking them to offer themselves. Think of the life we would breathe into our premeal prayers if we routinely reminded ourselves of what the mashed potatoes and gravy really meant.

Because of the significance of food as wealth and as worship to God, even simple meals took on meaning. In biblical times, eating together implied a close relationship; it implied family (Ps. 41:9). If you didn't like someone or wished to remain apart from a person socially, you did not eat together (Gen. 43:32). To miss a family meal communicated anger or alienation (1 Sam. 20:34).[5] The solidarity of the family meal even expanded to the guest-host relationship in the biblical narrative. Almost every act of hospitality culminated in a meal. Strangers, even enemies, were to be included at the family table (Matt. 26:20-25).

So important were meals that they were used in deliberate and ritualistic ways to seal covenants between two parties. Some scholars even suggest that the Hebrew word for covenant, *berit*, derives from a rare Hebrew verb *bara*, meaning "to eat."[6] *Covenant* described contracts or solemn vows between two human parties or agreements between God and the people. Four major covenants in the biblical narrative had meals as part of the ritual that sealed the relationship. The implication was that after eating together, the two parties functioned as family.

In the Bible narrative then, food functioned in four ways: as an essential part of healthy physical life that God graciously provided; as a form of worship through rituals and offerings; as a source of wealth; and as a means of social and contractual bonding. Layered within those functions, food was also assumed in the practice of hospitality, itself so cherished a value that even strangers became family around the table.

Got Milk?

So why doesn't it feel like any big deal when I gather around the table with family and friends? Oh, it happens occasionally—a Christmas Eve dinner by candlelight; the picnic overlooking Crater Lake; the one night my friends and I sat at the table, pushed back the dirty plates, and talked for five hours. Those were special moments. But usually meals are simply something to endure at my house. The four-year-old spills his milk, the phone rings, and I'm too tired to appreciate the Kraft Macaroni and Cheese. Conversation centers on keeping our elbows off the table. Where's the worship in this?

Several factors work against us in our North American culture. Food isn't as hard to get as it is in other societies. It's cheap, fast, and easy to make or have made for you. Food doesn't seem as sacred when you can buy it at the store two blocks away for a fraction of what you earn. We throw away food scraps that others would fight over in another part of the world. We have never known true hunger and don't break our backs providing the abundance we do have. Given these facts, what celebration or sense of awe is there in the traditional six o'clock supper?

It's a wonder, with all the abundance and convenience of our food, that we don't share our meals more often, but we don't. Sharing a meal is almost a lost art in North America. When we do eat together, it is almost exclusively our friends or extended families who are invited. Seldom do we sit at table with strangers. Does this mean that we really don't practice the full spectrum of hospitality? If we show kindness to the stranger but don't welcome her to the table, do we fall short?

Food preparation
Food preparation is extremely time-consuming for rural African women, because it involves far more than cooking. Women must first grow and harvest their crops. During the millet harvest in Zaire, women manually cut the heads of grain, pound them with a large wooden mortar and pestle, and then winnow to remove the chaff. For all this work, they return home at the end of a long, hot, dry day carrying one dishpan of grain on their heads.[7]

Is there something special that happens when we eat with friends or strangers? Do our actions at the table constitute worship?

Offering Food as an Offering

The Old Testament is replete with food stories. One story stands out, however, as an example of how offering food to the stranger became an offering to God. The story is found in Judges 6:11-22.

The Old Testament judge Gideon had a lot of doubts

about his particular situation. But he was certain about the importance of food for his life and the life of the community. That's why he was doing a most peculiar thing— he was threshing wheat in a wine press.

It was an awkward practice at best. Normally threshing floors were located in exposed areas so the wind could easily blow away the chaff. But Gideon's winepress was a hole in the ground. As he beat the grain, dividing the ripe heads from the chaff, dust flew into his face and into his mouth. He had to tolerate this miserable task because it was the only way to keep the harvest safe from plunderers, specifically the Midianites.

The Midianites had been a thorn in the side of Gideon's people for some time. The situation seemed hopeless, reducing men to such things as threshing in wine presses. Things were so bad that when the angel of the Lord appeared to Gideon with good news, he responded with words of doubt. "But sir, if the Lord is with us, why then has all this happened to us? And where are all his wonderful deeds that our ancestors recounted to us, saying, 'Did not the Lord bring us up from Egypt?' But now the Lord has cast us off, and given us into the hand of Midian" (Judg. 6:13).

Gideon felt so hopeless about the plight of his people that he could not recognize the supernatural being before him. God could not possibly be with them if God allowed this sort of thing to happen. The Lord seemed to ignore his unbelief. Gideon was charged to go in the strength he had and save Israel from Midian's hand. It was an urgent call. God Almighty commissioned him.

Gideon was still not convinced. "But sir, how can I deliver Israel? My clan is the weakest in Manasseh, and I am the least in my family" (Judg. 6:15). Was he a member of a small group with scanty resources within his tribe or the youngest member of his family? His family was wealthy enough to have at least ten servants (6:27), and he was old enough to have a son capable of bearing arms (8:20). Was Gideon only asserting the obvious—that any person called directly to serve God is by the nature of the calling unworthy? For whatever reason, Gideon was tentative about the call. The task seemed overwhelming and frightening.

It was a calling so huge, a mission so important, that Gideon felt that he had to be sure about the messenger who brought this calling, the stranger who stood before him. He asked for a sign: "If now I have found favor with you, then show me a sign that it is you who speak with me" (Judg. 6:17). The sign Gideon envisioned involved hospitality. "Do not depart from here until I come to you, and bring out my present, and set it before you" (6:18). The angel agreed to stay.

It would be a long stay for this messenger, for Gideon was going all out for the meal. He prepared a kid and unleavened bread from an *ephah* of flour—a long preparation. It was also a big meal. An *ephah* of flour would make many cakes for just two people, and a whole kid is a lot of meat. Here was a man representing a besieged people so afraid their grain would be stolen that they threshed it in semi-privacy bringing this enormous amount of precious food to this mysterious stranger. We don't know all of the details, but surely this had to be an extravagant affair. If Gideon was supplying that much food, then he was surely working very hard to make the meal just right. When my children can hardly wait for their restaurant food to be served, I say, "Well, they had to butcher the cow, you know." We laugh at the visual picture of some fry cook killing the cow. But here it was no laughing matter. The kid had to be killed, and the bread had to bake. All those hours of waiting, smelling the warm aroma of fresh meat and bread pouring forth from the tent had to drive that poor angel crazy (an angel from our culture, at least).

Gideon put the meat in the basket, its gravy in a pot, and together with the bread took it to the angel. The messenger of God then asked him to do a strange thing. Gideon was told to take the meat and the cakes and put them on a stone. The sauce that he had so carefully prepared was to be poured out over the rest of the food. Now for Gideon this probably didn't seem so strange. The food was an offering poured out to God. Yet I wonder if he might not have had just a twinge of hesitation as he poured out that rich gravy onto the rock. He had worked so hard to prepare this gift. This food could have fed his family for days. But the angel said pour, and pour he did. Steam rose from the hot broth, and the smells of baked bread and meat rose in the air like heavenly incense.

The angel took a staff and touched the meat and cakes. Fire leaped up from the rock and consumed the food. The wild smell of the food was now matched by the violent sight of the shooting flames. The food was gone. This was the sign Gideon asked for, the miraculous proof that this was the Lord.

The sign was so effective, in fact, that Gideon now feared for his life. Convinced that he had surely entertained the messenger of Yahweh himself, Gideon cried out in terror. He believed that to see God or a messenger of God meant death. "*Shalom,*" was the Lord's reply. This word signified peace and security. The gift Gideon brought, the worship he offered, had been accepted. Gideon's unbelief and need for a sign had been forgiven.

Hospitality as Worship

Hospitality, demonstrated by the food offering, was an important element in Gideon's encounter with God. Gideon showed weakness in his lack of faith and need for a sign, yet he graciously offered a precious piece of himself. It was not only the food, but also his gracious preparation of it. Though he was skeptical about the divine nature of the stranger, he offered it anyway. Gideon would again need signs for his ever-encroaching doubts (Judg. 6:36-40), but this step of hospitality began the journey whereby God worked through him to save the Israelites.

We can learn from Gideon's act of hospitality and apply his faith to our own times of doubt as we encounter strangers. Several principles, applied to our simple meals with others, can bring about a fuller experience of worship.

1. Don't forget the salt—or the faith.

Gideon struggled with his faith. The Midianites made it hard to believe that God was still in control. Yet he had faith enough to ask for a sign. He had faith enough to offer a stranger some food. He had faith enough to pour out this food in an impractical gesture of offering.

Many times our meals and our hospitality will call for that same faith. We take great risks at times to invite strangers to sit at table with us. It is downright scary. We feed them, going to a lot of work, and nothing seems to come from it. No one appreciates our efforts; no real ministry seems to happen. We might as well have poured the meat and gravy on a rock.

Hebrews 13:2 admonishes us to "not neglect hospitality to strangers, for by doing that some have entertained angels without knowing it." It is the "without knowing it" part that is so hard. Yet that is what worship is all about. We pour ourselves upon the altar, like the gravy on the rock, in a foolish, impractical act of complete adoration. We give up control; we give up the need to understand it all. We do it for love. When we share our meals and our lives with strangers for this reason, not knowing all the whys or hows, God sees and accepts that as our offering, our worship.

2. Expect the food to burn.

When we see our meals as acts of worship, our attitude toward all the hard work and preparation starts to change. Cooking is one thing I used to hate because there were never any lasting results. You cook this wonderful food, you slave for hours, and then—poof, in twenty minutes, it's gone. What a waste of time! Why spend precious time making a soufflé when tuna sandwiches will serve the same purpose! Protein is protein.

You can say the same thing about homemade valentines, handwritten letters, and handmade quilts. They are frivolous, time-consuming, and inefficient things—which is exactly why I love to receive them and love to give them

---

At Home in Guatemala

"During a visit to Guatemala, a friend took me to the home of a K'ekchi' Indian farmer. When we arrived, we found that he had been sick. His illness, however, did not dampen the welcome he gave us. He invited us into his small house and pulled up wooden chairs so we could sit and visit.

"Later in the morning when he was feeling stronger, he led us around to the back of his house to show us his animals. While we were there, his wife came and caught a chicken, an indication that we would have lunch before leaving.

"An hour or so later, his wife invited us into the kitchen. In the center of the room an open fire burned on the earthen floor. Over this fire she had prepared *caldo*, a spicy chicken soup. Now she used the same fire to cook tortillas.

"We sat on a backless bench with soup bowls before us on another bench of equal height. There was no table in this kitchen. Neither were there any utensils for eating. We used steaming hot tortillas to ladle up the soup. The woman did not sit to eat, but continued to quietly pat out tortillas, occasionally adding a chuckle or a quiet word to the subdued conversation.

"No prior invitation. No table, No utensils. No dinner music. Broth with only one bony piece of chicken. Hospitality? Indeed. And some of the finest I have ever experienced. The savory flavors of the *caldo* and fresh tortillas satiated my appetite. The gentle rhythmic patting of tortillas soothed my spirit. The warm smiles penetrated our language barrier, making me feel honored and at home."[8]

away. Their very frivolity and pointless effort speak volumes about the feelings we have for the people we give them to. Sometimes love must be expressed in extravagance, in foolishness, in wild abandon!

The meals we prepare for others should be seen as gifts of love. This doesn't mean that every meal should be a seven-course extravaganza. We should also guard against fixing fancy meals for the wrong motivation—to show off our culinary skills or to demonstrate how perfect we are. But every meal, whether simple or grand, takes on new meaning if we view it as an offering. Our food becomes more than food; it becomes one way of expressing our love for each other, and in that, our love for God. It doesn't matter, then, that the meal we spent four hours to prepare is gone in twenty minutes. It is an offering. It is intended to be placed on the altar and burned.

3. Sit down when you can.

While there is a place for both the sit-down meal and the party buffet, our meals move closer to worship as we choose more intimate ways of eating together. Food in the ancient world held a sacred meaning that is almost lost in North America, yet even for us there is that sense that eating together implies a deeper relationship. We don't feel comfortable eating in front of just anybody. What if something gets stuck in our teeth? We intuitively know that eating together lets down your guard. In ancient traditions, some of which still flourish in the back hills of the Appalachian Mountains, the act of eating together can turn enemies into friends. If you invite the enemy to sit at table with you, he puts down his gun for the day. The feuding stops.

Not every meal needs be an intimate, life-changing event. We can't live in that kind of intensity all the time. But we can choose to take small steps toward intimacy, especially with the strangers we welcome. In doing so, we become more vulnerable, more open to new relationships, and more open to the Spirit's work in our lives.

4. Appreciate the pudding.

Our meals will take on a more worshipful atmosphere if we remind ourselves of the sacredness of food. We who grew up on farms can still appreciate the incredible efforts of farmers and food producers and the knowledge and hard work of canning and gardening. Our children, for the most part, don't have that understanding. They, and we, can also forget what food means to a mother whose child is starving. In an act of sheer absurdity, we turn on the six o'clock news and watch scenes from Somalia while munching our hamburgers.

We have forgotten the sacredness of our God-given food. We have forgotten the interdependence of all living creatures and our dependence on God. David did not forget. Once on the battlefield, he casually asked for a drink of water from the Bethlehem well. David and his men were twelve miles from this well, which was behind enemy lines. David simply longed for water from his childhood well; he did not expect his men to fetch this water under such dangerous circumstances.

But fetch it they did. Three men, in an act of supreme loyalty, broke through the camp of the Philistines to bring David water from this pool. Twenty-four heart-stopping miles later, they presented themselves before their leader, flask in hand. David was in shock. He did the only thing that seemed right to do. He took the precious water and poured it out on the ground. "The Lord forbid that I should do this. Can I drink the blood of the men who went at the risk of their lives?" (2 Sam. 23:17). David could not drink it, for the men had risked their lives to get it for him. That made the water as precious as blood

to him. Blood, according to Israelite belief, is life itself
and therefore belongs to God. So when David poured the
water on the ground, it was a sacrifice, an offering to God.
He did not forget.

When we lived in Oregon, I watched migrant workers,
many of them resident aliens from Central America, work
the strawberry and blueberry fields. Their hourly wages
were pennies next to my salary. Did I ever refuse to eat
those berries, sick at the thought of the injustice? Did the
red juice of the berries ever remind me of blood?

We eat simple vegetarian meals at my house about
twice a week. We don't do it to upset the protein market
in North America. We don't do it to save money necessarily. We do it for ourselves, as a symbolic gesture toward
those who don't have the luxury to choose to eat meat.
We do it for our own benefit, reminding ourselves of the
sacredness of food. It is a way to help our children see a
broader world. It is a way to help us enjoy the wonderful
food we do have.

We must not forget.

A Little Ice Cream Is Good for the Soul

Biblical hospitality is an act of worship. Particularly in
the act of eating together. As we sit down and share the
stuff of life, we share ourselves. We bond in new ways,
experiencing the Christ in each other. Our food becomes
more than food when we share it as Christians. It becomes
an event of grace. "Where two or three are gathered in my
name . . ."

Perhaps children understand this better than we do.
This story from an unknown source speaks volumes:

"Last week I took my children to a restaurant. My six-
year-old son asked if he could say grace. As we bowed our
heads, he said, 'God is good, God is great. Thank you for
the food, and I would thank you even more if Mom gets

us ice cream for dessert. Amen!'

"Along with the laughter from the other customers nearby, I heard a woman remark, 'That's what's wrong with this country. Kids today don't even know how to pray. Asking God for ice cream! Why I never!'

"Hearing this, my son burst into tears and asked me, 'Did I do it wrong? Is God mad at me?'

"As I held him and assured him that he had done a terrific job and that God was certainly not mad at him, an elderly gentleman approached the table. He winked at my son and said, 'I happen to know that God thought that was a great prayer.'

"'Really?' my son asked.

"'Cross my heart,' he replied. Then in a theatrical whisper he added, pointing to the woman whose remark had started the whole thing, 'It's too bad she never asks God for ice cream. A little ice cream is good for the soul sometimes.'

"Naturally, I bought my kid ice cream at the end of the meal. My son stared at his for a moment and then did something I will remember for the rest of my life. He picked up his sundae and without a word walked over and placed it in front of the woman. With a big smile, he told her, 'Here, this is for you. Ice cream is good for the soul sometimes, and my soul is good already.'"9

Ice cream is good for the soul sometimes. Especially when we share it in the sacred act of hospitality.

Additional Reading

Whitcomb, Holly W. *Feasting with God: Adventures in Table Spirituality* (Cleveland, Ohio: Pilgrim Press, 1996).

Notes

1. Joetta Handrich Schlabach, *Extending the Table: A World Community Cookbook* (Scottdale, Pa.: Herald Press, 1991), p. 168. Story by Margaret Reimer, Leamington, Ont.
2. Schlabach, p. 191.
3. "Unclean and Clean," *Anchor Bible Dictionary;* David Noel Freedman, ed. (New York: Doubleday, 1992), 6:729-745.
4. "Canaan, Religion of," *Anchor Bible Dictionary*, 1:831-837.
5. "Eating and Drinking in the Old Testament," *Anchor Bible Dictionary*, 2:250-254.
6 Ibid.
7. Schlabach, p. 153.
8. Ibid., p. 86.
9. Story from an anonymous source on the Internet.

CHAPTER 7

Hospitality: The Giving and Receiving of Honor

Do not put yourself forward in the king's presence or stand in the place of the great; for it is better to be told, 'Come up here,' than to be put lower in the presence of a noble. —Proverbs 25:6-7

Now why should I do this mentoring program, really? My friend across the table gave me that cynical look. I had just asked her to join some of us in a hospitality ministry at an inner-city elementary school. I gave the usual reasons—these are high-risk kids, the mentoring is relatively easy, and it's only a ten-minute walk away.

She was interested, so we discussed the connections between hospitality and spirituality. As hosts, we receive a gift, I told her. Sometimes the gift is physical, sometimes it is the surprise of a new friendship, and sometimes it is the gift of being stretched. Practicing hospitality helps in the process of spiritual renewal and conversion. We meet Jesus in the people we serve. Our hospitality becomes a form of worship for us; our welcome serves as a sweet offering to God.

She was not yet convinced. Most people she knew practiced hospitality for different reasons. We feel pressure from our local congregation to have the visiting missionaries spend the night at our house. We entertain our friends right after we get new curtains for the entire downstairs. Being hospitable has its own rewards. It's a great reputation to have.

"What does Jesus say about hospitality?" Her question startled me. I assumed I had to talk her into this ministry by listing all the benefits to her. But that's not what mattered to her. What mattered to her was following Jesus. If Jesus said to do it, then that was what she would do because that was her identity. That's who she was.

Is there merit in saying we practice hospitality because we are commanded to? Because it is part of being a disciple? Was hospitality ever mandated by Jesus? Did he ever spell out how this hospitality is supposed to look?

Good questions.

The Mandate

Luke 14 presents the clearest statement Jesus makes on hospitality. In a poetic mix of narrative and parable, Jesus spells out what real hospitality is and what our motivation should be in practicing it. Jesus puts a new slant on why we do what we do and how we get the strength to do it.

The stage is set for this discussion because Jesus had been invited to a banquet. Banquets were big in Hellenistic culture, and their importance seeped into Jewish meal traditions. For the Greeks, banquets were more than just wonderful food and a nice place to recline. They were the most common settings for philosophical discussion, our equivalent to the college coffee-house phenomenon. They were important events—the intellectual center—complete with their own prescribed rules and expectations. Banquets provided the setting where dignitaries (anybody who was anybody) discussed the current issues and enjoyed the frivolity of strong drink and rich food. Jesus was invited to the Jewish version of this event, which usually toned down the frivolity part and emphasized the serious discussion. That Luke pictures Jesus so often at table implies that he intends to present Jesus as philosopher as well as a prophet.

The banquet in Luke 14 was not just any banquet. Luke gives us many hints that this banquet was earmarked for trouble. First, Jesus was going to the house of one of the rulers of the Pharisees. Typically this group opposed Jesus. Second, the event transpired on the Sabbath. Both meal settings and Sabbath settings had earlier been scenes of conflict. Putting them together alerts the reader that there will be conflict. Add to this tension a whole village watching from the sidelines. Ancient hospitality blurred the public and private lines much more than in North America today. Everyone, in one way or another, was attending this banquet. Luke gives clues about the tension: "They were watching him closely" (v. 1); "When he noticed . . ." (v. 7). Both parties had their eyes open, watching for discrepancies. Jesus was indeed a guest in this house, but it is doubtful that he was truly a welcome guest.

So Why Do We Do It? Reason One

So why did they invite Jesus in? He was obviously a controversial character, probably the subject of many earlier banquet conversations. He was a traveling teacher in need of hospitality and, by this distinction, worthy of such accommodations. Were the Pharisees inviting Jesus in to enhance their own status? Using hospitality to gain influence was common practice among the Greeks. Reciprocity was the standard among both Jews and Greeks. Those who received hospitality were indebted to the host and expected to give back equal or greater hospitality at another time.

A clue to the motive for inviting Jesus in can be found in the man who had dropsy. The text is unclear about whether this man had also been invited to the banquet. Was he a guest, or did he just happen by as one of the public bystanders? If his dropsy was obvious enough to be noticed, then by strict Levitical standards, he was unclean (Lev. 13:2). These Pharisees probably upheld such rules, making this man an unwelcome guest. Was Jesus really any more welcome?

If they did welcome the man with dropsy, then their intent was not true hospitality. They were not interested in this man finding healing. Knowing that, Jesus posed a question to these lawyers and Pharisees, a question that framed for them, and for us, a definition of hospitality: "Is it lawful to cure people on the sabbath or not?" (Luke 14:3). They were silent, so Jesus took the issue to a new level—a legal argument. "If one of you has a child or an ox that has fallen into a well, will you not immediately pull it out on a sabbath day?" (v. 5). It was a complicated question because the law was ambiguous concerning when an animal should be pulled out of a pit. The example of a child is much less ambiguous, of course. Jesus knew what he was doing. If their Jewish practice allowed them to help an animal in a pit on the Sabbath, why couldn't they respond to a person in need?

The Pharisees were silent. This response was strange, not only because silence was taken for consent in legal matters, but also because the rabbinical tradition was very clear about the impropriety of healing on the Sabbath. Why were they silent? Were they thinking of their own son in a pit? Did they see this man with dropsy, really see him, for the first time?

The issue was more complicated than just healing this man. His condition was chronic, not acute. He could come on other days to be healed. The Sabbath was too important to break for such nonemergency healings.[1] The price of healing was too great for them. It would change their beloved tradition. They saw this man in need, and his need touched them to the point of silence, yet the cost of healing this man or inviting him in and making him an equal partner was too great. This act of healing threatened the status quo. It was too much to ask.

We face similar situations today. In our medical practices, we deal with many chronic patients. Some of these people experience permanent healing, and some linger in their illness. Hospitality to those who remain chronically ill is a lifelong commitment. What about people who put themselves in chronic conditions by their lifestyle choices—the diabetic who won't eat right and exercise or the emphysema patient who still smokes? What about the people who use the emergency room for nonemergency reasons? What does hospitality mean in these situations?

Modern medicine can oppress the very people it tries to help. Physicians have massive power over their patients. Hospital regulations strip patients of everything that defines who they are—their clothes, their jewelry, their teeth, their freedom. Some of these regulations are there for good reasons. Nevertheless, in the regulating process, the medical professionals feel overwhelmed by the need, and the people in need feel powerless and invisible. Where does hospitality fit into this?

Jesus said that the man with dropsy was more important than the tradition of Sabbath. He didn't debunk Sabbath; he redefined it. He didn't answer all the immediate questions, either for them or for us. But he set the priority. Hospitality supersedes tradition.

So Why Do We Do It? Reason Two

Having laid the groundwork, Jesus turned to the heart of the matter. He noticed the scramble for seats when everyone arrived for this banquet. Places close to a special guest or to the host were honored seats. Placement at the banquet equated status.

Knowing this, Jesus said, "When you are invited by someone to a wedding banquet, do not sit down at the place of honor, in case someone more distinguished than you has been invited by your host; and the host who invited both of you may come and say to you, 'Give this person your place,' and then in disgrace you would start to take the lowest place. But when you are invited, go and sit down at the lowest place, so that when your host comes, he may say to you, 'Friend, move up higher'; then you will be honored in the presence of all who sit at the table with you" (vv. 8-10). It sounded like good advice, real common sense, and much like other wise sayings from the wisdom literature (Prov. 25:6-7). Given the culture's emphases on shame and honor, the advice was all the more appropriate. How true, the Pharisees thought. One must be careful how one receives honor.

Receiving honor was at the heart of their hospitality. With reciprocity in mind, these rulers gave lavish feasts to those who, first of all, would be impressed, and second, would return the favor with special privileges and loyalty to the host. Banquets helped define who was who, and how far up the social ladder everyone was. It seemed so wise, then, to participate in this kind of hospitality. You invited your friends, solidified relationships, and bettered yourself. The advice Jesus gave complemented the accepted cultural system, or so it seemed.

But Jesus was not finished giving his advice: "For all who exalt themselves will be humbled, and those who humble themselves will be exalted" (Luke 14:11). Jesus took his worldly wisdom, his good advice, and turned it on its head. Jesus was not addressing the appropriate way to get honor; he was exhorting them not to seek honor at all. The Pharisees were throwing parties and receiving hospitality only to enjoy respect in the eyes of their fellow guests. But the way to receive respect, Jesus said, was to not seek it at all. In humbling ourselves, God exalts us.

Don't do it for your own glory, Jesus said. Choose the last place. Take this last place, not so that in some strange ironic twist you will be honored, but because you really do want others to have the better seat.

Because you really do care about the man with dropsy.

So That's Why We Do It! Reason Three

Status, honor, priorities, reward? Jesus continued his line of reasoning. "When you give a luncheon or a dinner, do not invite your friends or your brothers or your relatives or rich neighbors, in case they may invite you in return, and you would be repaid. But when you give a banquet, invite the poor, the crippled, the lame, and the blind" (Luke 14:12-13). Jesus blatantly opposed the conventional patterns of reciprocity found in their hospitality. He also provided an alternate principle. Invite the very ones who cannot give you status by their coming. Invite the ones who have nothing to offer to you but themselves. Invite the ones who really need the hospitality.

Do it for them, not for you.

His words sent shock waves to his listeners. Jesus was not talking only about forsaking a cherished way of social stratification. He also was talking about downward mobility. He was talking about bringing unclean people into your house, people who would defile you. Jesus was talking about others laughing at you or scorning you. He was talking about the inconvenience of beggars and blind people at your table. Jesus was talking about seeing everyone as your equal and demonstrating that with your hospitality.

Jesus was talking about turning the world upside down—hospitality as a subversive act.

But an act that was not without reward: "And you will be blessed," Jesus said, "because they cannot repay you, for you will be repaid at the resurrection of the righteous" (Luke 14:14). There was honor to be had. There was reward for providing hospitality, but it was different from the promise of a reciprocal banquet gathering. It was more than the respect in the eyes of your fellow guests.

It's that big banquet at the end of the age.

The Pharisees knew about that big messianic celebration, so one of the guests responded to this high standard of hospitality: "Blessed is the one who will eat bread in the kingdom of God!" (Luke 14:15). The dinner guest spoke with the assurance of one who would someday attend this end-time feast. Rather than confirm that, Jesus launched into another story of rejection and challenge. Yes, there would be a reward, but not everyone who thinks he's getting a chunk of that reward will actually get it.

The crowd gathered close for the next story. There was a man who gave a great feast. He invited many people. On the day of the event, the master sent his servant out to call people to come in. But each one he called had excuses not to come. One had bought a field, another bought some oxen, and a third had just married. Upon hearing this, the master grew angry. He sent the servant out again, this time to "bring in the poor, the crippled, the blind, and the lame" (v. 21). They gladly came, but there was still room. So the master sent the servant out of the city limits to invite everyone he could find. The banquet table was finally full, but not with the people first invited.

Both the Pharisees and Jesus knew that this was not just any banquet, but the banquet at the end of the ages; and more than that, it was a picture of the kingdom of God. This kingdom banquet was for everyone. The excuses in the story—buying land, buying oxen, and having just married—were close parallels to the reasons a person gave to excuse himself from holy war, as stated in Deuteronomy 20:5-7. But this was more than holy war, more than just any banquet. Not only was everyone invited, everyone was expected to come.

Again we can see the emphasis Jesus put on hospitality over tradition and on hospitality motivated by love instead of status. The master of the household stepped out of the traditional framework and out of his comfort zone to invite the uninvitable ones. He did not invite "the poor, the crippled, the blind, and the lame" (v. 21) because they would give him status, but because he wanted his table full. This, Jesus implied, was not only how hospitality should function, but this was also the essence of the messianic banquet, the messianic mission.

A Connection to Wealth

There are more layers of meaning. Every excuse given for not coming to the banquet has a direct connection to wealth or relationships. The purchase of a field or ten oxen represents a great financial investment. Marriage implies a relationship commitment. All three excuses reveal entanglements in possessions and relationships that close people off from God. They had been invited, they knew about the banquet, and they had probably agreed to come, but at the last minute they couldn't make it because they had other, greater commitments. Not urgent commitments, but commitments that represented their own interests over the call to the kingdom.

There is a connection between our relationship with God and our wealth. There is a connection between our ability to be hospitable and our wealth. When God calls us to come in and taste God's hospitality, do we have excuses? When God calls us to help extend that hospitality to others, do we have excuses? Do those excuses have anything to do with our wealth?

A Connection to Discipleship

The parable in Luke 14:15-24 is about hospitality, but it is also about discipleship. The call to join the banquet is a call to relinquish all possessions and all relationships that have taken priority over God. The banquet invitation must relativize all other claims on life. The event is so important that the excuses do not apply.

This connection grows stronger when seen in the context of the rest of Luke 14. Jesus continued the emphasis on discipleship with his stunning word about hating our families and even our own lives, about bearing our crosses, and about estimating the cost of building our discipleship tower before starting. We must give up other things to come to God's banquet. The reward is there, but so is the cost.

Christ's words about how to be hospitable were also words about how to be a disciple. God's call to hospitality is one of the specifics within the general call to discipleship. Hospitality is an essential part of being a disciple. It is a piece of the pie.

A Connection to God's Generosity

All this talk of discipleship makes biblical hospitality sound hard. Not only should we be hospitable to our neighbors, but we also have to be hospitable to everyone, especially "the poor, the crippled, the blind, . . .the lame" (Luke 14:21), and the weak. We are called to this arduous task, but we can't even do it to impress our church family. It's a mandate; it's a part of discipleship. We sigh with the heaviness of it all.

But back to the story. If we look beyond the excuses for not coming, and the persons who refused to come, we find the hedgerow people, the homeless people. They are staring, wide-eyed and open-mouthed, at a buffet that is beyond description. It's not just the food. It's the linen tablecloths, the fresh flowers, the crystal goblets, the music, and the laughter.

It's a party, and God is the host.

Before the discipleship comes the party. Before we have to find within ourselves some strength and right motivation for all this hospitality we are supposed to do, we go to this wonderful party, God's party. Look how many times a feast follows repentance. Jesus told a despised tax collector, Matthew, to follow him. That meant leaving behind all his money, his job, his status, everything. Where did they go? To a celebration party! (Matt. 9:9-11). The banquet is the end-time banquet, but it is also the best symbol for our relationship with God, a relationship that begins as soon as we drop the excuses and enter the door.

It is in that party that we find the strength and motivation to throw our own hospitality parties. As we experience God's generosity, that generosity flows through us, transforming us. We realize how much we are loved. That overwhelming love from God to us enables us, in small ways, be Christ the host to the poor and weak in our hedgerows.

In our hospitality, we reenact the kingdom. Christine Pohl says, "The motif of the meal together is the closest symbol of the kingdom."[2] Over and over, Jesus explained the gospel in terms of eating together, in terms of an invitation to a banquet. When we offer hospitality, especially to people who do not know the love of Christ, we begin to explain it to them, not only with our words, but also with actions that touch deep regions of the heart.

The Stuff of the Kingdom

It's Thursday, 5:30 p.m. Not quite the end of a long week, but I feel like celebrating anyway. Thursday nights are always fun because on Thursday nights we go out to eat. No, not Olive Garden. No, not Red Lobster. Not even Wendy's or McDonald's. No, Thursday night belongs to—Belmont.

A new one-of-a-kind restaurant? Hardly. It's the community room of Belmont Mennonite Church, an inner-city congregation in Elkhart, Indiana. It is one of a kind, but it will never get written up in a gourmet magazine. But on Thursday nights, it hops. Atmosphere that is out of this world (really), food that is fun, and service that is great.

It's usually sloppy joes at a serve-yourself table under fluorescent lights and Sunday school-classroom decor. But let me get back to the atmosphere part. Something special happens at Belmont on Thursday nights. Something that doesn't happen just anywhere. Something that truly is out of this world.

Usually the first ones in are the community folks. Many walk from their homes—a beautiful variety of young and old, dark-skinned and freckled, pigtails and rattails. The neighborhood. Maybe I shouldn't see some of these characteristics automatically, but I do. If you're here long enough, though, you begin to stereotype other characteristics too. Like how they know how to laugh and have fun. Like how loose they are with the stories of their lives. Like how the church people don't talk as freely about themselves.

The church people come a little later. I put myself in this category. We tend to walk in late because we just had an important meeting or phone call, or we were just relaxing with our kids. We aren't quite sure how to relate if we come early. We are not all uptight, at least not all of the time. But we all relax more after we get there.

The meal costs one dollar or two dollars depending on your age. The menu is simple—lasagna, grapes, iced tea—made by one of the community ladies. She stands behind the food, giving you bits of trivia about the recipe or about what all happened as she tried to get the food around this afternoon. Whatever the food is, it's in one big pot. Everyone partakes from the same big pot.

After getting your food and putting your money in the basket, you look for a table. Tables for six fill the long, narrow room. If you're smart, you pick a table with the community people. Those are the happening tables.

Every time I sit at a community table, I am sized up in thirty seconds and asked the most pertinent question of the day. Maybe I'm an easy read, but my neighborhood buddies seem to know me better than most of my acquaintances at work. Honesty is the ground rule, and I have learned better than to try to be somebody other than who I really am at these tables. As they say, "You can smell a fake a mile away."

Maybe that's why some people don't go to Thursday suppers at Belmont. It can be a little disconcerting. If you only sit with people you know from church, you feel like you are compromising. If you sit with people you don't know, people from the neighborhood, you may feel uneasy. You have to deal with the fact that you have more money than some of them do. That you live in different worlds. Not only do you have to sit with people who see things differently, but you also have to sit with the ugly stranger inside you who is uncomfortable with people who are different.

I am still one of those people, one of those with the ugly stranger inside. I am learning the hard way. I began coming to these dinners being so pleased with myself; I was the sacrificing minister who was going to bless these neighborhood folk with her presence.

Puhl-e-e-e-ase.

They are very patient with me as I work through this. They don't slam me when I am patronizing or when I pre-

tend that I'm just like them. They put up with the bravado, knowing that eventually I'll admit this experience
feels weird. Which, as you know, is the first step toward
making it feel normal.

They teach me how to laugh. They teach me how to
relax a little and just talk about the weather if there's nothing else to talk about. No one's taking notes on how great
the conversations are. They help me meet the ugly stranger
inside myself, come to terms with her, and make peace.

Now it's not all peaches and cream—or sloppy joes
and carrot sticks. Sometimes the conversation really is
boring, and sometimes the people I'm sitting with,
church or community, are whiny and irritating. There are
flies, and I hate flies around my food. My kids are running
around, acting squirrelly, and I can't concentrate on what
little good conversation there is. I start to think Olive
Garden thoughts.

But these are my people. This is where I belong.
People who were once strangers are becoming friends.
There is joy here, celebration here, joy that you're not
going to find at the Olive Garden—no matter how good
the bread sticks are.

In the mystery that is God, our simple meals become
banquets. Everyone is welcome, and there is deliberate
welcome for the ones deemed less worthy by the larger
society. Status boundaries are transcended, needs are
met, and wealth is shared. People begin to feel like family, sitting around the table together. And the host? The
host receives nothing more than the honor that only God
can give—the honor to one who has humbled himself.

This is the stuff of the kingdom.

Notes

1. Luke Timothy Johnson, *The Gospel of Luke* (Collegeville, Minn.: Liturgical Press, 1991), 226.
2. Christine Pohl in a lecture series on hospitality at the Associated Mennonite Biblical Seminary, Elkhart, Ind., February 18-19, 1998.

CHAPTER 8

Buying Friends

*You prepare a table before me in the presence
of my enemies; you anoint my head with oil;
my cup overflows. Surely goodness and
mercy shall follow me all the days of my life,
and I shall dwell in the house of the Lord
my whole life long. —Psalm 23:5-6*

I'm ashamed to say that I didn't want to put out the fine
china. It's not like I had to—there was no stipulation
that we dine in some fancy way. Yet I seemed to hear God
saying to me, 'Put out the fine china.' I was puzzled by
this. These were people who weren't used to fancy stuff. I
had no desire to impress them. But this was a special celebration. Every other time my family celebrated this kind
of thing, we got out the china. For anybody else, I wouldn't
have hesitated. But this time, I was hesitating.

"Why? Was I afraid their rowdy kids would break a gob-
let? Was I afraid of making them feel inferior by my fine
china? I thought and thought about this.

"I decided to treat them like I would my own family. I
realized I really was afraid of my things getting hurt. In my
mind I could see stains on my linen tablecloth, scratches
on my new dining room table, and dirty fingerprints on
my wallpaper. I didn't want my things ruined. I cared

about my things more than I cared about my guests. And I knew I'd never get over this unless I set that china out."[1]

"I didn't want my things ruined." I can empathize with those feelings. I have them myself. I remember the student who ruined the Life game I took for us to play together. I am her mentor in an inner-city school. I had given the game to my daughter Erin for Christmas. It was a precious possession to her, and she loaned it to me in faith that I would take care of it. The Life game represented something beyond itself to both of us. It got bent by a little girl who really didn't know better. At best, I have ambiguous feelings about taking the game to her. Should I leave all my nice stuff at home? Should I only share the things that are replaceable? The Life game is replaceable too, but it is the thought of it, the trust my daughter placed in me.

Hospitality involves sharing our possessions, sharing our wealth. Maybe that's why practicing true hospitality is so hard to do sometimes. There's no guarantee that our things won't get stolen, broken, and messed up. At best, we have to wash the bedsheets after our guests are gone. At worst, we pay higher electrical bills and need to replace the carpet. There will be a monetary cost to our hospitality in terms of food, transportation, and depreciation. We live in such an affluent society, but what if there isn't enough food to go around and enough money to cover the bills?

How are hospitality and money connected to each other? How does hospitality play into the overarching call to stewardship?

Using Your Money to Make Friends

Once I caught my daughter giving her money away. When I asked her why she was doing it, she said she was buying friends. Only her tender age of five years kept me from sheer panic. How did my daughter come up with that idea? Did she realize the harmful effects, the manipulative nature, and the self-esteem issues that emerge when people try to buy friendships? No, she just had some money and thought that would be fun to do. She had plenty of friends, she informed me, and if one can buy toys, she reasoned, why not friends?

Her idea is not so far off. Jesus made the same point in Luke 16:1-13. His parable was equally disturbing to his listeners. What was Jesus trying to say with his story of the dishonest steward?

The parable began with a rich man. He had a manager—a steward—who kept the books and was in charge of bill collecting and managing the rich man's possessions. The master discovered that his steward had mismanaged his funds. When confronted, the steward didn't defend himself; the allegations were true. The master fired him, but the master ordered him to get the books in order for the next manager's benefit.

That was a crisis for the steward. He knew he wasn't strong enough to dig ditches or do any other kind of manual labor. He was too proud to beg. No one else would hire him as a steward; his reputation was ruined. He looked down the long road of poverty and starvation. The journey did not look pleasant.

Suddenly it came to him. He knew what he had to do. Taking the books he was to get in order, he called in his master's debtors. "Quickly," he said to each one, "change the amount that you owe my master. Cut your bill in half!"

The debtors couldn't believe their good fortune. The steward counted his blessings too. His master's debtors were now indebted to him! According to the code of reciprocity, those debtors now owed him. He was due a share of their wealth, their friendship, and their hospitality.

He used the master's money to buy friends.

Christians throughout the years have scratched their heads over this parable. What is the application for today?

Was Jesus recommending that we be dishonest like the steward?

One scholarly approach suggests that the steward was only deducting the interest from the principle bill. Charging interest among the Jewish community was forbidden by Torah (Exod. 22:25; Lev. 25:36). The steward, then, was merely doing the right thing; the master was the dishonest one. Another view holds that the deductions were the steward's commission. He was not hurting the master, then, but only himself.

But Jesus called the steward dishonest. In his explanation after the parable, Jesus talked about trustworthy and untrustworthy individuals. The steward told the debtors to change their bills quickly. There was something shady going on. So what was Jesus trying to affirm in this story?

It was certainly not an affirmation of dishonesty. Jesus said, "Whoever is faithful in a very little is faithful also in much; and whoever is dishonest in a very little is dishonest also in much. If then you have not been faithful with the dishonest wealth, who will entrust to you the true riches? And if you have not been faithful with what belongs to another, who will give you what is your own?" (Luke 16:10-12). Those who do not use money with integrity here on earth will not get a chance to handle heavenly treasure. Everything depends on the quality of our hearts and our souls. Whether in small matters or large, our hearts will do the same thing. Our hearts are not divided. Being good stewards with *our* resources, resources that really belong to God, is essential.

But it's more than just using our money with integrity. Jesus was pushing his followers to use money and possessions shrewdly and wisely, with the same urgent purpose that the dishonest steward had—to buy a welcome, to buy our hospitality.

We *are* to use the Master's money to buy friends.

From Riches to Rags

Sound strange? Look at the next parable in Luke 16:19-31. Here we see two opposites—a rich man, opulent in purple linen, and Lazarus, a beggar with sores. The rich man feasted, not just at weddings and on special occasions, but every day. The only comfort Lazarus received came from unclean dogs that licked his painful sores. Every day Lazarus sat at the rich man's gate. Every day the rich man had an opportunity to show Lazarus hospitality, to use his wealth to welcome this poor beggar. Yet the days passed, and the rich man ignored Lazarus. He enjoyed his rich feasts alone.

Both men died, and both went to their eternal rewards. Lazarus rested in Abraham's lap, welcomed into perfect rest, peace, and abundance. The rich man, however, found himself in a torturous place, a place of burning and awful thirst. His was not a welcoming, hospitable home. He sat in hell.

At first glance, this scene looks like the great equalizer, nothing more. Those who receive "good things" during their lives will receive a torturous existence in the life to come, and those who suffer on earth will be received into abundance and blessedness in the afterlife. There are no other determining factors of morality.

A closer look suggests more complexity than the rich simply reaping suffering and the poor reaping eternal comfort. Seeing Lazarus in his bliss, the rich man called out to Abraham for mercy. He wanted Lazarus to touch his finger in water and bring even that little bit to cool his tongue. Later he asked Abraham to send Lazarus back to earth to talk to his brothers so that they might repent and avoid the torture he experienced. Here was a man who had not yet learned his lesson. The rich man still saw Lazarus as an inferior being, someone to use as a servant, someone who could fetch water or send a message back to earth. His heart was still as hard as stone.

The rich man did understand, however, that hearts could be changed. He realized that he did not land in hell simply because he was rich, but because he had not repented. His brothers, still alive, had that chance, especially if someone would go back from the dead and warn them. They still had a choice; their fate, like his, was not sealed by a mechanical reversal of rich becoming poor. They could still provide a welcome for themselves by showing hospitality to the poor among them.

And so can we. The words of Jesus ring true for us, too. We are to use our money, primarily through acts of hospitality, to ensure our eternal welcome. But will we? The rich man's brothers were unlikely to repent of their ways, said Abraham, even if Lazarus were to go back from the dead and witness to them. They already had all the evidence they needed through Moses and the prophets, whose words exhorted Israel to care for the poor. If those words were not convincing, a resurrected Lazarus would not be either.

Someone greater than Lazarus has been resurrected to carry this message. Will his words, his life, and the Holy Spirit working in us transform us so we will use our money to build the kingdom? We know that we are to use the Master's money to win friends and to provide hospitality for ourselves in eternity. Many times our use of the Master's money results in acts of hospitality. So we practice hospitality, not only as a response to God's hospitality to us, but also as a way to be welcomed in heaven. In practicing hospitality, we gain hospitality.

The Power of Money

Between the two parables about money and hospitality, Jesus made this emphatic statement: "You cannot serve God and wealth" (Luke 16:13). Some translations use the word *mammon,* which means "something to rely on." Here Jesus personified this sense of ultimate security as an idol. To serve this idol was a rejection of God. The Pharisees sneered at the idea that one cannot serve both God and mammon/money. They harkened back to their interpretation of Deuteronomy 28, where one is blessed financially if one obeys God. So Jesus continued the theme of idolatry with a key word: *abomination.* "You are those who justify yourselves in the sight of others; but God knows your hearts; for what is prized by human beings is an *abomination* in the sight of God" (Luke 16:15). In Deuteronomy *abomination* usually refers to idolatry. The Pharisees understood Jesus well. He was clear that something about money could make it an idol.

Jesus knew of a power that would try to win the hearts of his followers. That power would make them believe that the possessions they used were really theirs. That power would tempt them into believing they could serve God and the power side by side, with divided loyalties. Jesus also knew that the power could be so feared by believers that they would avoid using it for the glory of God.

Jesus understood the godlike power of money. It competes with God for control of human living. If we're not watching, it can begin to control us, become an idol for us, and be a master over us. This is true whether we have a lot of money or not much money at all.

Christians tend to view money in one of three ways— as evil, as good, or as neutral. All of these are harmful ways to look at money because they do not address its god-like power.

Some Christians see money as evil. Stay away from it, they say. Get rid of it. This idea of money as evil has biblical support, such as the story of the rich ruler in Luke 18. Other texts raise questions, however. What do you do with people like Abraham and Job? What do you do with the many rich Bible personalities who were faithful and with the many wealthy Christians today who are courageous ministers with their money? To hold something at arm's length is to fear it, and to fear something is to give it power—more power than it deserves. The parable of the dishonest steward emphasizes that our money and possessions are to be used, not feared, even if their use gets complex at times.

Other Christians see money as good. They give it the status of a god, not because they fear it so much as because they out-and-out worship it. The Pharisees in this Luke 16 narrative fit into this category. Jesus condemned them for believing that money, as opposed to God, brought them security and gave true meaning to life.

Most Christians view money as neutral. It's a tool, they say, just a piece of paper. It's what you do with it that counts. It *is* just a piece of paper, but it represents so much more. If you look past the paper to how we view and use money, it can't be neutral. To say that it is gives it even more power.

Money has a godlike power. It is power, security, and control. If you don't believe it, try burning a fifty-dollar bill. It's hard to do. You start to put the bill in the flames, and you think about everything that bill could buy and all the good that bill could do. You instinctively draw back. Just thinking about burning fifty dollars makes my stomach churn.

Mark Vincent proposes seven reasons why money threatens to unseat God from our life's throne. Knowing these reasons may help us in our struggle to be faithful.

1. Money outlives us.

Money was here before we arrived. Money will live on after we are dead. "You can't take it with you," we always say, but you can do some powerful things with it after you die if you leave some money behind with your name attached to it. You can give it to your children or your church. You are, in a limited way, immortal if you have money that will do things for you after you die. Even if you leave an anonymous gift, the gift still outlasts you.

2. Money's circle of influence is greater than ours.

Money goes places we cannot go. It touches people's lives in ways that we cannot touch. I have never had the opportunity to visit Japan, but I have a television and VCR built there. I've never been to Europe, but our mutual fund invests there. I've not yet visited Venezuela, but our family supports mission work there.

3. Money is mysterious.

There is something incomprehensible about the way money works. Economists are schooled in the science of educated guessing, little more than meteorologists of money. They monitor trends, production, interest rates, and GNP. They build models that predict what is to come with ever-increasing sophistication. But no one understands the whole. No one has the omniscience to get it right every time.

4. Because of the first three reasons, money occupies the realm of things we are tempted to worship.

Money resembles what we know about God. God outlives us and so does money. God is more powerful than we are and so is money. God is mysterious, as we know money to be. Humans are always tempted to worship the things that share those characteristics.

A quick check of human history shows that we have worshiped fertility, natural forces, death, governmental leaders, money, and God. Science and rationality have unlocked the mystery of most of these items with the exceptions of money and God. (Now, of course, we worship science and technology.) Science doesn't take away all the fear of things like death and tornadoes, but at least we no longer sacrifice our children to prevent them. But we just might sacrifice our family relationships or welfare in pursuit of a few extra dollars an hour. In our era, money remains a major competitor with God.

5. Money mimics everything God promises in the New Jerusalem.

It seems, on the surface, that money can get us every single promise that God has ever made us. Take, for example, the wonderful promises in Revelation 21—22. Here John describes a beautiful city coming down, the New Jerusalem. This city is full of jewels and gold; even the gates are made of pearls. A magnificent river, lined with trees bearing fruit twelve months of the year, flows through the city. God says there will be no more poverty, no more sickness, no more dying, and no more tears. It is a picture of beauty and abundance.

Money, we say, can give us all that here and now. Money can buy us jewels and pearls. Money can keep us well fed and well dressed. Money can even extend our lives with good health care. It would seem that we don't have to wait for the New Jerusalem to come down. We have it all right here and now.

But it's a trick. Money can buy a house, but not a home. Money can buy jewels, but not happiness. Money can buy food, but not laughter around the table. Education, but not purpose in life. Toys, but not a spirit of playfulness. Money can buy extended health, but not eternal life.

It's a trick.

6. Money is something you wield.

Money is capable of great good or great evil, sometimes at the same time. You can hurt and harm just by spending a dollar. For instance, you might subscribe to a cable or satellite system so you can learn to be a better gardener, but your entertainment provider also welcomes income it gets from carrying adult channels. Maybe you get your mortgage from a local bank because of your commitment to your community, but some of the investment decisions made by the bank board contradict your religious convictions. You might decide to participate in a boycott against an unscrupulous company that mistreats employees, but the first thing the company does when the boycott takes effect is lay off the workers you wish to help. In the end, you are the one who uses money, yet you cannot control all of the results. You wield money, and there is always something sloppy about it. Sometimes the money scalpel slips and becomes a sword.

7. Everything can be economized.

Whatever is pure, whatever is noble, whatever is right, even whatever is of good report—all have an economic cost. Do you wish to plant a church? There are expenses to do so. Do you want to send a missionary, train a pastor, form a choir, or spend time with your spouse to nurture your relationship? Do you want to be a musical family, read the work of a literary genius, or be hospitable? It costs you something. Money has many tentacles, and they are deeply wrapped around everything holy.[2]

The Test of Idolatry

Money is powerful. Jesus said that it is mammon—its power can rival God's. We will serve one at the other's expense. Just because we are Christians, we aren't immune to the temptation to revere money as a god. We are just as likely as our unchurched brothers and sisters to get in the stranglehold of the money god.

But as we practice biblical hospitality, as we let go of our possessions in our welcoming, we begin to shake the demon loose. We begin to be trustworthy in the "small things." We begin to see that we are just stewards instead of owners in the first place.

Hospitality helps dethrone the false money god.

The desert monks were famous for their hospitality. No one was turned away from their doors. Their welcoming had a direct correlation to their attitude about their possessions. According to Basil the Great, "The bread in your cupboard belongs to the hungry, the coat hanging unused in your closet belongs to the [person] who needs it, the shoes rotting in your closet belong to the [person] who has no shoes, the money you put in the bank belongs to the poor. You do wrong to everyone you could help but fail to help."[3]

For the desert monks, hospitality was the test for idolatry. To be free *from* possessions is to be open *with* them. If we really believe that our so-called possessions are God's and that God is our only source of security and joy, then it matters not whether we have possessions or go without. Our freedom from care has direct correlation with our freedom to share. Why not? We don't need the money to sustain our lives. God is doing that. If we really believe that God's love for the town drunk is our ultimate proof of God's love for us, we don't need our possessions to guarantee our worth either!

Hospitality helps dethrone the false money god. Through hospitality, we can take the godlike power of money and make that power work for God. Here's what Vincent's reasons look like when money is used in hospitable acts:

1. Money outlives us.

When we provide hospitality, we spend money on food and lodging needs. The food and electricity we buy to be welcoming is gone by the time the visit is over, but the love the purchases represent may last forever. The relationships, the miracles that happen as a result of our hospitality, have a lasting effect. "The food I gave her didn't even last the weekend. But the friendship we forged will last forever."[4]

2. Money's circle of influence is greater than ours.

Many times we give such simple gifts, gifts that cost us very little. But when we give them in the name of Jesus, something happens. God takes those small gifts and multiples their worth. "All I gave was a couple dollars. It was nothing. I didn't really feel like I was hospitable at all. Yet those few dollars meant the world to him."[5]

3. Money mimics everything God promises in the New Jerusalem.

Money and the possessions we buy with money are shallow imitations of the riches God can give us. When we use our money in ways that honor God, however, God takes our small physical offerings and uses them to help bring about the New Jerusalem. God uses them to bring shalom, to bring salvation. "The funny thing is that all I gave was some money for his transportation. But because I gave it with prayer, with a desire to do God's will, the bus fare turned into something that eventually brought salvation. What happened to him and to me was much more important than him getting where he needed to go. It was his salvation."[6]

4. Money is something you wield.

Money can be used for great evil or, at the very least, it

can contribute to some complex ethical situations. But choosing *not* to use money for this reason also carries great power. "It's all a matter of being at the right place at the right time. I think I was looking for an opportunity to minister to someone because of the Forty-Day Experiment. I have opened my home to (and fixed dinner for) people before, and they never talked about suicide. I could have easily said no to her coming. But my simple dinner led to her opening up about her feelings [of suicide]. What if I hadn't obeyed?"7

5. Everything can be economized.

"Always before I had talked to her. Now I couldn't. I just didn't have time. I felt kind of guilty, but without sacrificing my family, what could I do? So I just stopped over and delivered a lace collar. The only hospitality I could do that day was this thing I had bought. But you know what? Later, I find out that she loves lace collars and collects them. She cried over my gift. And I cried, realizing that the Holy Spirit prompted me to buy this simple thing. That doesn't mean I should only buy things for people and not talk to them. But God worked through my gift."8

The Priestly Role

God does work through our gifts. God wants us to use our money and possessions in ways that build bridges between people and God. We are to use the Master's money to buy friends for God. To create access.

Creating access to God is the priestly role. The Levites in the Old Testament interceded with God on behalf of the people. With their offerings and sacrifices, they formed the bridge. They did it imperfectly, but it was an important role. The dishonest steward was also acting as a priest, though in a secular way. Through his cleverness, even though it was dishonest, he brought the debtors and

the master together. He made it possible for the debtors
to pay their bills. He introduced them to the generosity of
the master, even though the master was not intending to
be generous. The steward was creating access.

Our Master intends to be generous. His generosity was
so great that he himself became the sacrifice, the gift. By
giving away the Master's money and love, we extend that
generosity. We connect the debtors to God.

"But you are a chosen race, a royal priesthood, a holy
nation, God's own people, in order that you may proclaim
the mighty acts of him who called you out of darkness
into his marvelous light. Once you were not a people, but
now you are God's people; once you had not received
mercy, but now you have received mercy" (1 Pet. 2:9-10).
Peter reminds us of our new identity. He calls us the royal
priesthood. Like the Levites of the former times, we are to
create access to God for the ones around us. We are to
build the bridges. We are to be like the dishonest steward,
only so much better, for we are to buy friendships not for
our own sakes, but for the sake of those we meet.

That's why we hold our money and possessions so
freely. We don't give out of a sense of duty or obligation.
That motivation is a short-lived and heavy burden. We
don't give just because we're on some spiritual high,
which is fine in itself but is also short-lived. We give
because of who we are. We give because we are priests for
God. Our hospitality grows out of our identity.

When our hospitality grows out of our identity, some
good things start happening. We don't have to worry
about being manipulative in our giving or about whether
we have the right motivations. It doesn't matter if our hospitality looks unsuccessful by the world's standards. It
doesn't matter if we see no results. As we begin to hold
our possessions lightly, we begin to dethrone the false
money god. In doing so, we force ourselves to rely more

and more on God, until it doesn't matter whether we have possessions at all. We do make new friendships, but not so we will receive reciprocal hospitality from those we serve. Most likely, we will be hospitable to those who have nothing to offer us in return (Matt. 25:31-46). But what a welcome we will have in heaven when we see the ones for whom we built the bridges waiting for us there!

As we give in hospitality, we break free from mammon. As we give in hospitality, we create friends in "high places." As we give in hospitality, we are transformed into a new identity, into the priestly role, a role that sets us free from duty and obligation and the need to feel just right before we give.

Some early Christian monks understood this well. "Abba Macarius, returning to his cell, finds his goods being stolen. Thereupon he helps the thief load the wagon, and, with complete tranquillity, waves as the thief drives away with all his earthly possessions. When asked, he simply quotes 1 Timothy 6:7: 'We brought nothing into the world, and we cannot take anything out of the world.' Then there is Abba Euprepius, in discovering that the thieves robbing his cell have overlooked something, he runs after them, giving it to them as a gift."[9]

Hospitality can set us free. Free from being possessive with our possessions. Free from the stranglehold of the money god. Free from energy-draining motivations.

Free to not worry about the china.

Notes

1. Excerpt from the Forty-Day Experiment journals.
2. Mark Vincent, "The Power of Money," unpublished essay.
3. Quoted by Robert M. Brown, *Spirituality and Liberation* (Louisville, Ky.: Westminster Press 1988), p. 93.
4. Excerpt from the Forty-Day Experiment journals.
5. Ibid.
6. Ibid.
7. Ibid.
8. Ibid.
9. Douglas Burton-Christie, *Word in the Desert* (New York: Oxford, 1993). Quoted in W. Paul Jones, "Hospitality Within and Without," Weavings 9 (February 1994): 228.

CHAPTER 9

Breaking Down Barriers

Now a bishop must be above reproach, married only once, temperate, sensible, respectable, hospitable, an apt teacher.
—1 Timothy 3:2

There comes a time when hospitality gets complicated. It's more than expecting surprises, good or otherwise. It's the kind of thing you don't expect at all. It's the phone call at three in the morning. The enemy at the threshold of your door. You're standing there in your stocking feet, stunned. Caught off guard. Beyond surprise.

These are the times when God calls you to a hospitality that goes a step beyond tuna sandwiches and tea. There's something deeper, something bigger going on. This act of hospitality, should you accept the call, would shake up the status quo. It would challenge the powers that be. It would upset the social structure.

Even more, it would shake up—you.

Sometimes God uses hospitality to go a step beyond providing food and lodging for strangers. God uses hospitality to break down barriers of injustice. What do you do when the enemy is at your door?

"On our front door is a plaque that reads 'Peace to all who enter here.' One night that statement was challenged. At two in the morning, we heard a thump in the living room just outside our bedroom door. As we awoke, we saw that the living room light was on, and we knew someone was there. As Ray opened the door and looked out, he saw a man hurriedly leaving through the front door. Ray waited a moment to make sure no one else was in the house, then ventured out to the front porch. He could see no sign of the man or a car. The TV was gone, and the stand knocked over. The police came quickly in answer to our call, but no trace of anyone could be found.

"How did we feel? Surprisingly calm, collected—and above all, thankful. Not only was there peace on the door, but peace was in our hearts as we reflected on the unwelcome and unexpected guest. Although he came to take from us, he did not come to harm us. Our insurance bought us a new TV and a new front door. But most important we experienced once again the gracious care of the One who is both giver and caretaker of all we are and have."[1]

Guess Who's at the Door

Philemon also had to decide what to do with an enemy at the door. Before this moment, he thought he had seen it all. As the gracious host of a house church in Colossae (Philem. 2), he had known some really strange situations. Hosting gave him the opportunity to show hospitality in many settings—to strangers who might be spies, to itinerant preachers, and to the Sabbath gathering every week. He lived up to the task; he had a reputation as a refresher of souls (v. 7) and a beloved brother whose love and generosity were well known (v. 5).

Philemon's ministry was so important that Paul referred to him as one of his partners. The word *partner* here was not a lightly used term. It implied an almost formal arrangement where local hosts partnered with Paul in his itinerant ministry. Paul counted on these hosts to supply lodging and food, with a clear understanding that their role was as essential as his was in spreading the gospel.[2]

Philemon was a great host. He knew the significance of hospitality and had committed himself to this ministry. His generous heart welcomed everyone who came to his door.

Until now.

For now, standing at the door, dripping wet and shivering with cold, was his fugitive slave Onesimus. Philemon stepped back, stunned. Whatever kept his voice from calling some other servant to come and tie up Onesimus, he'd never know. But part of it was the shock. Didn't this slave realize that he could be killed for leaving? Philemon had long ago given up hope of ever seeing this man again, and now here Onesimus stood in the doorway.

Anger flashed through Philemon. The whole town laughed at him for losing this no-good slave. He sat up nights worrying about the other slaves running too. The grief Onesimus brought him, the frustration! And now he was *here?*

Onesimus extended his hand. In it was a letter. "From Paul," he whispered, not daring to glance up.

Onesimus in Elkhart

I am not as well known as Philemon for my hospitality. "Refresher of souls" is not the first phrase given to describe me. I feel more comfortable with the identity of peace advocate. I have not done everything, or even close to everything I could do to change unjust structures, protest war, and work for peace, but I have done my share. I understand the significance of peace work and have committed myself to this ministry. There wasn't an enemy I couldn't love.

Until now.

The phone rang in my new little office. I was proud of my office. I had been there only three weeks, and things were already beginning to make sense and feel like home. My family and I had moved from Oregon to Indiana—a big move, especially for my daughters. But we were adjusting so well. Everything was going so smoothly.

The phone rang again. The call was from my husband, Del. The new little office suddenly looked dreary and foreboding. Someone had beat up Tara, our oldest daughter, at school.

We tried not to panic. She was not hurt badly. It appeared to be a random act of violence. She was a new kid in an inner-city school. We tried to figure out what happened. Maybe she was doing something offensive unintentionally because she didn't understand her new cultural setting. Maybe this was a freak incident that wouldn't happen again.

Two days later it did. The same girl waited for Tara to get off the bus, threw her down on the ground, and started kicking her in the head. Teachers were right there and stopped the girl as fast as they could, but Tara was shaken to the core of her being, and so were Del and I.

Tara and Erin did not want to go to school. They had nightmares of being attacked on the playground; they dreaded getting off the bus. I felt an overwhelming sense of hatred in my heart.

Back in Colossae

Philemon was known for his hospitality. It was his gift, his specialty. But now the screw turned. Philemon, the expert in hospitality, was bidden to receive his own runaway slave. The letter Onesimus handed him asked for this welcoming. But to welcome a man who had greatly wronged him?

I prided myself on my ability to love my enemy, but now I actually had one. Could I learn to love and forgive?

The letter Onesimus held came from the apostle Paul, who at that very moment sat in a prison in Rome. In his flight away from Philemon, Onesimus had found Paul. Was he *trying* to find him? Possibly he knew about the Christian faith from hearing Paul speak. Perhaps he was anxious to meet this Christian named Paul because of the faith in action that he had seen in Philemon.

So why did he run away if Philemon was such a good Christian master? Was there a relationship problem between the two, or did Onesimus rashly steal something or misappropriate funds and then feel like he had to flee? We don't know, but he did flee. And in his flight, he found Paul.

Philemon looked at the letter in his hand. Paul knew it would be difficult for Philemon to forgive Onesimus and to accept him back. The letter was Paul's intercession for Onesimus. Knowing this, Philemon opened the letter. While primarily addressed to him, it was meant to be read in front of the whole congregation. At first glance, this letter looked similar to other letters Paul had written. But there was a different nuance here—something between the lines. The excessive politeness made Philemon chuckle. What was Paul up to? His letter exuded a softness, a mixture of pressure and pleading that touched Philemon's soul.

Paul spoke of Philemon's love for all the saints and his act of refreshing the hearts of the believers. Then, getting to the point of the letter, Paul reminded Philemon of his authority over him: "For this reason, though I am bold enough in Christ to command you to do your duty, yet I would rather appeal to you on the basis of love" (Philem.

8-9). Later, Paul stated that he would not remind Philemon of the debt that he owed him. Of course, in mentioning what he would not do, he brought the debt to Philemon's attention. But here again, the reminder of the debt, like the offhand reminder of Paul's authority, was a light touch. Paul was sending Onesimus back with no guarantee for the slave's safety from Philemon: "But I preferred to do nothing without your consent, in order that your good deed might be voluntary and not something forced" (v. 14). He made it clear that the decision was in Philemon's hands.

I too was treated with gentleness. I sat in my Christian peacemaking and spirituality class at seminary and squirmed as I heard about the connections between personal spirituality and our love for the enemy. Finally, in tears, I told the class what had happened. I told them about my feelings of hatred and that I was not ready to do anything yet but hate this child I had never met. I felt guilty for my inability to forgive her, but my classmates put their arms around me, prayed for me, and affirmed my honesty. Give it time, they said.

Philemon continued to read the letter: "I am appealing to you for my child, Onesimus" (v. 10). Philemon had to chuckle again. Paul was shrewd to wait as long as he could to state the slave's name, to get to the heart of the matter. But Paul's intent was no surprise to him; Onesimus was standing right before him.

The surprise, though, was in the way Paul described Onesimus. "My child" and later on "my own heart" were terms of endearment Paul used. Something must have changed, Philemon thought as he looked at Onesimus. "I am appealing to you for my child, Onesimus, whose father I have become during my imprisonment" (v. 10). Onesimus had become a Christian. Onesimus was now a brother in the Lord.

The identity change went even deeper. "Formerly he was useless to you, but now he is indeed useful both to you and to me" (v. 11). Paul was playfully using the name *Onesimus* as a pun here. *Onesimus* meant "useful." This slave, for whatever reason, had become useless to Philemon. But now, through Christ, Onesimus had become useful again, both to Paul and Philemon.

Philemon could easily visualize how Onesimus was useful to Paul. He was undoubtedly Paul's legs and hands while Paul sat in prison. Perhaps he even spoke on Paul's behalf during evangelistic meetings. But how could this runaway be useful to Philemon and, as the letter went on to say, even more dear and useful than before?

How Could She Be Useful to Me?

That was the essence of the question that weighed heavy on my mind. What would I do with this situation? How could any good come out of it? How could I get rid of the lump of hatred that gnawed at my soul?

I knew I had to meet the girl who had beaten up Tara. I had to put a face to the name. I had to come face-to-face with the source of my hatred. She's just a little girl, I thought. How hard could it be? So I set up an appointment to meet her. I had no intention at that time of ever taking her into my home or in any way being hospitable to her. That was asking too much. But another idea was forming in my mind and in my prayers.

"Have you ever considered being this girl's mentor?" a good friend of mine asked me. The logic was so clear. "You have hateful feelings toward her. These are feelings you will never get rid of unless you get to know her as a person," she said, and then more gently, "until you can see her as someone God loves."

I was nervous as I waited in the office. The social worker was there too, in case things got too scary for either of us. Then she walked in—a fifth-grade girl, almost my height and strong enough to take me down, a girl who could not look me in the eyes. "Sondra,"(not her real name). I spoke her name. "I'm Michele."

There was no response. I looked at the social worker, who nodded for me to continue. But I didn't know what to say. I prayed a quick prayer and plunged in. "Sondra, I know you don't know me. I'm Tara's mom. I'm here because—well, I have some pretty hard feelings toward you for beating up Tara. But Jesus told me—do you know about Jesus?"

She nodded her head.

"Well, Jesus told me that I must love the people that I—really dislike, so that's why I'm here. I can't love you like I want to unless I get to know you. And I want to learn to love you, Sondra. Will you let me be your mentor, your special friend? We could see each other every week. Sondra, could I be that kind of friend to you?"

There was a long silence. Then Sondra looked straight at me and said, "Yes."

The Greater Good

Philemon found himself staring at a new man. He looked like the old Onesimus, but the letter said he was a different man, different in the same way that he himself was after Christ transformed him.

When I first looked at Sondra, I saw a new person too. I had never seen her before, but I had imagined her as some dehumanized creature, some beast who went around attacking people. But she was just a girl with deep, sad eyes.

Just being faced with a new reality was not enough for Philemon. Gently persuading, Paul continued with his reasons why Philemon should take back his slave Onesimus, not only without punishment, but as a brother in the Lord as well. It was for the greater good, Paul reasoned. "Perhaps this is the reason he was separated from you for a while, so that you might have him back forever, no longer as a slave, but more than a slave, a beloved brother" (vv. 15-16). The slave's wrongdoing and flight from Philemon, here positively described as his separation, brought about his salvation as he met Paul. Paul didn't excuse the wrongdoing, but he asked Philemon to see the wrongdoing in a different light. God used the circumstances for greater good. Through his experience, Onesimus began a relationship with God. It was such a complete and dramatic conversion that he even came back to Philemon.

God also used the situation to bring about good for Philemon. Now Onesimus returned to Philemon as a brother in Christ—not just as a slave or even a repentant slave. What this meant in terms of Onesimus's slavery is uncertain. Did Paul ask Philemon to free him or just to forego punishment? The difference is less important than we may think. Even if Onesimus were freed, he was not economically free to leave Philemon. Without resources of his own, Onesimus probably would have remained, even as a freed man, under Philemon's care and as little more than a servant.

The real benefit to both Philemon and Onesimus was that their new relationship superceded all social barriers. Whether Onesimus remained Philemon's slave or not, the way they treated each other would change. That was Paul's goal. The options were clear. Philemon could free Onesimus or just take him back as a slave and a brother. But Paul was clearer still; he wanted Philemon's heart to change. He wanted Philemon to see Onesimus as his equal and as his brother in Christ. Paul wanted Philemon's heart to break open to a new level of understanding and a new level of being.

When my daughter was beaten up, my first reactions were to escape the situation. Should we send our daughters to a private school? We had the resources, if we decided we really wanted to do that. Even meeting Sondra did not immediately make it clear what we should do. My nightmares and feelings of hatred got worse right after I met her. Now in my dreams at night, I could actually visualize the face of the one beating up my daughter.

But as I established my mentoring relationship with Sondra, as we began a friendship built on trust and genuine care for each other, I could glimpse God's greater good. I don't believe that God caused my daughter to experience the pain she did, but God used that negative situation to transform Sondra.

God used that negative situation to transform me.

Hospitality Has a Price

Paul, knowing that every act of hospitality had an economic element, used the business language of the day. "So if you consider me your partner," he said, "welcome him as you would welcome me" (v. 17). Here he was referring to a *societas,* a trust that Paul and his supporters pledged to each other. It was a contractual agreement stating that everyone involved gave property, possessions, time, and talent toward some common goal—in this case, spreading the gospel. Everyone benefited. Because Christ was a part of this fellowship, this *koinonia,* Christ multiplied the benefits. Somehow, in a mysterious way, this partnership implied Christ's presence, creating a synergy that was otherwise unexplainable. Paul proposed that this partnership go into effect in this situation. Because Paul and Philemon were partners, Paul could ask for hospitality from Philemon. That hospitality was to be given to Paul through Onesimus.

As a partner, Paul could also ask for the entire matter

of Onesimus, outstanding debts and all, to be charged to his account. It seemed to be a ludicrous offer, considering that Paul was a wandering tentmaker in prison at the time. To balance everything up, however, there was that little matter of Philemon owing his very life to Paul. Philemon had to laugh again. But Paul was serious about paying the debt. He wrote this part of the letter with his own hand, as legally binding. He understood that hospitality, on both a physical and a spiritual level, had economic ramifications. If Philemon were to free Onesimus, what did that mean financially?

I too feel the cost of my hospitality to Sondra. Weekly trips to Dairy Queen with three girls add up. But the cold cash is easy to give up compared to my time. Invariably, some crisis at work makes me question whether I really can give an hour to Sondra. Yet even here, the mysterious presence of Christ multiplies the benefits. There is always enough time. Sometimes I even find time to spare.

Breaking Down Barriers

Paul was about the business of breaking down barriers. He was not openly debunking the whole institution of slavery, though the injustice and pain of this slave's situation were real for him. He asked one man to do the right thing, even to free this slave. Paul asked Philemon to change his heart toward Onesimus. He asked Philemon to see Onesimus in a new way. But they both knew that if Philemon accepted this call from Paul, this call from God, it would abolish slavery—though maybe not during that century or the next. In the deepest part of who they were, they knew that if Philemon forgave Onesimus and accepted him as a brother in Christ, the slavery in Philemon's house would come undone. Dignity and equality would mark their relationship, and that would have ripple effects throughout the household. It would be a new era in this household, where slavery would not carry its sting, where even the less radical social arrangement of patron and client would soften. It would be the beginning of the end, the kingdom of God among them.

"When you value the least ones in our society, you shake up the system," says Christine Pohl. "When you receive them as worthy individuals, those who have been labeled unworthy by society, you participate in a counter-cultural act. By your hospitality you make them visible. Before they were invisible, so the injustice being done to them was invisible."[3]

Paul could have demanded that Onesimus return to Rome to help him in Philemon's place. He could have kept Onesimus with him and sent the letter through another messenger. But Paul was about the business of breaking down barriers and healing relationships. The real issue was not so much slavery as it was reconciliation between brothers. But that reconciliation was the first big step toward tearing down the institution of slavery.

God was about the business of breaking down my barriers too. I could have limited my number of visits with Sondra and called it good. I did my duty. I could have given money to some inner-city organization that helped people like her. But God wanted to help me too. God wanted to change my whole worldview. God wanted me to see this girl and the others in her neighborhood through different eyes, to see them as "beloved sons and daughters" like God does.

And I do. I love Sondra. Our relationship is rocky at times. Sometimes I want to give up in utter frustration. I see only the failures, the overwhelming hopelessness of a home life filled with physical abuse, neglect, and drugs. And like Philemon, I'm scared of what this means for me. Now that I've taken the heart of this child as my own, I also have to step into the pain. I must open myself to the hopelessness. I can't just walk away—ever.

I see the world differently because of her.

From my mentoring relationship, a mentoring program began at Associated Mennonite Biblical Seminary in Elkhart, Indiana. Students and staff spend time each week with local elementary-school children. We work with violent children that no other mentoring program will accept. We practice hospitality as we read with them at school, take them to Dairy Queen, and even bring them into our homes. We visit the principal when they are suspended. We attend the awards ceremony when they get "Most-Improved-Attitude" for the first time. And we see the world differently. We receive from these children more than we give. We confront the stranger in ourselves, the stranger called racism. We conquer the fears inside us for our own children, the fears that the world truly is falling apart for lack of love.

The mentoring program at the seminary will not abolish racism or discrimination against poor people. Sometimes I wish it could do that and fast. I get as frustrated with my own ministry as I do with Paul for not condemning slavery right out. But when we meet with these children, we begin a process that nothing can stop.

Hospitality as the Means to a Very Good End

For Philemon the first step was hospitality: "Welcome him, as you would welcome me." See him, said Paul, as you see me. Paul was seeking forgiveness for Onesimus. He wanted Philemon to see his slave differently and form a new relationship with him. Those requests were the weightier matters for Paul, the real goals. The medium he used to achieve these goals, however, was hospitality. The new equality of brother to brother, whether Onesimus was freed or not, played itself out in hospitality.

The same is true for us. Hospitality is an effective vehicle for stopping injustice and confronting racism. Our welcoming puts teeth into our words and into our living. If the convictions aren't quite there yet, our acts of hospitality foster the very heart changes we need to make. Forgiveness, reconciliation, and the breakdown of social barriers imply hospitality. In turn, hospitality can help nurture our fledgling forgiveness, reconciliation, and fight against prejudice.

Our hospitality breaks down barriers more effectively when we are intentional in these ways. Following the example of Philemon, we need to first practice our hospitality in community, and second, to pay close attention to the balance of our values and the needs of our guests.

1. Hospitality in community.

Paul addressed Philemon in the midst of his community. In his letter, Paul referred to other members of his family and to the household of faith; the letter was intended to be read at their next meeting. Others were to know of the request Paul made, especially the other slaves who would be present for that reading. What would they choose to do? Would Philemon lose his means of supporting himself and his family? The church family had to wrestle with the economic ramifications of Philemon's decision. Would the congregation support him if he chose to free this slave or if the others left him too?

Philemon had a tough decision to make, and Paul insisted that it be made and followed through *in community*. The fact that Philemon could not make a private decision may sound manipulative to our modern, individualistic ears, but Paul knew what he was doing. Changes that break down barriers are not made easily and do not come without a cost, both economic and otherwise. The decisions about to whom we offer hospitality and to what extent are hard ones to make. Community was a vital link for Philemon in his hospitality ministry. It provided safety, discernment, and accountability.

Hospitality in the midst of community happens frequently in the biblical narrative. Many times in the Old Testament, strangers were met by the city gate, a public place where safety was more guaranteed (1 Kings 17:10). Safety was not the only issue. Community helped provide the resources needed for hospitality. When three servants of Cornelius visited Peter (Acts 10:21), Peter needed to give them food and lodging. But he was a guest of Simon the Tanner. The relationship between Simon and Peter was so well established that Peter the guest could easily transition into Peter the host. Community worked as a partner with the host.

"We can't effectively practice biblical hospitality outside the context of community," says Christine Pohl.[4] God's abundance is most fully experienced in community. That abundance is clearly needed in hospitality. In a world bent on a scarcity mentality, where everyone grabs for oneself because there's not enough to go around, God's abundance says there is plenty for all. In a world where strangers are viewed as potential threats, God provides a family of believers who supply safety and discernment. In a world where hospitality costs money and effort, God's abundance flows as the community shares the burden of care for the stranger.

2. The balance between our values and the needs of our guest.

A second concern in providing hospitality is the tension between being open to our guests and preserving our own values and identity. For Philemon, his welcoming of Onesimus challenged his understanding of his rights as a slave owner. He knew he should treat this man well, but how well? Should he welcome him unconditionally?

Should he confront him with his wrongdoing? Would Onesimus steal again? Should he merely forgive the debts Onesimus owed, or should he hold him accountable?

My dilemma with Sondra pressed the same questions. How much should I let her socialize with my daughters? Were my children safe? At first, Tara set the boundaries firmly; I could meet with Sondra, but she was not to come to our house. Those boundaries softened eventually, at Tara's request. Sondra was welcome at our house or the three of us went to the mall together or sat in the park and talked.

Boundaries continue to be an issue, however. Sometimes Sondra lies to me. She lost her library books and failed to show up when she promised she would. I don't know when to treat her like a special guest in my home and when to tell her to stop ruining everything in my house. I know I need to be open to her way of doing things and to love her more than my things. But sometimes I feel like a doormat that she uses to wipe her feet. Because she is a child, I usually move quickly to a parent role. Here hospitality means helping her learn some proper behaviors. Sondra is blessed with the gift of sorting out her own values in a safe place because I present her with my values, and at the same time, I communicate to her that she is loved for who she is.

Some situations are not so easy to discern. When smokers visit a nonsmoker's home, what does hospitality mean in terms of their habits? Is it hospitable to lovingly help them quit a dangerous habit? No smoking signs and annoying glares aren't welcoming. Yet if we really care about them, can we ignore the threat to their health? What difference does it make if they are strangers passing through or our family members?

How welcome do visitors really feel at our church? Is it okay if they want to introduce a new way of worship?

When should the church be open to change, and when is the change too threatening to its identity as the royal priesthood?

The whole concept of hospitality is built around the idea that we are not to own, but to serve each other and to create the space where guests can feel at home with us and with themselves. This means that we must be receptive to them. Reaching out to others without being receptive brings more harm than good. When we say, "You can be my guest if you believe what I believe and do what I do," we offer hospitality at a price. That isn't a true welcome.

But, Henri Nouwen says, "receptivity is only one side of hospitality."[5] The other side is confrontation. Being receptive doesn't mean that we become doormats, allowing guests to do anything they want to our homes or to us. True welcoming space has to have boundaries, for everyone's sake. Welcoming our guests while hiding who we really are and what our values are is like welcoming our guests to an empty house. They get to do anything they want, but it's lonely. There's no point of reference, no one to talk to, no one to bounce ideas off of, and no point of orientation. It begins to feel like a ghost house. Says Nouwen,

> When we want to be really hospitable, we not only have to receive strangers, but also to confront them by an unambiguous presence, not hiding ourselves behind neutrality but showing our ideas, opinions, and lifestyle clearly and distinctly. No real dialogue is possible between somebody and a nobody. We can enter into communication with the other only when our life choices, attitudes, and viewpoints offer the boundaries that challenge strangers to become aware of their own position and to explore it critically.[6]

There must be both receptivity and confrontation, and they must be balanced carefully with love. Flexibility is called for, and two different guests may call for two different responses on the same issue. The Holy Spirit must be our guide as we extend our welcome.

A Vehicle for Change

This balance of receptivity and confrontation found in hospitality is an effective way to work with controversial issues in the church. What would it mean to highly value the ideological strangers in our midst? How would we talk about things differently if we saw those strangers as guests—guests who need both freedom to be and the chance to hear our values and boundaries? If we practiced hospitality principles, such as nurturing ourselves in God *and* listening to the guest, challenging the status quo *and* allowing the guest to be host and bring us a gift, wouldn't we break new ground in speaking the truth with love?

At the very least, we would begin to value the process. Hospitality implies process. You don't know what the guest will do, you can't control the situation, and there's always give and take. The guest is supposed to bless you as well as receive from you. The guest can be, must be, loved by you without needing to be just like you. The joy and blessing of hospitality, the truth of hospitality, comes not from some end result, but from the experience itself. In the actual process, *koinonia* happens, Christ is present, and the gifts multiply. Surprise.

The experience of young adults in our churches is a case in point. Many in this age group are testing the faith of their childhood. They question the traditions and the theology that before they took for granted. This is an important process which, if successful, reshapes the faith handed to them and makes it their own. But the questioning itself pushes the boundaries of church identity. What does it mean to be hospitable to these young adults?

"On certain issues, I'm just quiet," says one young adult. "I have questions about Jesus and God and the infallibility of Scripture, but those are things I can't bring up in church, except in my Sunday school class, because some people would come unglued. I'm not where they're at, but I sense that if I don't conform, I'm out. I don't want to be out. I just want time and a safe place to work on these issues in my mind."

One North American conference on young adults compared the church to a refrigerator. The questions posed for the larger church were these: "Are young adults allowed to go to the fridge and take whatever they want to eat? Or is the fridge off limits? Is there anything worthwhile in the fridge?" In my own house, I get irritated when my eleven-year-old offers our fridge to her friends without limits. I know that soon, very soon, I will just be glad they're at my house—period. One must be a comfortable guest to open up the host's refrigerator. This action symbolizes a move toward ownership. But the young adults don't want an empty fridge either. They really prefer home cooking. They like having the hosts around more than we may think.

There are no easy answers. Flexibility without loss of Christian identity is key. Sometimes boundaries must change because of the needs of the young adults. Sometimes liberality is called for. Sometimes the most loving thing to do is to set boundaries. Each person calls for a different response. Each is a special guest. This doesn't mean that truth changes. It's just that the truth is so much deeper than a black-and-white, right-or-wrong answer. There is truth in the process too. We arrive at truth by going through the process. We are called to hospitality, which means being receptive and confronting—all for the sake of our guest.

Hospitality breaks down barriers. That is the deep nerve that hospitality touches. Hospitality is a concrete response to the enemy at the door or to the enemy at church. The answers are never easy, but the framework for hammering out the answers is. Practice in community. Practice both receptivity and confrontation.

And most important, says Paul, welcome them as you would—Christ.

Notes
1. Excerpt from the Forty-Day Experiment journals.
2. John Koenig, *New Testament Hospitality: Partnership with Strangers as Promise and Mission* (Philadelphia: Fortress Press, 1985), p. 79.
3. Christine Pohl in a lecture series on hospitality at the Associated Mennonite Biblical Seminary, Elkhart, Ind., February 18-19, 1998.
4. Ibid.
5. Henri Nouwen, *Reaching Out: The Three Movements of the Spiritual Life* (Garden City, N.Y.: Doubleday, 1975), p. 69.
6. Ibid., p. 70.

CHAPTER 10

Two Sides of the Same Coin

*Welcome one another, therefore, just as
Christ has welcomed you, for the glory of
God. —Romans 15:7*

What happens when we welcome them "as you would welcome me" (Philem. 17)? What surprises await our guests and us when, in the name of Christ, we show hospitality? We know from the Scriptures and from our own personal experiences that we meet the Christ in the strangers we welcome. God, the ultimate Stranger, visits our homes and hearts as we invite in the strangers among us. Can the inverse also be true? Can our guests see Jesus in us in a way made clearer by our hospitality? If our hospitality can be a link connecting people to Jesus, then our small acts of welcoming take on new meaning. For some of our guests, this would be a first-time introduction. What a truly delightful surprise to be a small part of connecting our guests with the Supreme Host, the one whose welcome never ceases to refresh!

"During the Forty-Day Experiment, I got a call from a young woman who expressed interest in volunteering with our church's tutoring program. We talked for awhile on the phone, and she mentioned that she had just moved into town from Canada. I asked her if she had found a church home since she moved to Meridian. She said, 'No,' with a tone in her voice that said, 'I didn't know I was supposed to be looking for one.'

"I invited Cindy to come by the church and look around the tutoring program and visit awhile.

"She came one afternoon and met the tutoring program director. She saw the church: sanctuary, office, nursery, and the whole thing. I invited her to worship services.

"'I'm kind of angry with God right now,' she said. 'I don't know when I was last in church.' She mentioned that since her husband's death, she had a lot of questions about God. As I looked at her, I felt great sadness. She was so young to be a widow. She was so far from home. What had life been like for her?

"Cindy told me about her husband who was from Meridian. She explained their unlikely meeting in Canada on a search-and-rescue operation. She described their passionate, short, and stormy life together. 'She's so young to have been through so much,' I thought. Touched by her pain and her honesty, I asked if she would like to come by the church office some day to talk. We agreed to meet again.

"As I drove home that afternoon, I pondered her story. As she talked about the search-and-rescue work she and her late husband had done, I remembered Tommy, a friend of mine who did search-and-rescue work. For several years, Tommy and his immense dogs lived next door to us. He loved to dazzle us with stories of searches for lost children and criminals. He ran his dogs on our farm. My husband, Duane, and he became friends through the years. We offered our farm as a place to stage training searches.

"My most vivid memory of Tommy was the evening I left a pot of chicken on the stove while we talked down by the lake. It was an unusually frank conversation about God. Later, when I returned to the smoky kitchen, I considered myself fortunate. There was no fire, and I had the exhilaration of sharing my faith. I wondered if Cindy had ever run across Tommy in her work with search-and-rescue.

"During our next meeting, she talked more about her spiritual journey. Though she had grown up in church and taught Sunday school, she wondered if there was a God and knew she had never really known him. She talked about her late husband. If there was a God, how could God allow a good man to be killed at work? If she believed in God, did it mean she had to believe her husband went to hell when he died? Yet it seemed with the unexplainable events that kept happening in her life, there had to be a God.

"As she talked, what began as a trickle of recognition swelled until it hit me like a wave. Tommy had been killed in a work-related accident after he moved from our neighborhood. Cindy's late husband must have been our neighbor, Tommy. All the details fit.

"I asked her. Yes, it was true. Her late husband was Tommy. We sat in stunned amazement. There was an air of reverence in the room. 'This,' I said, 'is one of the reasons I know there is a God.' She shook her head in a mixture of disbelief and belief.

"Later as I sat across from this lovely young woman from Canada, I wondered aloud about the possibilities of us ever meeting. She said there was no chance. She never went to church. Of all the people in Meridian, she had gotten to know me, someone who lived right next door to her late husband. She said that, even though she was confused about God, she knew God had planned for our paths to cross."[1]

Cindy's story is a beautiful tale of openness, a story of

people who trust in a God who sends strangers into our lives, a story of sharing faith in a way that loves the stranger. It is a story of hospitality and evangelism.

Hospitality is an important key in our call to make disciples out of all nations (Matt. 25:31-46). It is an important element in doing evangelism with integrity. It is, in fact, a component of evangelism, the part that says, "Welcome, you're home."

Hospitality and Evangelism in the Early Church

Hospitality was equally important for the early church. The sheer number of hosts and guests in the Luke and Acts narrative, with many persons named primarily because of their hospitality, implies great importance. Jesus, the Messiah, came to earth and found no place of welcome. Yet he, the wandering prophet, became the abundant, party-giving host (Luke 14). The book of Acts ends with Paul, banned from the synagogue and under house arrest, yet still welcoming all who came to him (Acts 28:30-31). Hospitality played a key role in spreading the good news.

The house church

The believers themselves gathered in homes to fellowship, pray together, share possessions, and eat the Lord's Supper. Meals were of particular importance. In Luke, Jesus used many parables around the theme of eating; and in Acts, the believers ate together regularly (Acts 1:4 and 10:41). Several important things happened at these meals. Lessons about the kingdom were taught, repentance was celebrated, and physical needs were met as the believers shared what they had. Most important, with great joy and awe they celebrated the death and resurrection of their Lord as they took the bread and cup.

Imagine what the house church must have been like.

As host, you would prepare your meager dwelling as best you could. Many people would work to squeeze into the main room of your home. Most of these people would bring food—the house would soon smell wonderful with the scent of freshly baked bread—but others would come hungry. You would be prepared. New persons, strangers, would also show up at your door. If they were not escorted by some of your friends, you would have to make a decision. Were they looking for something to report to the authorities? You would allow them in for the worship to hear the joyous laughter and the fervent prayers, but not for the Lord's Supper. You wanted to provide a welcome, but the eucharist was sacred and easily misunderstood by people who did not know or accept the whole story.

Of course, your own new friends would come too for the first time. They had observed the gatherings for some time now. They questioned you about the sharing of food and possessions, the party atmosphere, and the unity that seemed to exude from people who came from such different backgrounds. You just smiled and said, "Why don't you come over and see for yourselves?"

Lodging for itinerant preachers

The necessity of the house church made hospitality very important to evangelism. Hospitality was also crucial to evangelism because of the needs of the wandering prophets. Jesus was the primary example of a wandering prophet, but many others followed. These disciple preachers literally left all to follow Jesus in this way, teaching about Jesus wherever they went. They were homeless, penniless, and in need of lodging at night. Here the home owners of the early church stepped in. The Christians who had not sold everything to follow Jesus opened their homes and shared their possessions for the sake of these itinerant preachers. They provided extended lodging, meals, and short-term job opportunities. For example, Priscilla and Aquila shared in Paul's mission as they offered him lodging, food, and an occupation (Acts 18:2-3). They also understood the role of the traveler, for their own ministry took this course in later years.

Connecting people

Finally, hospitality functioned as a person-to-person link that was crucial to the mission of the early church. No doubt this happened many times as established believers introduced new believers into the circle of faith. There was always risk involved because persecutors were everywhere, sometimes in disguise. Two disciples, however, did small acts of welcoming that changed the course of Christianity. The person they wanted to introduce to the larger church, the person they staked their own reputation on, had been a persecutor, one of the worst.

The persecutor? Paul. The disciples who risked their own necks to connect Paul to the wider church? Ananias and Barnabas. We can only imagine what a bewildering task they were called to. Ananias was the first adventurer of the faith. The Lord gave him a vision with specific instructions to go to the house of Judas and ask for Saul of Tarsus. But Ananias was hesitant. He knew exactly whom the Lord was talking about. He also knew he was on Saul's hit list. So Ananias questioned the Lord about the risk in showing hospitality, but the Lord was emphatic. Saul had been chosen to carry the gospel to Israel and the Gentiles. Ananias was to welcome him into the family of believers.

With incredible faith, Ananias went. Knowing what Saul needed so badly, he touched this man whom he had earlier feared. Without requesting an explanation of this supreme turn of events, Ananias said healing words over

Saul. God worked through these gentle acts of welcoming, and Saul regained his sight. Continuing the welcome, Ananias baptized Saul. He fed him. There at the table together, sharing bread, were two former enemies.

Luke, who gives such stunning detail in the previous account (Acts 9:10-19), grows silent over the next obvious event in the lives of Saul and Ananias. Surely Ananias took Saul to the next house-church gathering. He struggled to keep his friends from fleeing the premises. He promised safety and begged them to trust this stranger because they trusted him and because they believed in the God of miracles. But the first few meetings had to have been tough.

What was tough for the Damascus Christians was tough for the Jerusalem fellowship as well. "When he had come to Jerusalem, he attempted to join the disciples; and they were all afraid of him, for they did not believe that he was a disciple" (Acts 9:26). So Barnabas took the risk and made the introductions. This was not your typical let's-get-to-know-each-other party. Barnabas told Saul's conversion story and how the Lord had used Saul in Damascus to preach fearlessly in his name. How much risk Barnabas really took we can't know. Did he know Saul well? Had he experienced Saul's preaching himself, or was he taking the word of fellow believers in Damascus? Under any circumstances, it was a big risk. But because he took that risk, his hospitality became a vital link to the mission of the early church; much of that mission pulsated through the life of Paul.

In the early church, then, hospitality went hand in hand with evangelism. The two made up the two-sided coin of mission—private and public, house church and synagogue. The host stood equal to the itinerant guest.

At least, most of the time.

Sometimes there was a tension between those two parties—the resident believer and the itinerant preacher. Luke seems to hold up the role of the preacher in the Gospel of Luke, where many examples of selling everything you have and giving it to the poor (Luke 18:18-30) molds the norm for disciples. In Acts, however, the resident believers, those who have not sold everything or who at least still have homes in which to host the fellowship, take the main stage. So what is Luke trying to say? Which role is the most important? Whose example should we follow?

Luke proclaims for us that both roles are important. In a parable in Luke 17:7-10, Jesus described a landowner who probably had a small plot of land and only one slave. The slave worked in the fields all day, plowing the ground and looking after the sheep. Then he came home and waited on his master at table. That was culturally permissible behavior for both the slave and the master. Both would think it absurd for the slave to sit down and expect the master to wait on him. That was just not how it was done. The master would not thank the slave, for nothing above the call of duty was done. The servant was not treated inhumanely; he had his allotted time to eat and drink. But his time of refreshment was after the master's because he was owned by the master. His time and energies were not his own.

At first glance, this is a parable about our own duty toward the demands of the kingdom. We too have no special claim on God, no matter what we do in the fields or at table for our Master. We never go above and beyond this duty. We do not do any special favors for which God needs to thank us. There is no special merit in our obedience.

These are wise teachings from this small parable and worthy of our consideration. However, another interpretation rests beside this one that helps resolve the tension between resident believers and itinerant preachers. Paul Minear notes three ministry components, three apostolic activities that dominate the parable: plowing the fields, watching the sheep, and waiting table. The first two would be job requirements for the wandering preacher. Plowing the fields is synonymous with teaching and preaching the gospel. Watching the sheep has a pastoral flavor to it. But waiting table is distinctly an act of hospitality, the role of the resident believer.[2]

Now comes the surprise. If Luke was here addressing as a primary audience the itinerant disciples, this parable sent them spinning. Instead of the expected response of a superior status in the body of believers after the hard labor of evangelism and on-the-road discipleship, the itinerant preachers found themselves waiting table as well! It is, says Minear, "a distinction between field work and housework which was the source of conflict among the apostles in the post-Easter church."[3]

The parable was not saying that the itinerant preachers also had to function as hosts. There were many ways to divide the work of the kingdom, as there are today. The point, however, was that there was only one work. If the wandering prophets must participate in waiting table, then the resident hosts must also become missionaries and leaders. No one carries a superior role. All are only "worthless servants," merely doing their duty to the Master. "All that you were ordered to do" (v. 10) implies the presence of only one ministry, a ministry where hospitality and evangelism work together to spread the good news.

There is only one work.

Throughout Luke-Acts we can see that house owners and wandering prophets worked side by side. Barnabas and Paul, the resident believer and the itinerant, worked together for the gospel. Paul's own far-reaching ministry blossomed under the hospitality of Barnabas. The many steward parables Jesus told, all aimed at disciples with possessions, suggest too that this stewarding, centered in hospitality to the stranger, was an important ministry and a test of faith. The kingdom was to be built, *is* to be built, by the joint efforts of those in evangelism and those in hospitality.

Partners with Mission

What about today? Do we as resident believers see our ministry as being as important as that of our pastors or those working in foreign mission fields? Do we view our simple acts of hospitality as mighty acts of grace where God moves, convicts, and changes lives?

We should.

What would happen to the church in this day if we saw ourselves as partners with God on a mission to save the world? Paul partnered with Philemon and other resident believers to build a supporting network of hospitality that spanned a wide area of ministry. They saw their work as integral to Paul's work. So did Paul. What would happen to us if we would recapture that sense of purpose in our acts of welcoming?

Hospitality is an important key to our mission initiative today. It is so important that when neglected, our evangelism becomes perverted and manipulative. When the two work together—present-day house church hosts and itinerant missionaries—both evangelism and hospitality are done with integrity, and the kingdom is built.

Two sides of the same coin

Evangelism has a bad reputation in some circles. Some have experienced it as manipulative and degrading. The message they have heard is "You're welcome if you conform to our standards." The hospitality that is extended to unchurched persons comes with a price, the price of doing things my way. Even when this message is not explicitly spoken, the implications of some evangelistic techniques suggest it. Passing out tracts or working to get people to come forward without any follow-through sends a message that we are more concerned with numbers than with people. Altar calls are not wrong, but when altar calls come without the nurturing attitude of hospitality, their effectiveness is diminished. New believers get mixed messages.

Evangelism without hospitality also affects believers. As a reaction to this aggressive evangelism, many Christians have become hesitant to make their own convictions known. They don't want to hurt anybody's feelings. They don't want to manipulate anyone into becoming a Christian. They instinctively know this kind of evangelism is not true hospitality.

But neither is silence. Indifference to the needs of others is just as unwelcoming as manipulative evangelistic techniques. The true host doesn't offer refreshment in an empty house. Likewise, spiritual hosting cannot be devoid of values and beliefs. Henri Nouwen says, "We can enter into communication with the other only when our own life choices, attitudes, and viewpoints offer the boundaries that challenge strangers to become aware of their own position and to explore it critically."[4] Our guests need our boundaries—flexible, loving boundaries—as much as they need our food and lodging!

To truly extend welcome in a way that honors God, hospitality must balance receptivity and confrontation. We must share our beliefs, especially our faith in God, with the guests in our home. They need to hear those words and see our faith played out in our lives. But we must share our faith in a way that is true to our faith, in a way that does not force, and in a way that is motivated by love. We must never extend hospitality for the sake of church growth. If we extend true hospitality, we will share our faith and the church will possibly grow, but that is not our motivation. Our hospitality must always come from the love we feel for our strangers, powered by the love we feel from God.

Receptivity and confrontation are two inseparable sides of Christian witness. Nouwen says, "Receptivity without confrontation leads to a bland neutrality that serves nobody. Confrontation without receptivity leads to an oppressive aggression which hurts everybody."[5] Balance between the two is crucial.

Early Church Hospitality

The early church had a wonderful balance of receptivity and confrontation, a balance that played itself out in the value of hospitality. Early Christians had a plan for welcoming new believers in a way that was truly hospitable without sacrificing the integrity of their commitment to be Christian. It was a tough balance to be an alternative yet welcoming community in a hostile environment. But when you face death every day for your faith, as these early Christians did, it had to be both. The newcomers, in order

---

A View from the Road by Noah Kolb, conference minister, Iowa-Nebraska Mennonite Conference of the Mennonite Church

"Hospitality is primarily a gift from the heart. It is an invitation to be at rest and peace in their presence. It is like coming home. It is a place where I can be myself and don't have to stay in a shirt and tie. While some Christians are gifted with hospitality and leaders are called to be hospitable, I believe at the core of the gospel is the invitation for God's children to experience and practice hospitality. . . . Most pastors come as strangers. The congregation opens their hearts and hands to receive strangers, to accept them just as they are, and to extend to them a place in the family. . . . Congregations who are best able to express hospitality to the pastor may be best able to extend a welcome to those outside the church who are seeking a place to belong. In other words, hospitality may be one of the primary tools of evangelism. . . . Isn't hospitality one of the best ways to reach our neighbors, colleagues, and those in need around us?"

to be trusted, had to demonstrate their commitment. At the same time, the life of early believers was so difficult that their hospitality had to be genuine, almost divine, or no one new would venture through the rugged ordeal of joining. The lives of the Christians had to be so different that their neighbors asked, "Why do you live the way you do?"

This balance evolved gradually, emerging more fully as persecution increased for the Christians. The early post-Easter church baptized new believers immediately. But within two hundred years, the church developed a plan for nurturing and training inquirers. When someone showed interest in the Way, the church put the inquirer through a period of questioning. In these rough times, membership had to be defined clearly. If the inquirer passed, the church bent over backward to show hospitality for the next three years, as the person underwent a time of learning and testing. The church was very active in the welcoming process, providing mentors and spiritual directors for the inquirers. Much time was spent in prayer and study of the Scriptures and lessons in moral behavior. The whole church was involved in the hospitality.

After three years, if the inquirers were deemed ready, the church held a special time of welcome and confrontation. The new believers fasted and prayed during the Lenten season. Exorcisms were performed every week. During Holy Week, the inquirers washed themselves every day and held to a strict fast. On Easter Eve, the entire community gathered for an all-night vigil. Members told the whole story of the gospel as together they waited for the dawn. When the sun broke through, the initiates were taken to a separate house where they were immersed three times, anointed, and given new garments to wear. Sweet smelling, they returned to their new family to take communion for the first time, where milk and honey accompanied the bread and wine.[6]

What a welcome for those early believers! The touch of tender hands as the older ones anointed these new ones. The aroma that filled the room, the feel of the new, fresh garments—the hospitality extended to the whole person. Even the weekly exorcisms were wonderful gifts of hospitality for those who were addicted to evil. And the welcome did not stop at Easter. Instruction and mentoring continued until Pentecost, when the new believers were sent out to do ministry.

The early Anabaptists practiced a similar balance between receptivity and confrontation. Their central belief that baptism should be an outward sign of a person transformed by God was itself a radical, status-quo-shaking act of welcoming. Baptism was the public sign of the personal decision; it was a welcome-to-a-new-family ritual. But baptism was also a decision that insisted on confrontation. "Are you willing to die for your faith?" was the question implied in the pouring on of the water. For this reason, many Anabaptists delayed their baptism for a period of preparation, a time to think and count the cost.

Like the early church, the early Anabaptists also took upon themselves the burden of hospitality to the new believers. Persons seeking to join the movement promised nothing until they were baptized. Yet in the preparation time, many hours were spent teaching them how to pray and read the Bible and how to live together in community. It seemed like a huge time-and-work commitment on the part of the gathered body, but think of the grief and work they saved by not having problems later on down the road.

True hospitality, a hospitality that balances receiving people for who they are and presenting these same persons with our own values and faith, must be practiced as a key component, an integral part, of evangelism. We must follow the lead of our spiritual ancestors and find ways of receiving without controlling and confronting without judging. We must find our true motivation for evangelism in our love for the strangers among us.

Hospitality helps create community

Community is an essential part of our faith. Throughout Scripture the church is called to live as a gathered community of persons who celebrate together, support each other, seek accountability together, listen to and challenge each other, forgive and heal each other. "God has called us to witness our inward sense of unity in outward ways; the life of the church and the experience people have within it are to manifest the oneness we find in the Spirit," says Parker Palmer.[7] When people look at the church, the thing that usually matters to them first is not our doctrines or our worship, but rather how we live together.

Community and evangelism touch each other in two ways. Some people hear and believe the Word first. They experience conversion; they repent of their former ways of doing and being; they make a complete turnaround that affects every part of their life. But because this is just the beginning of the journey, the first step of Christian discipleship, they need the loving support and account-ability of a faith community. So the second natural step is joining the faith community. Hospitality from those already in the community can be an important link in their faith development.

For others the reverse is true. Our community life attracts them to Jesus. They look at us in amazement. They see how different we are, how diverse our origins and opinions, and yet how we love each other. We work together. We stay together in spite of the differences. The witness of our community life together gives indisputable proof that something powerful is here. Seeing that power at work, they desire that same love themselves.

But what if our community doesn't attract people to Jesus? What if the neighbors and strangers among us look and see squabbling and pettiness? What if they see a disjointed group of people who really aren't community at all? It's obvious that a little hospitality within the community is in order here, not the tea-and-cookies kind, but the kind that says, "I'm going to listen to you and respect who you are."

I believe the greater problem with our faith communities lies not in the open-air fighting we do (which may be very healthy), but with the very closeness of our communities. The irony is that the very thing that draws many people to our Christian circles is the same thing that repels them once they get close enough. Our closeness may also communicate that we are closed in. How can we really be community and yet always have open doors?

Let's take a look at one scenario. Some new people in the neighborhood want to join my church. They grew up in a different theological background, but they feel more at home with much of my church's beliefs. They are particularly attracted to the community life. They love the fact that we all know each other and that we do so many things together. The Relief Sale that we help support is delightfully fun for them. They even revel in our ethnicity; they are interested in our history. They think it's great that we have some understanding of where we came from.

My community welcomes this couple and their children with open arms. We are friendly to them and seek to include them as much as we can. But the very thing that attracts them also puts them outside the circle. The very thing that they want so much to be a part of, they can't be a part of completely, no matter how hard they try, because they don't have the same last names. They don't catch the inside jokes.

The community attracts, and the community repels.

So what is the problem here? Is ethnicity itself the culprit? I used to believe that, as a young pastor, and I worked hard to downplay that aspect of community life. I did so, however, with a heavy heart, for I am proud of my heritage, and there are pieces of truth in the old traditions. But upon reflection, I found I could not abandon my ethnicity at all, just as I cannot abandon my freckles or curly hair. It's part of who I am, who we as a community are. We cannot be other than who we are.

The problem is also larger than the individual members of the community or even the neighbors who try to join community. The concept of community itself is vital. Community and the hospitality it implies are biblical mandates, the arena through which God has chosen to bring abundance.

There's something else afoot. It's how we define community that hurts us. In his book *In the Company of Strangers,* Parker Palmer talks about the myth of intimacy. Inherent in that myth is the idea that the church community is a bastion of warmth and intimacy, a place of close family relations. Church as family is a fine idea, but church as the ideal family can be very harmful. Says Palmer, "When an idealized image of family is imposed upon the church, our experience in the congregation becomes constricted. Now the church—where we might experience creative conflict, heterogeneity, and freedom for innovation—becomes dominated by the expectation of closeness and warmth."[8]

My imaginary neighbors and my imaginary community both suffer from the same disease. We see the larger society as a fragmented, disintegrating mess, and we want an alternative that is the opposite in every respect. Instead of conflict, we want comfort; instead of criticism and competition, we want affirmation and good will; instead of nameless wandering, we want identity.

Instead of strangers, we want intimacy.

But to get that kind of "family," we have to be really careful whom we let in. Unlike the early church, we are more concerned with who will fit our intimacy needs than who will really follow Jesus with their lives. People who are like us, who believe the same things we do, and who grew up like we did are okay. We want people who feel like family, people who won't rock any boats. We can't have conflict in the church. So how can we really welcome strangers into our midst? They will change our identity—and if that happens, then maybe we won't be community anymore. Patrick Keifert says, "When we think of our congregations in such intimate terms, as family, we are apt to exclude those who do not fit into the family. More often than not, those excluded are persons of a different race or class. As a result our churches abet and exacerbate the injustices due to race or class. Even when we include those who are clearly different or other, we demand that they are only truly welcome if they enter by way of intimate, personal relationships with the heads of the family."[9]

God did not call us to that kind of family. That's not even a realistic picture of our own biological families. We call ourselves sisters and brothers in the church, but do we really allow each other to act as we do with our own brothers and sisters? Family members fight; family members grab for power; family members can come from the same home and yet be very different from each other. There are times when families are strangers to each other.

The problem with many church communities is that they buy into the myth of intimacy: everyone needs to be warm and intimate. To protect the myth, we set up unreasonable and inhospitable standards for acceptance into the community. Many times we expect the same level of intimacy in our larger community that we experience in our small groups. That expectation is not fair to strangers who want to join us. Pride in an ethnic origin is great, but it should not be the community norm. Living together without conflict is wonderful, but don't expect that to be the standard for true community life. We need some degree of familiarity, but not to the extent that we all have to have the same background and think exactly alike. We need healthy, constructive fights; we need the differences strangers bring to us. Without new perspective, we lose the fresh wind of the Spirit who pushes us to grow beyond our narrow worldview.

When strangers come into our midst, we feel threatened. They might sing the wrong kind of songs. They might question our theology and point out some of our weaknesses. They might, by their very presence, make us uncomfortable because of different social or economic positions. Their different backgrounds might dilute our pure identity. They will, invariably, change who we are. That feels like a threat to the community.

What feels so threatening is our only hope of survival. Strangers keep us from making our wonderful ethnicity into an idol. Strangers save us from the stranglehold of the myth of intimacy, that high expectation no community can ever truly attain. Strangers force us to look at and deal with the conflicts that are there anyway, just under the surface. Most important, strangers, because they are different, show us a new face of God.

Hospitality and Evangelism in a Pluralistic, Postmodern Society

If it is true that hospitality is a key element of evangelism and that our communities actually suffer from their lack of strangers among them, what specific things can we begin working on to incorporate hospitality into our mission?

Hospitality and Evangelism in Arlington, Texas

"I was waiting for the police to come and carry out the eviction notice," Virginia Maanani related. "I had no place to go and was trying to get the nerve to call the Department of Human Services and have them come get my two girls and give them to families who could provide for them. After struggling and struggling, I was down to one can of pinto beans and one can of green beans and coming eviction."

"Then the knock on the door came. I opened it a crack and set my foot against the door so that no one could get in," explained Virginia. "And there was this skinny lady smiling from ear to ear, and as she talked, she pushed on the door until she was in and moving over to the kitchen table to talk to me."

"I want to start a Bible study in your apartment," said Tillie Bergen, the smiling skinny lady.

"All right," replied Virginia, inwardly laughing to herself that any minute she wouldn't be in her apartment.

"Do you have any needs?" asked Tillie, still smiling.

"Do I have any needs?" mimicked Virginia, sensing an opportunity to send her visitor running. "Okay, here are my needs," challenged Virginia. "I owe money to the landlord. I'm waiting to be evicted any minute. The electricity has been turned off. I have had no phone for six months. The car died. And we have almost no food."

"I'll be back," said Tillie.

"Two hours later a knock on the door came, and it was Tillie with two bags stuffed with groceries and two more needing to be brought in," Virginia related. "There was a whole chicken and fresh milk sticking out of one bag and a sack of candy bars sticking out of another, and we had been living on canned food. The girls grabbed the candy bars and ran!"

"You're special," said Tillie, and gave Virginia a hug. "I'll be back tomorrow." Virginia thought she would never see her again.

But Tillie came the next day and asked, "How much is your rent?" When she left to pay the rent, she gave Virginia another hug and told her she was special and that she would be back

the next day. When the next day came, Tillie arrived with a pound of coffee, a receipt for Virginia's paid electricity bill, and time to sit and drink a cup of coffee. When she left she said, "I'll see you tomorrow. You are so special."

"It took a year and a half of Tillie's coming every day, having coffee and telling me I was special before I believed it," said Virginia. "But in the meantime, we did start Bible study in my apartment—church really. Everyone in the apartment complex was invited, and some Sundays we had as many as 70 in every corner of the apartment and some listening through the windows."[10]

1. We can see our acts of hospitality as important ministry tasks, equal to the tasks of pastoring and evangelism.

We need the physical and spiritual acts of hospitality to keep the other ministry tasks from seeming hollow and possibly manipulative. Our simple gifts of welcoming bring integrity to our words of witness. What we do and who we are in the marketplace speak as loudly as the Sunday morning sermon. We must never forget that.

2. Welcoming committees must see their roles in a new light.

All of the welcoming details—signs about where bathrooms are, name tags for the ushers, a follow-up visit from someone from the church—are acts of ministry. They are important ways of showing welcome and must continue. But these actions are only the tip of the iceberg. A congregation can wear name tags and bake bread for visitors and be as friendly as can be, but still never draw a stranger in. They will be friendly but not friends. The hospitality committee at church must work with the church leadership to help the congregation redefine who they are as a body. This committee must work to educate the congregation about their own need of the stranger. They must help the church take a hard look at their heart attitudes. If this doesn't happen, all the name tags in the world won't make any difference.

3. The congregation needs to reexamine its welcoming rituals.

How do church rituals, especially initiation rituals like baptism and communion, communicate both receptivity and confrontation? First, they must be intentional. There must be overt welcome and invitation to join the church. The congregation needs to call people to commitment, call people to join the church, call people to begin a relationship with Jesus, and call people to recommit their lives to God. The old tent revival movement understood an important concept when it called people to come forward.

But our invitation can't stop there. We must be intentional in our mentoring, our passing on of the faith. We need to tell the story in ways that fit the needs of the seekers. We can't dilute the message, yet we must make the message accessible to the ones joining us. We must do this in many different ways and at many different times of the year. Seekers may experience the confrontation in Sunday school, in the worship time, in a small group session, in a mentoring relationship, or in a variety of other places. The task may seem overwhelming, but to a congregation who sees their main goal as welcoming the stranger, the time and energy needed for the task seem right.

The actual welcoming ritual of baptism needs to be tailored to fit the experience of the people being baptized. Allow them to help plan the baptism; ask them to pick songs and words that fit their experience. Make the language simple and accessible to all. Then, after one year, throw a party for all the newly-baptized. Celebrate their welcome into the kingdom again!

4. We must be sensitive to the special demands of a post-modern society.

Our pluralistic society frowns upon anyone who claims to know the truth. Absolutes grate against our sensibility. Christians find it difficult, then, to witness about Jesus. Hospitality is one answer to this dilemma. "Hospitality offers a way to be Christian and yet communicate in inviting ways to the society around us," says Mark Diller Harder.[11] Hospitality emphasizes listening to the guest and supplying the needs of our guests—including their need to hear our values and beliefs. In true hospitality, the guests know where we stand, yet are free to accept our values or move on.

Mark Diller Harder experienced this kind of hospitality on a native Canadian trip. "How does hospitality affect our interactions with other religions, worldviews? I was so struck on my native trip by the way our native friends shared their faith. It was so un-evangelistic, un-pushy. They always talked about 'this is my understanding' or 'this is how an elder taught me.' They would not try to prove their point or out-argue a different position, even when asked. They would simply say, 'I learned it this way.' All our teachings were done out of a mode of hospitality. And yet, they were extremely appealing and drew people in. Several of our hosts have done a wonderful job of integrating Christianity within their particular cultural history."[12]

5. We must encourage a transfer of leadership.

Real hospitality means ministry *with* people, not ministry *to* people. We can be very welcoming when newcomers first join our faith communities, but when it comes time for them to join the inner circle of the community, to be part of the power structure, many congregations start backing off. This story illustrates the point well:

"Our church did an excellent job of welcoming Becky. Becky was a struggling divorcee, and we took her in and nurtured her in many ways. She thrived on our love and hospitality, and as a result, started to pull her life together. She emerged with a tremendous gift for teaching, a gift that was greatly needed in our congregation. She also had some good leadership skills, particularly in administration. So naturally she began using these gifts in the church. But the door of opportunity slammed shut. For reasons she could not explain, she was denied the chance to be a Sunday school teacher or to work on the church council.

It was a great puzzle to her until one day it hit her. 'When I was struggling, you needed to take care of me. I needed it, and you needed it. When I became strong, you didn't want me anymore. You wanted someone you could take care of. I didn't fit the bill anymore.'"13

There are many reasons why we don't let new believers or young adults come into the inner circle of the community. They have new ideas that threaten us. They want to change that beloved carpet we picked out twenty years ago. They force us to share the power we worked so hard to get for ourselves at one time. We forget how we felt when we were the outsiders wanting to put that carpet on the bare floor in the first place.

But welcome lasts forever. We must welcome others because we love them, not because they fulfill our need to be needed. Hospitality says that we must share the ministry. To be a healthy church of the future, we must not only share ministry, but also actively cultivate the leadership skills of those who wait on the outside of the circle. Like Barnabas and Ananias, we have the opportunity to nurture the next Pauls.

Both Host and Stranger

In our postmodern society, we serve the unbelieving world best if we function as both host and stranger. Kiefert says, "When understood through the metaphor of hospitality to the stranger, the dynamics of confessing the faith in a cultural pluralism embody the confessor as both host and stranger. . . . As strangers we depend upon hospitality; among strangers, we are called upon to host . . . we live hospitably toward every stranger, refusing to domesticate our God, the gospel, the church, or even this neighbor we do not know. Rather we appreciate the irreducible difference of the stranger."14

Appreciating the difference does not preclude witness.

It demands it. In our incredibly diverse world, with our unique mission of reconciliation, the task is impossible except through Christ. We seek to reconcile people, not by erasing diversity or by creating an ideal community, but by "holding fast to the recognition that Christ alone, as the presence of God for us, can reconcile us, by grace through faith."15

A congregation can infuse hospitality into its mission in many ways. We can see our hospitality as an important ministry calling. Welcoming committees and other church leaders can help the congregation see its great need for the strangers in their midst. Rituals such as invitations to faith and baptism can become more intentional in their welcoming. Congregations can bring their message to a pluralistic society in an inviting way through hospitality. Leadership can be developed in young adults and new believers.

We can be like Barnabas and Ananias. Their efforts and our efforts, empowered by the Holy Spirit, will reap huge rewards. That was the experience of many in the Forty-Day Experiment, including the story of Cindy, with which we began:

"I gave Cindy a copy of *The Message* and tried to explain how the New Testament was put together. She said she would withhold judgment until she had read the book. We laughed and agreed to meet again, which we have done several times since then. I don't know what all will come of this. But Cindy knows I love her. And she's beginning to believe that God loves her too."16

Additional Reading

Stutzman, Ervin R. *Welcome! A Biblical and Practical Guide to Receiving New Members*. Scottdale, Pa.: Herald Press, 1990.
Finger, Reta Halteman. *Paul and the Roman House Churches*. Scottdale, Pa.: Herald Press, 1993.

Notes

1. Excerpt from the Forty-Day Experiment journals.
2. Paul Minear, "A Note on Luke 17:7-10," *Journal of Biblical Literature* 93 (1974): 85.
3. Ibid.
4. Henri J. M. Nouwen, *Reaching Out: The Three Movements of the Spiritual Life* (Garden City, N.Y.: Doubleday, 1975), p. 70.
5. Ibid.
6. Marlene Kropf in a lecture on rituals, hospitality, and the early church, given at the Associated Mennonite Biblical Seminary, Elkhart, Ind., January 1998.
7. Parker Palmer, *In the Company of Strangers: Christians and the Renewal of America's Public Life* (New York: Crossroad, 1981), p. 118.
8. Ibid., p. 120.
9. Patrick Keifert, "The Other: Hospitality to the Stranger, Levinas, and Multicultural Mission," in *Dialog* 30 (Winter 1991): 37.
10. Robin Scott, "Mission Arlington," *The Lookout* 110 (11 January 1998).
11. Mark Diller Harder, written communication, February 1998.
12. Ibid.
13. Excerpt from the Forty-Day Experiment journals.
14. Keifert, p. 41.
15. Ibid.
16. Excerpt from the Forty-Day Experiment journals.

CHAPTER 11

Remembering Who We Are

*So then you are no longer strangers and
aliens, but you are citizens with the saints
and also members of the household of God.*
—Ephesians 2:19

In some of our communities are certain persons who, by a sheer exterior definition, are labeled strangers. Whole groups of people, because of their color, religious beliefs, or economic status, are discriminated against because they are different. Wherever they go, they fight the unspoken or legal barrier that says, "You don't belong here. You are not wanted." They are aliens in a foreign land.

Such is the case in my own hometown.

"'Samuel' and his family have been in the United States for over five years since arriving from Guatemala seeking political asylum. Samuel has obtained citizenship and applied for permanent residency for his daughter and daughter-in-law. In February 1997, permanent residency was granted to the women, but in July of that same year, they were asked to go to Indianapolis for something having to do with their documents. They complied and traveled to Indianapolis. When they arrived, their permanent resident cards were confiscated, and they were ordered deported. One question had been answered incorrectly on the application. Lacking fluency in English, they had paid someone else to fill out the forms for them, but the Immigration and Naturalization Service (INS) official would not listen. They were immediately shipped to Chicago. Samuel and his wife and son went to Chicago to see them and take them a letter, but they were not even allowed to exchange letters. The two women were returned to Guatemala. Samuel's daughter cannot reapply for entry for ten years. Since the daughter-in-law has two preschool children who are United States citizens, she will be allowed to apply in five years. Five years. How fortunate to have children."[1]

I cringe every time I hear stories such as this one. This is a story from *my* town. The immigration officials here have deported undocumented persons several times during the past two years. *From my town.*

Perhaps the story of my town is different from the story of your town. Here in this city, many undocumented people work in the factories. There are other immigrants here who have permanent residency, but undocumented persons have no legal status as citizens or legal residents in the United States or Canada. So in this town, they are called *illegals.*

They are illegal because they reside here without express permission. So why *shouldn't* they be deported? That is a difficult question. The United States and Canada do have immigration laws that bar undocumented people. But what is the ethic behind them? What is the spirit of the immigration laws? The first immigration laws in the United States were intended to exclude "undesirable" people.

Most of the undocumented people who live in my town are from Central America. They have come to

Canada and the United States because the economies in their countries are collapsing. It is much harder to find a job there to support a family, making it worth the risk to cross borders illegally. They would come legally if they could, but the immigration laws and the quotas for legal immigration work against them. The *World Book Encyclopedia* entry on United States immigration admits, "Immigration laws favor certain individuals, including relatives of United States citizens, refugees, and people with skills needed in the United States Others may have to wait years, particularly in countries that have many people wishing to emigrate. Generally, no more than twenty thousand people a year may emigrate to the United States from any one country." Canada has a similar policy: "In 1990, the federal government announced a five-year plan to increase immigration, raising the annual limits from one hundred seventy-five thousand to two hundred fifty thousand. They have also made a decision to favor independent individuals (with skills) over dependents of citizens and resident aliens."[2]

There are currently an estimated 2,700,000 undocumented Mexican immigrants in the United States. At the rate of twenty thousand a year, how many years would it take for the backlog to be admitted legally?[5]

If it is difficult for them to come legally. If they have great financial need, why don't our countries allow them to come? There are many reasons, says Ron Collins, pastor of Iglesia Menonita del Buen Pastor.

Current Information and Statistics

About 5 million undocumented immigrants were residing in the United States in October 1996. The population was estimated to be growing by about two hundred seventy-five thousand each year, which is about twenty-five thousand lower than the annual level of growth estimated by the INS in 1994. These 5 million people made up 1.9 percent of the population.[3]

In 1990, the Canadian government introduced tougher immigration laws that allowed officials to reject migrants at the airport and order them to leave within seventy-two hours. New laws also allowed officials to deny amnesty for eighty-five thousand persons already in Canada claiming political asylum.[4]

Misinformation is a main reason. People believe that undocumented persons hurt the economy by taking jobs and collecting welfare, but those beliefs are not based on fact. Immigrants usually take jobs at the lower end of the pay scale. Unemployment at this level is extremely low, and, at least in my town, there is great demand for persons who will work at these jobs. Working-age documented immigrants are less likely to be on welfare than working-age citizens. Undocumented immigrants can't apply for welfare. Immigrants currently pay about $30 billion more in taxes yearly than they receive in government services. Furthermore, immigrants start 18 percent of all new small businesses.[6]

Economics may still be the reason for the apparent resentment toward undocumented immigrants, even if undocumented aliens actually aid the economy rather than harm it. Citizens in financial straits or out of a job are tempted to blame their troubles on some other group—undocumented immigrants become a handy scapegoat.

Many people in my community, however, do understand the true dynamics of the immigrant situation in our area. They know the undocumented people help create jobs and boost the economy. They know, as do the INS officials who carry out the raids, that the very people they are arresting and deporting back to Central America are the ones who are working and contributing to the economic base.

Yet the majority of our communities stand by and watch it happen. Even the prospect of greater good for all does not motivate us to take action to stop the deporta-

A Canadian at the United States Immigration Office

"Because I married an American, I too had to get resident alien status, even though we moved the next year to Canada. We too went to Indianapolis. We were the only Anglos in the room, and while we did have a specific time appointment, we were served immediately, while the rest waited in the room. We were also treated fairly and cordially, which wasn't the atmosphere for others. We've never felt so white, middle class, English-speaking, and powerful before."—Mark Diller Harder

tions. Why? What keeps us quiet in the face of this injustice? Is there something else going on here?

Maybe we have forgotten who we are.

Long ago, there was a group of people who were facing financial crisis. There was a famine in their land, and although they were wealthy people, people who were good stewards of the land, they were still in great need. So great was their need that they traveled to another country in search of help. They went to the king of the country and asked for land where they could start over. "They said to Pharaoh, 'We have come to reside as aliens in the land; for there is no pasture for your servants' flocks because the famine is severe in the land of Canaan. Now, we ask you, let your servants settle in the land of Goshen'" (Gen. 47:4).

Goshen—that's funny, that's the name of my town too.

Aliens in a Foreign Land

Pharaoh, ruler of the Egyptians, granted the land of Goshen to the Israelites. They prospered, and under the leadership of an Israelite named Joseph, all of Egypt was spared from the worst of the famine that swept through that country as well. The alien Israelites brought prosperity in every way to Goshen.

After Joseph and his generation died, however, a new king rose to power who did not know the story of God's providence to Egypt (Exod. 1:6-10). He looked at the strong Israelite nation that lived as aliens among them, and he feared them. "He said to his people, 'Look, the Israelite people are more numerous and more powerful than we. Come, let us deal shrewdly with them, or they will increase and, in the event of war, join our enemies and fight against us and escape from the land'" (Exod. 1:9-10).

Suddenly the land of Goshen, the land of salvation for the aliens, became the land of horrors. The Egyptians made slaves of the Hebrews and oppressed them with hard labor. But the more they oppressed the Hebrews, the more they multiplied and spread. The Egyptians began to dread these aliens. They ordered the Hebrew midwives to kill every newborn Hebrew boy, and when that order was not obeyed, the Pharaoh commanded that every Hebrew boy be thrown in the Nile River.

In the midst of this seemingly hopeless situation, God was working for the deliverance of these aliens. One brave Hebrew mother listened to God's voice and put her undocumented baby in a basket. Pharaoh's daughter found the baby, and Moses, an alien, grew up in the shadow of the palace. In dark Goshen, there was a glimmer of hope.

Thus began the story of the Exodus, the story of an alien people in a foreign land striking out for home after four hundred years. Aliens in Egypt, they were aliens in the wilderness for forty years, and then aliens in the old homeland (the new Promised Land)—Canaan.

The alien factor came into effect on several levels in the wilderness. The Israelite people as a whole were landless, nomadic wanderers, strangers to everyone they encountered. But among the Israelites themselves were other aliens, people who had left with the Israelites on their flight from Egypt (Exod. 12:38). The group that marched away in the middle of the night was a mixed crowd. The Israelites were strangers in exile, and among them were other peoples who were naturalized into God's people.

With the Exodus, the alien identity God gave to Abraham was now firmly established with the Hebrew people. They were pilgrims, wanderers, and strangers on the move: "Know this for certain, that your offspring shall be aliens in a land that is not theirs, and shall be slaves there, and they shall be oppressed for four hundred

years" (Gen. 15:13). The history of God's people is filled
with aliens. When there was a severe famine, Abram left
for Egypt to live there as an alien (Gen. 12:10). Later, at
God's command, he left his home to go to a far-off place
that God had promised him. He lived in Canaan as an
alien, never receiving this land as his own while he lived
(Gen. 17:8). He even had to ask his neighbors for a spot
of land to bury his wife, Sarah (Gen. 23:4). His son Isaac,
too, lived all his life as an undocumented person in a land
God promised his descendants (Gen. 26:3). Moses named
his son Gershon, meaning "I have been residing in a foreign land" (Exod. 2:22).

On and on, through the exile to Babylon, through the
stories of Ruth and of Jonah, all the way to Jesus, who welcomed the tax collectors and prostitutes to sit at table
with him, the motif of aliens continued. Cornelius
marked the entrance of the Gentiles into God's kingdom.
Peter urged his fledgling congregation, plagued by perse-

Ruth 2 as North America wishes it rewritten

2 And Ruth the Mexican said to Naomi, "Let me go to the factories and find work." She said to her, "Go, my daughter." 3 So she went. She came to the RV plant owned by Boaz, a relative of Naomi. 4 Just then Boaz came from South Bend. He said to the workers, "The Lord be with you." They answered, "The Lord bless you." 5 Then Boaz said to his supervisor who was in charge of the workers, "To whom does this young woman belong?" 6 The supervisor who was in charge of the workers answered, "She is the Mexican who came back with Naomi from the country of Mexico. 7 She said, "Please, let me work in your factory. So she came, and she has been on her feet from early this morning until now, without resting even for a moment." 8 Then Boaz said to Ruth, "Now listen, my daughter, do not come back to work. I am sorry that I can not give you work. 9 You are a foreigner and must go back to your country and to your people. 10 Then she fell prostrate on the ground. "Why have I not found favor in your sight, that you should take notice of me, just because I am a foreigner?" 11 But Boaz answered her, "All that you have done for your mother-in-law since the death of your husband has been fully told me, and how you left your father and mother and your native land and came to a people that you did not know before. But laws are laws and must be obeyed. 12 May the Lord reward you for your deeds, and may you have a full reward from the Lord, the God of America, as you go back to Mexico."[7]

cution, to consider themselves exiles and aliens in the world. (1 Pet. 2:11). Over and over again, God told his people to think of themselves as strangers. "The land shall not be sold in perpetuity, for the land is mine; with me you are but aliens and tenants" (Lev. 25:23). "For we are aliens and transients before you, as were all our ancestors; our days on the earth are like a shadow, and there is no hope" (1 Chron. 29:15).

The story of believers as aliens continued through the first three hundred years of the post-Easter church. Many Christians were not aliens by definition of their nationality, but because of their religious beliefs, beliefs that became crimes against the state. Thousands of Christians were thrown to the lions or burned at the stake in the name of the Roman emperor. With Emperor Constantine's conversion, however, the alien status suddenly changed. Christianity became the state religion, and people joined it to avoid persecution and to enjoy the benefits of this privileged status.

Twelve hundred years later, during the Reformation, many Christians became aliens again, as they proclaimed biblical truth over against the traditions of the official state church. The more radical groups—the Huguenots, the followers of John Wycliffe, and the Anabaptists—suffered the most from this new estrangement. Hunted down to be tortured and executed, their children branded illegitimate, their property confiscated, they were truly strangers in a foreign land.

The fate of thousands of these Reformers was the ultimate alienation of execution. C. J. Dyck says, "Church and state had been so closely linked in the medieval period that the state considered it a part of its duty to enforce the accepted belief of the established state church. If the church declared someone a heretic, that person was considered dangerous to the state and removed from society.

Anabaptists were considered heretics. . . . The treatment of prisoners was extremely cruel. They were broken on a torture device known as the rack to make them disclose the names of others, especially leaders. For those who remained steadfast, burning at the stake was the usual execution."[8]

Throughout the ages, those persecuted or made homeless for their religious beliefs depended on the hospitality of others for their survival. Abraham asked for kindness in the strange lands he resided in. The Israelites asked Pharaoh for the land of Goshen, and this land was granted to them in a beautiful act of hospitality. Although the welcoming turned ugly four hundred years later, even at the time of the Passover, the Israelites asked their neighbors for items of gold and silver. God softened the Egyptians hearts, so that the Hebrews took many precious metals and cloth into the wilderness, items that were later used to build the tabernacle for God. Under the caring hand of Boaz, Ruth the Moabitess was able to glean the leftover grain for herself and her mother-in-law, Naomi. She became an ancestor of King David and ultimately of Jesus.

The Reformers also felt the providence of God through the hospitality of those around them. Not everyone was out to kill the Huguenots, Hussites, and Anabaptists. Those who dared show them welcome often did so at the risk of their own lives. The movement could not have survived without the hospitality of sympathizers. Hospitality meant life to these undocumented, illegal groups.

Hospitality meant everything.

Identity Crisis

God's people knew what it meant to be aliens. In our own history, we can remember that our ancestors were strangers in a foreign land. In our modern day, we too can feel like strangers. We may not be desert nomads, but one-third of all Americans move in any given year.[9] Being an alien is our spiritual as well as physical identity, says the writer of the book of Hebrews. Knowing your identity as an exile and alien in this world makes all the difference in the world. "All of these [Abraham, Sarah, Noah and others] died in faith without having received the promises, but from a distance they saw and greeted them. They confessed that they were strangers and foreigners on the earth, for people who speak in this way make it clear that they are seeking a homeland. If they had been thinking of the land that they had left behind, they would have had opportunity to return. But as it is, they desire a better country, that is, a heavenly one. Therefore God is not ashamed to be called their God; indeed, he has prepared a city for them" (Heb. 11:13-16).

Knowing who you are makes all the difference. We are to think of ourselves as exiles and aliens on the earth. The writer of Hebrews gives us several reasons why we must see our identity in this way. If we understand our role as exiles, its affects our faith, our vision, and our final home.

1. Knowing who you are affects your faith.

If you see yourself as an alien in this world, then it is okay if you don't receive everything you're looking for. Abraham lived in a tent on land that God had promised him. He didn't receive the actual piece of ground though he walked on it every day. It didn't matter. With eyes of faith, he saw a better city. His son and grandson too lived as foreigners in their own land. They kept the faith; they believed in a spiritual world that was more real to them than the physical earth. They saw another city. When they admitted they were aliens and strangers on this earth, they admitted that there were better things to aim for than land to call their own. They believed the things they were promised on this earth would come—in their own time. We, as aliens and strangers in our world, are to be like them.

2. Knowing who you are helps you catch a vision.

Some people dwell in the past. They remember the glory years, the good old days when the world was just right. Some of the Israelites felt that same way as they wandered in the desert far from Egypt. Earlier, they had cried to God to free them from their oppression there. Now, on their journey in the wilderness, with the Promised Land nowhere in sight, they pined away for Egypt. "Remember the fleshpots," they said, "remember all the food we had" (Exod. 16:3). Looking back, they were romanticizing about Egypt; they were forgetting the bone-crushing, backbreaking slavery.

But those who have an identity as aliens and strangers, says the writer of Hebrews, never look back. To say you are an alien means you don't belong back in Egypt or even here in your present situation. No, you know there's something better ahead. You long for that better country. You don't look back, even if that means facing change, even if that means facing the strangeness all around you, even if that means facing the reality of what the good old days were really like.

3. Knowing who you are demonstrates your final destination.

God has prepared a special home for the homeless, says the writer of Hebrews. God is building a city for those who have chosen the identity of exile and alien. To feel like an exile, then, is a sign of faith. If we feel uncomfortable where we are, if our world seems cold and evil, it is not time to despair. It is time to start searching again—for that new city.

This doesn't necessarily mean we literally become exiles—unless God calls us to this vocation. If we all sold our homes, we could not show hospitality. It does mean that we take on the character of an exile. We think like an alien. We view our possessions like an exile would. No matter where we live, we take on the identity of an undocumented person because we don't really live here. This is not our final home.

I'm not saying that we try to escape the racism, materialism, war, and injustice of this world. God does not want us stuck in an ivory tower. The Israelites, says the writer of Hebrews, could have returned to their old land if they had wanted to (Heb. 11:15). Maybe they could have, but we can't return if the "lands" that we pine after are those "good old days" when everything was secure and safe. Those days never existed anyway, and even if they did, they're gone. The Israelites couldn't really return to Egypt either. It would have shown such a terrible lack of faith. It would have been such a slap on their identity. Their father was a "wandering Aramean" (Deut. 26:5). To live as sojourners was their calling. To live as sojourners was to live in faith.

It is the same with us. How odd that those very feelings of fear and not belonging are not feelings we should flee, but signs of God among us. Those giants of faith so praised in Hebrews 11 were praised because they did not want to go back but were longing for a better home. They rejected the need to feel at home because to them it was idolatry. It was trading in a dependence on God for security in home and familiarity. Parker Palmer says, "What a curious inversion—taking feelings of estrangement which we normally try to get rid of and calling them positive signs of vocation instead! . . . If we live in God, we will find ourselves on a pilgrimage; we will be taken to alien places where we are strangers and estranged. Only when we acknowledge that 'you can't go home again' will we be on the road to faith."10

"Therefore God is not ashamed to be called their God; indeed, he has prepared a city for them" (Heb. 11:16). This is why we suffer as aliens. This is why we cling to our identity as strangers in this world. We forsake the comfortable and secure so that God will not be ashamed of us, so that, in the end, we will be welcomed into that grand city where God will also dwell (Rev. 21:3). And what a glorious city that will be—a city where strangers will mingle freely, where all will be welcome, where each one will find comfort and rest and peace.

If we allow ourselves to be strangers now, if we allow the strangers among us to help us in our search for that city, if we refuse to settle for the comfort and security of this world, then God is proud of us. God claims us as God's own. That new city is ours.

City of Compassion

The Lord spoke to Moses and instructed him to build six cities of refuge—three cities beyond the Jordan and three in the land of Canaan. These cities were places where all killers, both innocent and guilty, could flee. Those accused of unjustifiable homicide were to stand trial before the congregation. If they could run to the city of refuge before they were killed, then they could plead their case. If found guilty of murder, they were slain by a near relative of the deceased. Those who killed another accidentally also fled to the city of refuge. They stayed in the city until the death of the high priest, after which they were free to go home without being slain. The cities were built as a refuge for the Hebrews and the aliens who resided among them (Num. 35:6-15) Their concept was simple. They were places of safety, places that helped insure justice.

We can build cities of refugee too, as we welcome strangers into our homes. God still wants places where people will not be judged unjustly. God still wants places of safety for all of us, including the aliens who reside among us. When we welcome those deemed unworthy of welcome, we lay the foundation of a city of refuge.

We also receive a foretaste of the city to come at the end of the age. As we interact with undocumented persons, we catch a vision for what could be. Our guests strengthen our faith with their own incredible testimonies and remind us of our own alien identities. But perhaps the most important gift they give us is the gift of compassion. The very process of strangers coming together and sharing with each other brings forth an outpouring of love that would not be there otherwise. Glimpses of the city of God have flashed across my kitchen table as we shared a meal together.

Perhaps the story of Victorino can explain this better. Victorino is a man from El Salvador who fled to the United States to escape the death squad. All of his brothers were killed by the death squad, an organization financially sponsored by the United States. He helped his family, a wife and ten children, to relative safety in a refugee camp in Belize, and then he headed north. Eventually, he found his way to the home of my parents-in-law, James and Gladys Hershberger.

James and Gladys had signed up for a program called the Underground Railroad. Like its namesake from pre-Civil War days, this organization helps undocumented persons get to Canada. Using homes like my parents-in-law's, aliens stay and work until they have enough money to cross the border and become Canadian citizens. Working with the Underground Railroad is not as dangerous as it was when slaves were running for the Mason-Dixon Line, but there are legal problems. For example, in the state of

Indiana, it is illegal to transport undocumented persons, a crime punishable by fines or jail. So Indiana residents who house undocumented persons can't transport their friends anywhere. Technically, it is not illegal to have aliens in your home, but some laws make it inconvenient.

Victorino stayed in the home of my in-laws for a year and a half. During this time, I spent Christmas with this wonderful man who became more than a guest to us. He became one of the family. Through Victorino, my worldview changed. As he told stories of the death squad and the torture chambers, stories of how a few rich families had all the power and how so many others were literally starving to death, I looked at my own wealth with new eyes. As I listened to him talk about his faith in God, I had to encounter the stranger within me, the stranger called prejudice.

I remember the first Christmas we all spent together. Christmas is an important time for the Hershbergers, a precious time to reconnect as a family. Some years, this is the only time we are all together. So I was not too happy when I heard that we would have a guest with us that year. Our inside jokes, the way we like to play cards till 2:00 a.m., the serious talks we have around the table—what would happen to all that when we had a person at the table who didn't know the jokes and didn't even speak the language? For weeks I fumed to myself. I had looked forward to a week of letting my hair down and just relaxing with family. And now this! How could I relax with a stranger in the house?

To a certain extent, my fears came true. At times it was awkward having Victorino in the house. I found myself being more careful with my words and trying to include him when I could, and that was not relaxing. His English was very weak, and his cultural expectations, so different from mine, threw us all off balance sometimes. But it was

Christmas, and when I looked into his dark eyes, I saw Joseph, looking for an inn or fleeing to Egypt. Somehow the awkwardness was okay.

Then something happened that changed everything for me. Toward the end of our visit, Victorino took my little girls in his arms. My girls, then ages four and two, had enjoyed playing with Victorino the whole week, so they gladly jumped into his lap. He held them for a moment and then started to cry. "My girls," he fumbled in English, "same age." Little Tara gave him a kiss on the cheek and snuggled on his shoulder. He looked lovingly down on her, but his eyes were seeing another little girl, two little girls, little daughters that he loved more than his own life.

It was a holy moment for me, a moment when the world stood still. All my life I had learned and said that we are all alike, that we are all just one people, that we all live and breathe and need to eat and rest, and that we all love our children. I knew that intellectually; I preached it from the pulpit; I believed that with all the determination I had. But now I *felt* it. I knew it in a different way. In that moment, that special, holy moment, I become more fully human. I found a love for others and an identity with others that I had never experienced before.

That man loves his children just as much as I love my own. That man aches for his family just as I do for mine. His heart tugs for the same things my heart yearns for. Knowing this, his exile becomes my own, not in any way close to the suffering he has gone through, but in a small way. His pain is mine. If that isn't so, if I turn my back and walk away, and if I refuse to take in his humanness as my own, I lose something.

I lose compassion. I lose a part of my soul.

Victorino is now in Vancouver, British Columbia, reunited with his wife and ten children. We visited him twice. With pride, he introduced us to his family and showed us the city and the place where he worked. My two girls played with his two girls, rolling around on the grassy lawn. Victorino proudly showed us his Canadian citizenship card. In that moment, I wished I could be a Canadian too.

There were tears when we left home for Oregon. We are family, and it's always hard to leave family. Every Christmas, Victorino calls. We're family.

The Gift of the Alien

Herein is the special gift of the undocumented persons in our midst. They remind us that we are undocumented too—in God's way of thinking. We don't belong here; we don't want to belong here. There's something far better than settling for this. Just like Abraham and Sarah, Ruth the despised Moabitess, the Israelite slaves, the unclean Gentile soldier, and the hunted Anabaptists, we long for a land, for a way of being that others cannot see. We don't give up hope when we die along the way. The time will eventually come when the land will be ours. We don't hold our possessions tightly, for they are a part of this world, not ours. They are mere shadows of the grand abundance to come. There is One who travels with us, who sojourns with us as we walk on foreign ground. The troubles we face, the estrangement we feel—it all makes sense when we think of ourselves as undocumented.

It's not supposed to feel like home on this earth.

But even though we are "undocumented," we are loved. Just like Abraham and Sarah, Ruth the despised Moabitess, the Israelite slaves, Cornelius the unclean Gentile soldier, and the hunted Anabaptists, we are loved. So we don't despair when we are rejected for the world cannot fully understand us. We don't worry if we don't have the most prestigious jobs or fanciest houses because those things give only a brief moment of satisfaction. We don't accept the world's definition of success so we are not bound to it. We are loved. There is One who travels with us, who weeps when we weep, and who gives us encouragement when the strangeness seems overwhelming. There is One who is not ashamed to be called our God.

That's what the alien comes to teach us. It is a priceless gift.

It is the gift of identity, a gift we must never forget. Many Christians forget this identity, and in doing so, they open the door to justifying violence and wars that kill their own brothers and sisters in Christ. When we forget that we don't belong to any certain nationality or race as much as we belong to God and God's people, then we fight to defend turf that isn't ours to defend. We put our greatest allegiance in temporary land and wealth and government; and to protect those things, we disobey the One who says, "Love your enemies" (Matt. 5:44). When we believe ourselves to be exiles and aliens, then our greatest allegiance goes to God. This identity clarifies for us when we are to obey our temporary government and when to heed a higher calling.

Even pacifists who claim a theology of peace have at times forgotten who they are. We don't participate in war, but we shun the neighbors around us because they don't make as much money as we do or because they are different. We shun them because they are strangers.

The Mennonite experience in Russia takes an interesting slant from the typical alien experience. This group went as aliens to the Ukraine and prospered so much there that they became the established community. Beginning in 1789, many European Mennonites immigrated to Russia to escape hardship and persecution. They were shown hospitality by the Russian government and the local people at that time. These aliens grew prosperous, and by 1850 they had developed a peaceful and secure community life beyond their dreams. They also had a rich spiritual life, as attested by their sacrifice as congregations to send their young people as missionaries and seminarians around the world. One thing, however, they neglected to do. As they slowly evolved from poor immigrants to wealthy landowners, they isolated themselves from their Russian neighbors. This was not true for every family, nor was it specifically taught in the churches that one should forget one's neighbor. But the isolation, the us-them attitude happened nonetheless. Imagine the displeasure of the Russian authorities when a delegation of five Mennonites came to discuss exemption from war, and two of them could not speak Russian.

Many Mennonites saw the error of their ways. They acted to bring about more involvement and assimilation, but it was too late. As Cornelius Dyck writes, "This involvement, however, was not sufficient to close the social, cultural, and economic gap that existed between the Mennonites and their neighbors. The peasants and many of the Russian officials were jealous of Mennonite achievements, piqued also no doubt by a certain Mennonite hauteur and condescension which they regarded as a feeling of superiority. . . . These attitudes, together with Mennonite wealth, brought great difficulty to the colonies with the coming of the Bolshevik Revolution in 1917. As German-speaking people, the Mennonites were suspect as enemies of the state in its war against Germany; and as prosperous farmers and businessmen, they were soon suspect as enemies of the revolution as well."[11]

What happened to the Mennonite communities during the Bolshevik Revolution was due to many factors other than their exclusivity. Angry peasants ravaged their villages and killed their sons and daughters for many reasons. All the terrible atrocities might have happened even if there had been no us-them attitude between the Mennonites and their Russian neighbors. But the question will always haunt the survivors and families of the dead: Would it have made any difference if they had not been so isolated?

Similar stories can be told of other groups of Christians. All of us, to differing degrees, have forgotten our stranger status. Every time we refuse to help an alien, we forget our own history when others broke the law to help us.

Recapturing Our Identity

Even though we may have forgotten in the past, it is never too late to start remembering again. Interaction with undocumented friends can help us remember. One such group in my town that works intentionally at this goal is the Neighbors' Deportation Response. This group matches churches, families, and individuals with another family who loses a breadwinner because of deportation. After the INS raids, families who lose an adult worker call a coordinator, who then consults a list to find a family who will help with food and rent for one to two months. A project of Christian Peacemaker Teams, this group helps many families who find themselves in desperate need.

Another group in Goshen calls themselves the Interfaith Hospitality Network. Here a number of area churches agree to take turns hosting homeless families. The homeless families spend several nights at one of the churches. Members from the church serve as hosts, providing food, companionship, and beds in the church building. These hosts also spend the night at the church, making sure their guests are comfortable and experience privacy and safety in their church basement home. The families usually only spend a couple of nights before they move on, either to another town to try to find a job or to another church. Walnut Hill is one participating church. "We believe in the need for the Network and also see the value of deliberately interacting with persons outside our comfort zone," says Jane Stoltzfus Buller, a member of the pastoral team at Walnut Hill. "It has been a real pleasure to use our building as a place where persons in temporary difficulties can find a warm, safe bed and food for their journey. We were also recipients of help when our church house burnt and many helped us."[12]

These are only two programs designed to provide hospitality to strangers in crisis. Undocumented aliens are by definition strangers in crisis because they are illegally residing in a place that is not home. They are not performing criminal acts; they are illegal because it is not possible for them in a legal way to provide food for their families. They are aliens in a foreign land.

There are some sad things happening in my hometown. But there are some exciting things happening in my hometown, too. Goshen, the land Pharaoh gave to the alien Israelites; Goshen, the place of misery as these same Israelites became slaves for four hundred years. Now it is *my* Goshen, a place that deports undocumented persons and a place that welcomes them—depending on who you are.

Depending on what your identity is.

Notes
1. Ron Collins, pastor at Iglesia Menonita del Buen Pastor in Goshen, Ind., from a press release.
2. "Migration," *Compton's Encyclopedia Online,* vol. 20, The Learning Company, Inc., 1997.
3. Immigration and Naturalization Service website.
4. "Migration," *Compton's Encyclopedia Online.*
5. Immigration and Naturalization Service website.
6. *MCC Washington Memo* 29 (May-June 1997): 1.
7. Ron Collins, press release.
8. Cornelius J. Dyck, *An Introduction to Mennonite History* (Scottdale, Pa.: Herald Press, 1993), pp. 110-111.
9. Parker Palmer, *In the Company of Strangers: Christians and the Renewal of America's Public Life* (New York: Crossroad, 1981), p. 61.
10. Ibid., p. 63.
11. Dyck, p. 185.
12. "Walnut Hill Partners with MMA to Assist Homeless," *Gospel Evangel* (March 1998): 2.

CHAPTER 12

Hospitality and the Lord's Supper

Do this in remembrance of me.
—1 Corinthians 11:24

Come on, Ruth, hurry up!" Marcus called to his wife from the courtyard to the barn. "We're already late!" Ruth scurried out of the barn, wiping dust and straw from her garments. Their master had assigned many chores for them to do today, and she could only move so fast. They could not leave until all the work was done, and even now, as they headed into the house, they were not sure if the master would let them go.

It was always this way when they wanted to attend the meetings of the Christians. Their time was not their own. Sometimes he did not let them go at all. But Ruth and Marcus really desired to go today, for the gathered body of believers would celebrate the Lord's Supper. Even though it happened with some regularity, this was a special time. Not every gathering would culminate in the special meal, but many did. It was a time of great joy and holy remembrance. It was also special because there was food there. Usually their partaking of the Lord's Supper was the most substantial meal of their week. They counted on this time of feasting, not only for its spiritual significance, but also as a way of sustaining their physical lives. For many reasons, Ruth and Marcus hated to miss out.

Today was a blessed day, for the master gave them permission to go. He gave them no food to share, but then he usually didn't. Even though she knew it would be this way, still Ruth lingered at her master's door, hoping that somehow the master would relent. Marcus read her thoughts. "Ruth, come. We must go."

They ran as hard as they could down the path to the house church. From far down the road, they heard the laughter and lively conversation of the believers already there. Panting and thirsty, they entered the open door. "Hello, Ruth and Marcus! Welcome, welcome!" Ruth sighed with joy. It was so good to be here among friends.

Marcus was not so joyous. The hands that clasped his own were warm and inviting, but they were also holding pieces of bread and meat. Something inside him winced. Were they so late that they had missed the meal?

A voice from a corner of the room called everyone to quiet attention. No, thought Marcus, the meal had not begun, for the invocation was about to be spoken. He tried not to think about the food he saw in the hands of his fellow believers; he tried to concentrate on the meaning of the broken bread and body. He tried to drown out his own hunger pains and his own doubts about the welcome he and Ruth received. "Dear Lord," he breathed in a whisper, "help me to understand."

With the last amen, the believers sat down for a full meal, largely donated by the richer members of the fellowship. Ruth and Marcus joined their friends, who lounged in every available nook of the house. People like Ruth and Marcus were grateful that their wealthier sisters and brothers opened their homes in such a generous way. "One of these days, we too will bring food to share," Ruth thought to herself.

Something was different about this meal, however. When the bread and meat were passed to Marcus and Ruth's table, there was hardly any left. They split an end piece of bread and two bites of meat between them, so those friends sitting close by would have other scraps for themselves. The same thing happened after the prayer over the wine. As thirsty as Ruth and Marcus were, there was no wine at all for them to quench their dry throats.

But at other places around the house, there were cheers of glee and hilarity. Others were lifting their wine cups high in the air, the same ones who greeted Marcus with bread in their hands. "I'm going home," Marcus announced loudly enough for most of the house to hear. "If this is what the body of Christ means, then I want no part in it." He walked out of the house.

Ruth stared at this group she knew so well, who had now grown deadly silent. Tears stung her eyes. The words tumbled out. "We thought—we thought that it was okay that some of us couldn't bring food. We thought that—we were all one body. What fools we were, Marcus and I. It's no different here than out there. I will go and join my husband."

Ruth and Marcus are fictional characters, but their experience was real in the Corinthian house churches. Paul wrote to the Corinthians about their practice of the Lord's Supper. The problem didn't rest with inappropriate liturgy or neglecting this ritual all together. The offense was much greater than that. In their practice of this holy meal, they were not practicing true hospitality. By their neglect of this important value, they were threatening the very life of the community.

No Praise for You

For Paul, hospitality and community were important elements of the Lord's Supper—so important that if hospitality was not practiced and community not nurtured, their gathering with the bread and wine was not the Lord's Supper at all.

> Now in following instructions I do not commend you, because when you come together it is not for the better but for the worse. For, to begin with, when you come together as a church, I hear that there are divisions among you; and to some extent I believe it. Indeed, there have to be factions among you, for only so will it become clear who among you are genuine. When you come together, it is not really to eat the Lord's supper. For when the time comes to eat, each of you goes ahead with your own supper, and one goes hungry and another becomes drunk. What! Do you not have homes to eat and drink in? Or do you show contempt for the church of God and humiliate those who have nothing? What should I say to you? Should I commend you? In this matter I do not commend you! (1 Cor. 11:17-22)

Paul did not mince words with the Corinthians. Without hospitality, the Lord's Supper did not truly happen. If the sharing didn't benefit all members, and if the entire community was not honored and nurtured, then the celebration, in Paul's mind, could not be that same event that proclaimed and remembered the Lord's death.

Paul was trying to teach the Corinthians that the Lord's Supper was more than just a ritual. In the meal and the surrounding hospitality it provided, three things happened—socioeconomic barriers came tumbling down, discernment about the true nature of the believers took place, and Christ came as a guest bringing either grace or judgment.

1. Hospitality builds up community by tearing down socioeconomic divisions.

In the Corinthian house churches, some believers despised and humiliated other believers. They did not wait for their sisters and brothers before they started to eat. At first glance, this seems like a fairly harmless departure from good manners. Did they set out to be rude? Were they well-meaning people who gradually let their worldly attitudes infect their actions? Paul did not see it as a harmless breach of etiquette. Understanding what lay under the behavior, he came out so strongly against this practice that he said that some had died because of their not waiting (1 Cor. 11:30).

It was a matter of the rich neglecting the poor. When the believers gathered for this special meal, the wealthy Christians provided most of the food. They also served as hosts, for they were the ones with their own homes. Their wealth affected their beliefs, which propped up another barrier. Some scholars believe the rich Christians represented the majority of the liberal party, that is, the party that found no harm in eating meat placed before idols (1 Cor. 10:23-33).[1] They probably represented a good portion of that group, for they were the only ones who could go out and buy any meat. All of these factors added up to a feeling that they, the ones who provided the food for the Lord's Supper, were more worthy than the ones who could not afford to do so.

They were also the first ones to arrive at the appointed house for the eucharist. Slaves and others who were free but indebted to a master had more time constraints placed upon them. Reading between Paul's lines, we can imagine this picture. The wealthier Christians waited around, lingering beside a table laden with food. What at first was an innocent taste here and there evolved into a quasi-feast where these Christians took the first—and the best—of the food that had been prepared. In their minds, this was justified because they were the ones providing the food and hospitality in the first place.

Their behaviors reinforced their attitudes of superiority. The believers who arrived later suffered more than just empty stomachs and dry throats. They felt the sting of their lower socioeconomic position. They saw the leftover food and thought of themselves as leftover people, surely not as important as their wealthier contemporaries. They felt despised and humiliated.

"It can be assumed," says Gerd Theissen, "that the conflict over the Lord's Supper is a conflict between rich and poor Christians."[2] The issue here was larger than hunger pangs and proper etiquette. The apostle Paul saw quickly that some Christians believed in a gospel that had no effect on their social standing and the privileges that accompanied the higher positions. There were exceptions among rich Christians, of course, and Paul elsewhere applauded their generosity and their ministry as they shared their possessions. Paul did not make a sweeping condemnation against wealth. He only warned of the tricks that wealth can play on minds and hearts. The very cross that the Lord's Supper represents is also a social cross, a death and resurrection where the weak and lowly, the foolish of this world, are lifted up. So every Lord's Supper must do likewise.

In true hospitality, worldly barriers of class and wealth come crashing down as each member is treated with equality and dignity. The apostle did not ask well-to-do parishioners to give up their economic advantage. If they wanted to feast in this way, they should do it in their own homes (1 Cor. 11:22). But the Lord's Supper was different. As the poorer members were treated with honor, they would eventually be thought of in a more honorable way. Behavior influences attitude.

2. The degree of hospitality at the Lord's Supper brings discernment and judgment.

Paul wrote,

> Whoever, therefore, eats the bread or drinks the
> cup of the Lord in an unworthy manner will be
> answerable for the body and blood of the Lord.
> Examine yourselves, and only then eat of the bread
> and drink of the cup. For all who eat and drink with-
> out *discerning* the body, eat and drink *judgment* against
> themselves. For this reason many of you are weak and
> ill, and some have died. But if we *judged* ourselves, we
> would not be *judged.* But when we are *judged* by the
> Lord, we are disciplined so that we may not be *con-
> demned* along with the world. (1 Cor.11:27-32, italics
> added)

The Greek word *krinen* (marked by italics in the passage quoted above) meant both "to judge" and "to discern," and even "to condemn." The message was clear to
these early Christians that there was something to be
rightly discerned here or there would be condemnation.
The proper practice of the Lord's Supper brought a new
understanding of what it meant to be part of the body of
believers. If the experience did not bring about this new
insight, then judgment would fall.

Paul had an important question: What does it really
mean to be community? Some of these Corinthian
Christians desperately needed to understand the mystery
of the body of Christ, made up of so many different people and yet one. Differences were not shoved under the
carpet but were transcended. Roles were reversed, divisions dissolved, and persons freed to serve God out of a
sense of calling instead of what society dictated to them.
That's how these Christians were to discern the body.

That's how we are to discern the body. Real community means that we see each other differently. More important, it means we see *ourselves* differently (v. 31). We see ourselves as an intertwined part of all others in our community. We look at our sisters and brothers and say, "I'm not separate from them. I can't use any advantage that I may have over them. I'm not better or worse than they are, just different. It isn't even a they-me situation. Just *us*."

Proper hospitality at the Lord's Supper helps bring that discernment. Intentional waiting for weaker sisters and brothers forces the issue—what does it mean to be part of this body? Who comes to table late and why? What are their needs, and what special gifts do they bring? The act of waiting causes a change in heart and a growing understanding of the mystery of oneness in Christ.

If that new understanding, learned through hospitality, doesn't come, then judgment comes in its place. Paul's statement that this inhospitable situation had caused some to die sounds stern to our ears, but it was a judgment for their own sakes. The Christians were being judged now in this way so they would not be condemned later with the world (v. 32). What could be more disastrous for the early church and for us today than to misunderstand our interconnectedness with each other? What could be worse than trying to love God without loving the brothers and sisters in our midst?

3. Depending on the hospitality given, Christ comes either as a guest bringing grace or as a guest bringing judgment.

The Corinthian Christians believed that Jesus was present in a special way as they participated in the ritual of the Lord's Supper. Paul agreed with his readers that the food and drink they took in had spiritual ramifications (1 Cor.

Hospitality in the Lord's Supper

In the ritual of the Lord's Supper, the physical act of hospitality is most clearly connected to its spiritual significance. Many hospitality themes are identifiable in this event. Here Jesus the Host/Guest brings full circle the theme of the wandering stranger, the stranger that God loves and cares for, the stranger who is God. In the four Gospel accounts, these themes can be identified:

1. The guest/host role is fluid. Jesus, the one born in a stable, the one who had no place to lay his head at night, now becomes most fully the grand Host. Yet even here, the roles merge. Jesus sent Peter and John to prepare for the Passover, to be the hosts. When they wondered at the details, he provided for their needs by telling them to follow a mysterious man carrying a jar of water. Jesus enabled their hospitality. He allowed them to participate in the hosting.

Jesus, however, was the real host. He not only served the bread and drink, but also alluded to these provisions as symbols of a provision far greater. As the host, Jesus would offer himself as the sacrificial lamb in the ultimate hospi-

tality, the hospitality of the cross.

2. The guest brings a gift. In the grand hospitality of this Supper, the Guest/Host gave the grandest gift: a kingdom (Luke 22:29). Dining with Jesus meant, not only eating bread and drinking wine that represented his body and blood, wondrous gifts in themselves, but also the promise of a partnership of kingdom building together, and at the end of time, the grandest feast of all.

3. Coming to terms with the stranger inside. The disputing disciples demonstrated that they could not yet fully understand and participate in the hospitality Jesus was offering them. Peter, in particular, did not know his own mind as he pledged to Jesus that he would go to prison for him or even die for him. It was a noble gesture, but Jesus knew that some hard lessons had to be learned before Peter was truly ready for that kind of loyalty.

4. The ministry of receiving hospitality. John's Gospel expounds on the table ministry of Jesus that night. Jesus not only served the bread and wine but also offered the hospitality of foot washing to his friends (John 13). This humbling act of servanthood was too

much for Peter. He could not bear for his Lord to wash his smelly, mud-caked feet. But Jesus knew that Peter needed to receive as well as give. Peter had to accept this loving hospitality from Jesus. It humbled him and prepared for other times when he would need to be on the receiving end again.

5. Seeing Jesus in the eyes of a stranger. Jesus was a stranger at this Passover table. Jesus and the twelve disciples had been with each other every day for three years. Yet after all these days and all his words to them, Jesus stood among them as a stranger. They still did not understand who he was. Had they known that this One came as a servant, though he was Lord, they too might have accepted their roles as servants. They might not have quarreled over who was the greatest. Like Cleopas and his friend on the road to Emmaus, their eyes were opened to spiritual truth as Jesus served them in this humble way.

6. Hospitality as an act of worship. This was more than just any old supper. "This is my body, which is given for you. Do this in remembrance of me" (Luke 22:19). The apostle Paul gave added emphasis: "The cup of blessing that we bless, is it not a sharing in the blood of Christ? The bread that we break, is it not a sharing in the body of Christ?" (1 Cor. 10:16). Christ is present as we celebrate the Lord's Supper. Different traditions disagree on the exact way that Jesus is present, whether the bread and wine that we partake literally become his flesh and blood. But all understand that in this simple act of sharing bread and wine, our acts of hospitality become acts of worship. We remember Christ's death. We participate in the divine mystery. Whether we fully understand it or not, we worship the One who died for us. We worship as we share with each other.

7. Hospitality as a sign of the kingdom. Jesus often used feasting as a picture of the kingdom. Nowhere is that more evident than in the table time of the Lord's Supper. This meal was a beautiful symbol of the abundance, celebration, and intimacy of the kingdom. The one loaf broken into many pieces symbolized both the oneness of the disciples and the brokenness of Jesus' body needed to achieve that oneness. This is how the kingdom of God should be, how the kingdom of God really is.

8. Hospitality and the god-like power of money. Part of the story of the Lord's Supper is the story of Judas, who on that night made plans to betray Jesus to the chief priests and teachers of the law. Why did he do it? It had to be more than the money, yet money was part of it. Judas accepted thirty pieces of silver for his help in handing over Jesus. This betrayal was not a direct refusal to be hospitable to Jesus, but it stopped Judas from being able to accept the overwhelming hospitality and love Jesus wanted to give him. The power of money so controlled Judas that he was blind to the One who wanted to provide all his needs—and so much more.

9. Hospitality breaks down barriers. The disciples argued among themselves, erecting barriers of superiority against each other. True hospitality cuts through the divisions of class, wealth, race, and prestige that we so quickly build. As Jesus humbly served the disciples, they saw not only a new face of the Master, but they got in touch with the new understanding of themselves as the one loaf, united in Christ.

10. Remembering our own identity as strangers. The Last Supper was a Passover meal. This meal remembers an important long-ago event in the lives of the Hebrews. They were slaves in Egypt, brutalized by hard labor and cruel masters. They were aliens in a foreign land. God heard their cries for deliverance and saved them. All they had to do was obey God and sacrifice a spotless lamb as the terrible death angel *passed over*. They remained aliens as they wandered in the wilderness, waiting to enter the Promised Land. In remembering the Passover now, the Jewish Christians, if their spiritual eyes were open enough to see it, did two things: they remembered how God loves and cares for the strangers and aliens, an identity they still carried; and they relived the symbol that pointed them to another spotless lamb, Jesus, who would also die so that they could escape the consequences of their sin.

Biblical understandings of hospitality are interwoven in the Lord's Supper. As we partake of the bread and wine in our own communities, let us also remember the importance of hospitality, love of the stranger, and the ministry of humbly receiving the guest who is always present among us—the Christ.

10:1-4; 11:27). But Paul wanted these believers to see that the supper was not magical in and of itself. The taking in of the bread and drink was not some automatic medicine.[3] The bread and the wine only had meaning as they pointed to right living. Paul goes on in 1 Corinthians 10 to show that these same forefathers and foremothers who ate the spiritual food also died in the desert because God was not pleased with them. They ate the sacred food, but they did not allow their hearts to be changed (vv. 5-11).

The Corinthians were also eating the sacred food, but they were not allowing their hearts to be changed. They divorced the ritual from ethical behavior. Some went hungry while others feasted. The spiritual meaning of the meal was lost on them, for it did not play itself out in their hospitality.

Perhaps some of Paul's readers argued with him in their minds. "But isn't Christ present when we partake of the food and drink?" they wondered. "Yes," Paul answered in 1 Corinthians 10:16-17. When believers remembered and were thankful for Christ's death by eating the bread and drinking the cup, they participated in the blood and the body of Christ. But there was one loaf, and though they were different, they all ate from that one loaf. Though they were many, they were one. If the Lord's Supper was not celebrated as true community, then it was not truly a memorial to the One who died to bring about reconciliation for all.

As in all acts of hospitality, Jesus the Guest/Host sits at the table with us as we partake of communion. If we welcome Christ in our welcoming of others, particularly the weaker ones among us, then his presence is one of grace and blessing. "But if Christ is not welcomed by his people in one another," says John Koenig, "that is, if barriers are erected to obscure or prevent this hospitality, then he comes to the supper as a judging host whose food and drink have the effect of punishing his guests."4 We lose out on the grace, we become sick and even die, when we partake of the Lord's Supper in ways that don't honor community.

And we lose out on joy. I remember the first time I received communion in a church that, only months earlier, had refused to license me as a pastor. The reason for this refusal was my gender. I had been called to be a pastor to a congregation that was not yet comfortable with women pastors. After five and a half years of ambiguity, I asked to be licensed. After a process that was very painful at times, we prepared ourselves to take a vote. We asked the persons in the congregation who were opposed to my licensing to stay on as part of the community. That meant, of course, that my husband and I would not immediately leave either, if the vote didn't go the way we wanted. I didn't worry too much about this because I felt confident that my desire to be licensed would be affirmed.

But my intuition was wrong. I was not affirmed. Like the faithful opposition on the other side of the issue, we didn't feel right about running away. This was our community, but the pain ran so deep. No matter how I looked at it, the rejection felt personal. I went to communion anyway, trying to hold my head high.

There at the table, a dear elderly lady came up to me, tears in her eyes. "Michele," she whispered, "I must tell you. I had to vote no for you because of how I believe. But I didn't want to. Oh, I didn't want to." I looked into her eyes, and I saw immense pain, a pain that matched my own, a pain that came from the gut-wrenching tension between faithfulness to God and love for me. In that holy moment, I felt a deep love for her. In spite of our theological differences, differences that had brought great pain to both of us and personal rejection for me, we were one. We loved each other. Together we were Christ's body.

People tell me I'm too generous to love these people as much as I do. But they are my people and I am theirs. Would it have been different if they wouldn't have allowed me to take communion? Would it have been different if I had not stayed in the community long enough to hear my dear friend's testimony? I knew in my heart that they loved me even though the vote had not gone my way, but her words and her tears broke through a wall that Sunday morning. I was able to receive her love and the love of the others in a deeper way than before. Communion helped facilitate this love—this value of community. We all valued community, we stayed committed to each other, we saw ourselves as a part of each other and still do.

Because I chose to stay, I experienced joy that morning. Joy in the midst of my pain. My family did eventually leave, partly because this congregation could not accept my calling. I continue to live with a sense of brokenness from that experience. But I left feeling their love for me, a love that goes so much deeper than "we love you because you're just like us." In one sense I didn't leave at all, for that congregation, all of them, are still family to me. What a wondrous unity we share, a unity not predicated on identical beliefs but on profound love and welcome for each other.

That is the church. That is Jesus among us.

Waiting for a Surprise

All of these things—breaking down the barriers that divide us, discerning the true nature of who we are in Christ and in each other, and welcoming Christ in our midst as we welcome the least among us—work together to bring us unity. As we begin to serve each other in hospitable ways, and as we show kindness to the weaker ones, the strangers, and the less desirable ones, our behaviors soften our hearts. We may not yet feel the unity, but as we begin to relate to our sisters and brothers in ways that value them, we come to know them and see them as Jesus sees them. Seeing them through the eyes of Jesus, we fall in love with them. There is unity.

This is why Paul writes toward the end of his admonitions on the Lord's Supper, "So then, my brothers and sisters, when you come together to eat, wait for one another" (1 Cor. 11:33). The unity comes as we wait for one another. The verb *wait* here is wonderfully ambiguous, as John Koenig explains, "On the most literal level it means 'wait until everyone has come.' But it can also mean (and surely does in this context) 'wait with positive expectations' or 'receive' as one would a guest or visitor. In other words, Paul urges his Corinthian readers to do essentially what he will later recommend to the believers at Rome: 'Welcome one another'" (Rom. 15:7).[5]

Waiting on each other is nothing more than hospitality. On the practical side, we don't start eating until everyone arrives. But there's so much more. We *wait* in anticipation of a pleasant surprise. We *wait* for one another in the same way we *wait* on a special guest. It is the surprise of new relationships. It is the surprise of a new way of understanding ourselves and others. It is the surprise of a changed heart. It is the surprise of unity.

A Symbol of Unity for Today

What do these words of Paul mean for us today? It must be more than instructions to wait for others before eating. If that's the extent of Paul's problem with the Corinthian church, my congregation is in good shape.

There *is* more to it. If we look below the surface, do we see barriers between people? Have we really discerned correctly who we are and what our role is in this body? Do our communion times symbolize both the cross and the Lamb's wedding feast? These are questions we must be asking. And our answers need to point toward the following tasks:

1. Nurturing a vital community life.

If Paul or Jesus came to our congregation in disguise for a length of time, would they feel at home? Would they see us working together in a way that builds up everyone? Being community means sacrificing some of our precious individualism, giving up some control. Being community means having respect across the generations. These are high goals but worthy ones.

One way to foster community is to emphasize the Lord's Supper as a celebration where everyone participates. That is, whenever the bread and cup are taken, they should be taken together as the whole community. It is popular now in some circles for married couples to receive communion during the wedding ceremony. My husband and I wanted to do this as part of our vows too. But my father-in-law, who married us, reminded us of the importance of community in the communion ritual. In our faith tradition, all are encouraged to participate whenever the Lord's Supper is celebrated. Conrad Grebel, one of the founders of the Anabaptists, said it best:

> Although it is simply bread: where faith and brotherly love prevail, it shall be taken of with joy. When observed in that way in the congregation, it shall signify to us that we are truly one loaf and one body, and that we are and intend to be true brothers one with another. But if one should be found who is not minded to live the brotherly life, he eats to his condemnation, for he does not discern the difference from another meal. He brings shame on the inward bond, which is love, and on the bread, which is the outward bond. . . . The Supper, however, is to be an

exhibition of unity. It is not a mass or a sacrament. Therefore, no one should receive it alone, neither on a deathbed or otherwise.[6]

A good friend of mine once missed communion because she had nursery duty that day. Usually someone comes during this special time and substitutes for the nursery workers so that they can participate, but this time it didn't happen. Just as she was about to leave, one of the elders realized the oversight and quickly brought the cup and bread. My friend was alone in the room, picking up the last of the toys. She gazed quizzically at the elements in the elder's hands. "Don't you want to take communion?" he asked. "Why would I?" she responded. "Nobody's here."

The Lord's Supper has no meaning outside the community.

2. Intentionally breaking down barriers.

Even though it might not be food and who gets what to eat, barriers surrounding this ritual do exist. Our communion time can be a microcosm of the barriers that divide the congregation in general. Some questions that church leaders—the people on the inside—need to ask are: Do we exclude people by our unspoken dress codes? Is our worship expansive and welcoming? Do we use language that everyone can understand and appreciate?

Many of our church traditions emphasize the importance of preparing ourselves before we participate in the Lord's Supper. We are encouraged to look honestly at our spiritual condition and make confession to God and others if needed. This is an essential step. So many times, though, we only focus on certain sins in our confession—those things that are only between God and us. Paul in Corinthians reminds us that the way we live out our beliefs in hospitality is equally important. Our public morality is as spiritually necessary as our private morality.

3. Measuring the level of joy in our gatherings.

If we are really proclaiming the Lord's death until he comes (1 Cor. 11:26), then we are emphasizing two of the most important foundations of hope we have as Christians. Through Christ's death, we are redeemed, bought back, saved from the angel of death. As we eat of his body and blood, we take into ourselves this life-giving source of hope and freedom from sin. We are not sentenced to a life of sin and its consequences, a slavery just as real as the slavery of the Hebrews in Egypt.

We look back on the hope of the cross each time we receive the Lord's Supper. With this same ritual, we also look forward to Christ's return. Every time we say the words and eat the bread, we remind ourselves that Jesus will come again and that when he does, all tribes and nations will come to the table for a Lord's Supper that is beyond our imagination.

The hope of these two truths gives us joy. Or at least it should. Is there joy in your communion? With the solemnity that comes from remembering the cross, is there also a profound joy? If it is not present, what barrier prevents it? If the Lord's Supper is not received in true community, with genuine welcome for all, it is not the Lord's Supper that we receive. Without true community, there is no joy.

There Is Joy

A few nights ago, I celebrated Maundy Thursday at my home church. It is an inner-city church that is intentional in its outreach to the neighborhood. This night was one of the fruits of that mission. We sat around small tables in a gymnasium that every other night of the week has rowdy teens playing basketball in it. We shared a simple meal of soup and bread. We talked and laughed together—my friend Pablo from Guatemala; a couple of seminary professors; Valerie, who wears a rat-tail and multiple tattoos; and Deon, who used to run with a gang. I am half-afraid to mention them in this way for fear that they will be taken as tokens or stereotypes. I mention them because they were all at one time strangers to me, different from me, but now are my friends. Real friends, not just people I'm supposed to be friendly to. I mention them because without them, I would be less of a person. These people, all of them, are pictures of Jesus to me. All of us, together, are a picture of the kingdom.

Toward the end of the meal, Valerie got up from the table and in silence gave each person an old-fashioned looking nail, painted red on one end. Her children helped her pass out these nails, one by one, until each hand in the room held one. Tears filled my eyes as I looked at my bloodstained nail. Her gift meant more to me than all the words spoken that night.

There were no barriers that night in that gym—only love and joy. It didn't matter what you wore or who you came with. We sang simple hymns that most could pick up. We offered the option of washing hands for those who had never tried foot washing or for those who weren't ready for the intimacy that it involves. We told the story of the Lord's Supper in a simple, respectful way that gave information to people who didn't know the story.

We all waited on each other. With our words and our actions, we proclaimed the community of the Lord's Supper. We proclaimed our unity and love for each other. We proclaimed the cross and anticipated the return of our Lord. In our hospitality to each other, Christ was present.

Ruth and Marcus would have approved.

Additional Readings
Stoffer, Dale R., ed. *The Lord's Supper: Believers Church Perspective*. Scottdale, Pa.: Herald Press, 1997.
Kreider, Eleanor. *Communion Shapes Character*. Scottdale, Pa.: Herald Press, 1997.

Notes
1. John Koenig, *New Testament Hospitality: Partnership with Strangers as Promise and Mission* (Philadelphia: Fortress Press, 1985), pp. 66-67.
2. Gerd Theissen, *The Social Setting of Pauline Christianity: Essays on Corinth*. J. H. Schutz, trans. (Philadelphia: Fortress Press, 1982), p. 151.
3. Koenig, p. 66.
4. Ibid., p. 69.
5. Ibid., p. 70.
6. Conrad Grebel as quoted in *The Lord's Supper: Believers Church Perspective*. Dale Stoffer, ed. (Scottdale, Pa.: Herald Press, 1997), p. 58.

CHAPTER 13

Strength for the Task

*Above all, maintain constant love for one
another, for love covers a multitude of sins.
Be hospitable to one another without complaining. Like good stewards of the mani-
fold grace of God, serve one another with
whatever gift each of you has received.
—1 Peter 4:8-10*

I hate to run out of food. It's bad enough if the potatoes
aren't salty enough or the Jell-O sags or the glasses have
water spots. But it is the ultimate shame if I run out of
food. I can picture it now. We are all sitting at the table
after the prayer, eyeing the food. The meat and the potatoes look good, but are they enough? We pass around the
serving platter, taking small helpings. As the host, I insist
that my guests take more, oh, please take more, but they
say they always take this amount. We all know better. I
smile weakly and take very little food myself. What little I
have, I rearrange on my plate so it looks like more. We
talk about the weather. I think about what I have in my
fridge that would not look like a leftover. The kids ask for
seconds.

I start to cry.

I don't know why I'm so afraid of running out of food. It has never happened to me. Even when I am surprised by guests at mealtime, the food fixed for five feeds seven or eight easily. One time we even made a meal of leftovers on purpose. It was one of those weird youth activities, going to different homes and raiding refrigerators. It was a strange conglomeration of ordinary stuff, yet a wonderful feast.

But the fear remains. If I'm honest, there's more to it than the food. It includes all my resources—my time, my money, and my sense of control. Sometimes I think I don't have enough of those precious commodities for myself. I think about the overwhelming task of hospitality, and I start to sweat. What if all these strangers come to my door, and I just don't have enough to give—physically, mentally, and spiritually? It's a great value, this hospitality, but it's too much.

Sometimes the best I can do is to be the guest.

The First Piece Is the Hardest to Pass

I can't help but think that the disciples felt this way too. At least once. Once on a remote shoreline without a sign of civilization anywhere.

As Mark tells the story in Mark 6:30-44, the disciples and Jesus got out of a boat on the beach and stepped into a sea—a sea of faces. The twelve and Jesus had hoped to get away from the crowd and get a break. "Come away to a deserted place all by yourselves and rest awhile," said Jesus (Mark 6:31). Too many people, too many conversations—why, even the most extroverted among them were exhausted. So they took the boat and set sail for a solitary shore.

Only to be greeted by this. Just when they thought they could not take anymore, here came the sea of faces, with the tide rising higher by the minute.

The afternoon sun was starting to dip toward the earth. The disciples were no dummies. They glanced at each other and then at the crowd and then at the sun. They had a big problem on their hands. They were in a remote wilderness with over five thousand people who hadn't eaten all day. Hungry people. No food.

They did what they thought was the hospitable thing to do, or at least the only viable act of hospitality they could muster with their lack of resources. One or two of the disciples walked up to Jesus and said, "This is a deserted place, and the hour is now very late; send them away so that they may go into the surrounding country and villages and buy something for themselves to eat" (Mark 6:35-36).

Send them away, Jesus. It's too much. We can't take care of all their needs, so they need your permission to leave and find some food wherever they can. It's too much for us, Jesus.

"You give them something to eat."

"What!" The disciples frowned in disbelief. Had they heard right? *They* were to provide the food? With what? It would take eight month's wages to buy barely enough bread. Where would that kind of money come from? Was that what Jesus wanted them to do?

"How many loaves do you have?" asked the Master. "Go and see."

"Five loaves—and two fish. Small loaves, Lord."

There was an awkward pause. The crowds were getting restless. Jesus was not giving them any of the profound words they had walked all day to hear. Instead, he was fumbling around with a couple of loaves and two smoked fish halves. Something needed to happen very soon, but what?

"Have them recline in groups of hundreds and fifties."

Okay, the disciples thought, we're doing something. What now? The crowd got quiet as the tall Stranger cradled the five biscuits and two fish in his hands and lifted them up to the clouds. He spoke the traditional Jewish blessing on these humble pieces and began to tear them in two.

"Peter, come here and take this. Andrew, here, come."

"What?"

"This piece of bread. Feed the people."

"What?"

"Here's a piece of fish too. What are you staring at? Go."

Peter took the piece of bread and the fish. He looked at Jesus for some sign, then at the seated people staring at him. Slowly he walked up to a little girl and tore the biscuit in two. "Here you go." His mind was racing with crazy thoughts. A little boy shoved his hands into Peter's. Peter broke the biscuit again and this time the fish too. Then another and another.

Peter looked into his hand. There was still half a biscuit and a piece of fish.

Hardly daring to breathe, he started passing out the pieces faster, still small pieces, but more and more. And more. "Look, look, everyone, the food doesn't run out! Do you see this? Look, there's still some in my hand. Here, take this, sir. You want more? You bet. There's plenty. Look, there's plenty! Jesus, look, there's plenty!" The pieces of bread and fish got bigger and bigger.

All over the field the disciples were breaking the bread and fish as fast as they could, then throwing chunks of it up in the air. Big chunks of bread and fish flying in the air. It was a party. "Here, take more. Please. Here, little one, hold out your shirt and I'll just dump it in. Isn't this fun? Hey, anyone need any more?"

Jesus just smiled.

When it was all over, the fields were dotted with pieces

of bread and fish. Piles of food covered the green grass. "Better collect it," the Master said with a smile. The twelve picked up twelve baskets. Twelve baskets overflowing with food.

"What a party, huh? Pass the fish."

"Haven't you had enough? Eight month's wages, who came up with that one?"

"If only we could have seen then what we see now."

Seeing Things Differently

The disciples did see an amazing turn of events, a big surprise, on that hillside. They saw Jesus, not only teaching the crowds and healing their sick, but also showing them hospitality. Hospitality in a miraculous way. It wasn't just the miracle of the multiplying fish and bread. Some other miracles were happening too. One might say the disciples could see with new eyes. So can we.

1. We can see the situation differently.

When the disciples saw the huge crowd of people, they saw a problem. They saw a mass of hungry people with no food in sight—a hopeless situation. Jesus saw people in need and seeing them, he had compassion on them (Mark 6:34). Jesus didn't see an impossible situation; he saw a miracle waiting to happen.

Eventually the twelve saw the opportunity too. They did have the resources to feed this mass of people. They had more than enough to feed twice as many people. They only had five loaves and two small fish, but because they had Jesus, it was enough. Because they gave their small resources to Jesus, Jesus multiplied those tiny offerings and brought abundance from out of nowhere.

We too have all the resources we need. All of the great pressures that hospitality brings and all of the risks and costs can never deplete what we have in Christ. Even if all we have are two small fish and five loaves of bread.

This mysterious multiplying showed up in many of the hospitality stories I've heard. For example:

"I was asked by the school to get some clothes for three boys who lived with their mother. Her finances did not allow her to buy clothes so their clothes were torn and dirty. A severe car accident further complicated things; the mother was not expected to live. Somehow, by the grace of God, she started to improve.

"Then the question came up, 'What will happen to the boys till their mother recovers?' We found a home, but their need for clothes was desperate. So I asked for clothes and cash for the boys in my church, Tabor Mennonite. To our sad surprise, the clothes for the oldest boy did not fit. I decided to give the caretaker thirty dollars to purchase two pairs of jeans. I had put the cash for the clothing in a separate purse and had written in a notebook how much was collected. When I opened the purse to get the thirty dollars, I first counted the money. I had fifteen dollars more than I had written down in the notebook. I counted again, and there really were fifteen extra dollars. I took the fifteen dollars out and put them in another purse. Then I took out the thirty dollars and gave it to my friend to buy the jeans.

"A few weeks later my friend came again and asked for more money for the two younger boys. I got out my little cash purse again and counted it. Now I had five dollars more than I had written down. I counted again. 'This money just keeps multiplying,' I said to my friend. 'I have never seen anything like it. First fifteen dollars more and now an extra five. It's a miracle.'

"The mother got married shortly after this, and I was able to give her the extra twenty to use for the wedding. It really is amazing to see how God increases the cash when you give in his name."[1]

2. We can see others differently.

Although the biblical text doesn't allude to this, I can imagine the disciples were somewhat annoyed at the large crowd that gathered on the hillside. I know what would be going on in my mind: "Why didn't they plan ahead? Why didn't they bring their own food? Who do they think we are, some kind of miracle workers who are going to take care of all their needs?" The disciples considered the crowd a nuisance to be dismissed before things got out of hand, but in their act of hospitality, their attitudes changed. They began to see the people as Christ did, as honored guests.

We too have a choice. Is the person in front of us an annoyance or a beloved guest? One Forty-Day Experiment participant had to make that choice. "It was the day before Christmas. I took the afternoon off to go home to prepare for our family's Christmas Eve supper. But on the way home, I realized I needed to buzz over to the variety store to find a stocking stuffer or two. It was crazy to do considering the long line and my busy schedule, but I determined to make one quick stop.

"I looked around a little, and then finally selecting my items, I got in the checkout line. The cashier rang up my items, and I dug into my purse to get my money. All of a sudden, there was a scuffle with the cashier and a customer. The two began hitting each other. The cashier shouted, 'You can't be behind my cash register!' The customer angrily retorted, 'I could have you arrested!' She was angry with the cashier but walked away. As I looked up, I recognized the unkempt customer.

"We grew up in the same church. She was born with a birth defect that had never been corrected. It affected her appearance. She was difficult to understand. Kids teased her at school, which naturally made her angry. Her lot in life was a difficult one. She married, but he too had problems. He was there, standing off at a distance, and she went to join him.

"The cashier commented to another cashier about how the customer had hit her. Without even thinking, I made some comment about this woman having problems, but didn't acknowledge I knew her. Finally, I finished paying for my things and started to leave, but something held me back. I stopped in my tracks. Maybe I should go talk to her, I thought. But other thoughts raced through my head. It's Christmas Eve. I have a big supper to prepare. I don't have the time or energy for this. How could *I* help the situation? I started out the door. But something didn't seem right. Maybe if I just talked to her, I could help her feel better. I turned around and went back inside. She and her husband were still standing in the same place.

"As I approached her, I greeted her warmly. She greeted me warmly too. We chatted for quite awhile, she asking about my family, she telling me that it was her birthday, that her case supervisor took her out for a birthday breakfast, that she and her husband were having problems, but they were working at it.

"Then she started to tell me about what had just happened. She saw a penny on the floor right behind the cashier. She stooped over to pick it up, saw another one, and attempted to pick it up, too. The cashier saw it as a threat, and the confrontation began. She said that the cashier hit her first.

"Did my presence there help calm her? I'm not sure. Was it the Christmas spirit that made me turn around and go talk to her? I'm not sure. Was it because I had asked the Lord to help me minister to someone that day? All I know is this. It felt right to be there. Somehow I know that God led me to that place to do that very thing."[2]

If our spiritual eyes are open to the gift of hospitality, we look for people who need a special welcome. We look for strangers who need to be loved. Grouchy old Mr. So-and-So is really a lonely person who has no one to talk to about growing old. The uptight saleslady is really just tired and overworked. The too-cool teenager is using the wild hairdo to help carve out an identity in a chaotic world. With the eyes of hospitality, we can see others as Jesus does.

3. We can see time differently.

The disciples did not expect to see a crowd when they got off the boat. They had planned for a retreat, just them, but they were greeted by masses of people who had great needs. So Jesus changed his schedule. He was flexible, using his whole day to care for their needs. "The good host takes time," says Gerrit Dawson. "Jesus said, 'They do not need to go away.' And he did not just mean that there was enough food. Even more, there was time to continue to host this multitude. His welcome made them feel that they were not an intrusion on his busy life but cherished guests. He gave them his words, which they longed to hear. He gave them his healing touch, which they ached to feel."[3]

The disciples were somewhat stressed by this. "The hour is late," they said. Lack of food was not the only thing on their minds either. They felt a lack of time. Their schedules were full, their energy resources depleted. Many Christians feel the same way. I would love to host some people, they say, but I just don't have the time.

Being a good host does take time. First of all, we have to simply be there when someone new comes to our church or to our door. Then it takes a relaxed sense of time to nurture relationships. We can't schedule appointments to get to know people; quality time presupposes quantity time. Finally, we speak volumes about how we love someone by how much time we are willing to spend with them. For many of us, time is our most precious resource. When we rush off to meet some deadline, we are communicating what is really important to us.

Time was a big issue for the participants of the Forty-Day Experiment. One person, partly through the greater sensitivity to ministry that the forty days of prayer brought him, decided to adopt a girl who had been placed in an abusive foster home. The hospitality afforded to this child will be lifelong. Many hours have already been spent listening, holding, and reassuring this girl that she is loved.

One high-school participant wrote about his time commitment in this way: "At our church we have tutoring and open gym on Thursday evenings. I helped tutor in the past but felt this year was too hectic to make that commitment. I believe God called me to get involved with this group, if not through tutoring then through just being there and spending time with them. It all started when I decided to eat at the church one Thursday. I wasn't even sure I'd stay, but I ended up helping with the open gym time. I found that I really enjoy it, and I think the kids are glad I'm there. . . . The craziest thing is that all I have to do is be there. My time translates into my love for these kids."[4]

Late-night calls were also common during the Forty-Day Experiment:

"It is 10:10 p.m. A knock at this hour? It's a fellow postal worker and his wife. I don't know them except as acquaintances. So what are they doing here at this hour? Beth, normally very quiet and shy, begins talking about their ten-year-old ADHD [attention-deficit hyperactivity disorder] son. The dam breaks, and she talks nonstop for two full hours! Apparently it has been a bad week with him and the other four kids and parents. We can surely relate! Beth needed someone who *knows* by experience. I know, too. There is no other source of comfort than to talk with those who have been there, done that. Tonight, at least, we are able to share the load."5

4. We can see God differently.

I can picture the disciples as they began passing out the bread and fish. Not sure there would be enough, they tore the food into tiny pieces and passed them out—tentatively. Their pieces represented their understanding of God. They were generous in accordance to the generosity and power that they had experienced in God. Theirs was a beginning understanding of a medium-sized God.

I am much the same way. I know, intellectually, that God does miracles and that God will provide all my needs in my hospitality to others. But I don't always know that in my heart. I have even seen miracles as amazing in their own way as feeding five thousand, and still sometimes I forget how great and big and generous my God is.

Our God is the God of leftovers. Many times we talk about God as the God of firstfruits, and that's very important. But what strikes me in this story are the leftovers—twelve baskets, one for each of the twelve disciples, one basket for each of the twelve Israelite tribes. Not only was there enough to go around, but thousands of pieces were left over. That is the kind of God we serve.

In the Old Testament equivalent of this story, the leftovers also make a profound statement. In the story told in 2 Kings 4:42-44, a severe famine was on the land, and the prophet Elisha faced the dilemma of a hundred hungry men and no food. When a man came bringing a firstfruits offering, Elisha received the offering and promptly ordered his servant to set it out before the men. Like the disciples, this servant protested: "How can I set this before a hundred people?" Elisha promised him that the Lord would not only make the offering enough for the people, but there would be leftovers.

Leftovers in a famine? Leftovers among people who hadn't eaten for days? Leftovers in a land of starvation? That is the kind of God we serve.

This is also the God who wants to provide for all of our needs as hosts. This is the God who wants to give us overflowing leftovers. So many times we attempt to be hospitable out of our own strength and resources. No wonder we get tired and feel used up. The miraculous abundance of the feeding of the five thousand is an abundance available for us as hosts too. We begin to receive this abundance through a regular diet of prayer and reflection, by being fed by the Great Host. It is only when we are inundated with God's generosity that we can turn around and welcome others in a generous way.

When we see God differently, we begin to see our giving differently. Why not give in an outlandish, extravagant way, if God is the one supplying the provisions for our needs? It's easy to give when you worship a God who has given everything for us—even his own life. "Gospel hospitality," says Gerrit Dawson, "begins by realizing that we have access to something people want and need. And what is it that Christians possess? Nothing less than everything, for we are held by Christ. 'For all things are yours, whether Paul or Apollos or Cephas or the world or life or death or the present or the future—all belong to you, and you belong to Christ and Christ belongs to God' (1 Cor. 3:21-23). Because God gives me love, I have love to give. Because God gives me food and shelter, I have food and shelter to offer. Because Christ welcomes me, I can give welcome to others. The cupboard is never bare. . . . Christ provides the nourishment, but our work is to prepare the house and welcome every guest."[6]

Seeing God differently also means we believe that God still does miracles. One Forty-Day Experiment participant said, "One experience was really humbling for me. On the way home from a doctor's appointment in Kansas City, my children and I were in heavy traffic. Ahead we saw a lady along the side of the road. As we got closer, we realized that she was on the outside of the guardrail looking to the street below. It hit me like a wave! She was trying to jump! My first impulse was to stop, but traffic prevented it without a real threat of an accident. From deep within I prayed, 'Lord, please don't let her jump. Please, Lord, don't let her jump.' It got very quiet in the car as we drove home.

"After we got home, Daniel came down from his room and told me he heard on the news about a jumper on Red Bridge Road. She had been talked out of jumping—our lady. When I told some friends about it, one said, 'Do you realize your prayer could have saved her?' On one level, that was hard to accept, very humbling, but then I thought, 'No, God still wants to work miracles today. We just have to see with the eyes of faith and respond to the Spirit's urgings."7

5. We must see ourselves differently.

One of my favorite phrases in the story of the feeding of the multitudes is found in Mark 6:41: "He . . . gave [the bread and fish] to his disciples to set before the people." It's one of those details that you can miss, but its application for our lives is tremendous. Jesus gave the bread and fish *to the disciples* to pass out. He did not do the task himself. Jesus could have snapped his fingers and presented the entire crowd with a full-course meal, but he didn't. He chose to feed the crowds through the twelve.

The true miracle in this story is that Jesus empowered the disciples to do the ministry. He taught them in this wonderful object lesson that they had more resources within them to do kingdom work than they ever thought possible. Yes, the resources were there because of him, but they were there within the disciples. Jesus chose to work through them.

Jesus chooses to work through us as well. He chooses us to share in the glory and in the blessing. He chooses us to be the fortunate ones to see the miracles, to see the impossible become possible, and to toss huge chunks of God's generosity to people because there is a never-ending supply.

He chooses you—and me. Understanding this has always been the biggest hurdle for me in my Christian life. Do I believe that God parted the Red Sea? No problem. Do I believe that God can still heal people, feed people, and save them from alcoholism, depression, and anxiety? Yes, I do. Do I believe that God can do all of these things through me? That's tougher for me to accept.

What happens if I fail to listen? If my faith grows weak? If I start to rely on my own strength? I have failed—miserably—in my ministry of hospitality, and I fear failing again. I feel like Elisha's servant, who accidentally put the wrong gourd in the stew pot (2 Kings 4:38-41). When the company of prophets began to eat the stew, they cried, "There's death in the pot!" What a horrible mistake!

But like Elisha, who quietly put some flour in the stew to neutralize it, God takes my blunders and brings good out of them. That does not mean I can be careless in my work because God will always cover my mistakes, but it does mean I can relax in the grace of God. I'm not the one ultimately responsible. I'm the one God has chosen to work through. But God is the one doing the real work, not me.

Seeing ourselves in a different light is crucial to the work of hospitality. We can have all the other elements— seeing the situation differently, seeing strangers differently, and even seeing God differently, but if we don't assume that God desires to work *through us*, the miracles don't happen. God will empower us for the task. God will take our resources and multiply them. But we have to believe in ourselves. Our faith in God has to apply to us as well.

We Must Expect Surprises

In all these different ways of seeing and of being, we must expect surprises. On the surface, that seems like an oxymoron, a contradiction of terms. If we're expecting something, then it isn't a surprise. If we know that certain events will happen, then we wait with expectation. We get surprised by the *unexpected.*

But hospitality is more than a happening, a tea party on a grassy lawn. It is a value, an attitude, and an expectation. Hospitality is a way of approaching life. We expect guests; we are ready to receive them. At the same time, we are open for anything to happen. We anticipate being welcomers, but we don't anticipate just how it has to be. We are ready for anything, ready for a big surprise.

We do anticipate the surprise to be a good one. Though our encounters with strangers are not always good ones, those experiences are the exception, not the rule. We look forward to our encounters with strangers with excitement. We expect to be blessed. I think that's what it is all about. That attitude changes our behavior. That expectation makes us more welcoming.

We expect to be blessed. We believe that when we love the strangers among us and when we welcome strangers around our table and into our lives, God is present too. One plus one equals more than two. One welcoming the other in the name of God also welcomes God. And our God is full of surprises.

Expecting surprises is not the only paradox we could use to describe biblical hospitality. We can talk about this welcoming as openness with boundaries or structured flexibility. In some crazy way, we accept our guests just as they are, but at the same time, we offer our values and faith as well as food and lodging. It works because we do it out of love. Other polarities, too, come into play—public/private, giving/receiving, physical space/heart space, and feeding the body/feeding the soul. Most important, our hospitality calls for a blurred role of guest/host. Our giving and receiving becomes indistinguishable as we enter into each other's lives.

The best way I can visualize these paradoxes is to put my hands together, palms up but fingers closed. My hands form a cup. The cup can be used for giving; I can scoop into a bowl of pretzels and hand them to my guests. The open palms symbolize the freedom I have with all my possessions. Whatever I have is for the taking. The cupped hands are also meant for receiving. My guest can become my host and place blessings into my hands. I am open to both. Yet my fingers are closed. There is some structure. The blessings that I give and receive don't fall through the cracks of a life without values or expectations. That is true hospitality—open to outcome, soft on people, and secure in who I am.

Surprised by Joy

The surprise I most expect in hospitality is the surprise of joy. Pure joy. I expect it, yet I'm usually caught off guard by it. I get distracted by the sink full of dirty dishes, or I get tired from the chore of making small talk, but then it hits me. Just when I'm about to get really annoyed, the joy catches me by surprise.

Another surprise is the surprise of conversion. Many of the Forty-Day Experiment participants expressed great surprise at what happened to them as they began to pray for the Lord to send hospitality opportunities. Perhaps Carrie Jo's poem says it best.

Carrie Jo Starts Praying

Carrie Jo starts praying.

Dear Lord. Help.

Life keeps pushing her hard. Not much seems to be happening. Not anything real dramatic anyway. And Carrie Jo really likes drama.

So, where are the miracles?

Now little changes. Small ripple really.

So, where are the miracles?

She starts listening, really listening to the joy, to the pain, and to the needs around her. She starts turning off the noise in her own head. Life's noise seems to grow softer.

Shhh!

People's souls, their still voices, come forth to her.

Is that Christ I see?

She starts hearing—for the first time.

Shhh!

Carrie Jo struggles. She doesn't have time for this listening. She has obligations and responsibilities, rehearsals and deadlines. Asthma! She can't breathe.

For heaven's sake, can't you see I have laundry to do?

The ripples become waves.

Students she has had no contact with for five or six years come and find her. She listens.

What?

Sidney talks of her father's death. Carrie Jo listens.

Oh.

Shannon's mom says that Shannon has found peace in Christ and is sober. Carrie Jo realizes that she is listening to a miracle.

Oh, yes!

Catherine calls again and again bouncing her hopes and dreams like balls off Carrie Jo's ears.

Oh my!

Joanne, Carrie Jo's baby, whispers to her, "I love you, Mama." Carrie Jo breathes deep.

I love you, too.

Carrie Jo hears—for the first time—deeply the world-weariness of her husband.

I love you, too.

She hears the coming of adolescence in the voice of her ten-year-old daughter.

I love you, too.

She hears her body's struggle to breathe. She listens to her own body in a new way. The breath of her life flows more freely. She feels a moment of wellness—for the first time in a long while.

I love me, too.

Suddenly, Christ is real and present to Carrie Jo in the everyday moments of life.

Surprise.

She witnesses and is witnessed to in the ordinary conversations of life.

Say that again.

She realizes that Christ is often singing to us and to her in the whispered stories of joy and pain played around us, around her.

Shhh! It's okay.

She realizes the holy healing power of listening.

Shhh!

As she listens to others, Carrie Jo feels in a new way Christ listening to her.

I love you, too.

The waves pound her heart.

I love you, too.

The laundry really doesn't matter anymore.[8]

That's the surprise. The laundry doesn't matter anymore. In hospitality, the work is hard, your food burns, the guests look intimidating, and you don't have the time. You have every reason to see this calling as a chore, not a blessing. Sometimes it is a chore. But—the blessing is there. Look again. Look hard.

Surprise.

Notes

1. Excerpt from the Forty-Day Experiment journals.
2. Ibid.
3. Gerrit Dawson, "Feasts in the Desert and Other Unlikely Places," *Weavings* 9 (February 1994): 34.
4. Excerpt from the Forty-Day Experiment journals.
5. Ibid.
6. Dawson, pp. 32-33.
7. Excerpt from a Forty-Day Experiment journals.
8. Ibid., Carrie Jo Vincent, adapted by Michele Hershberger.

Hospitality Enhancers

The following are ideas for nurturing and encouraging hospitality. These projects can be done alone, as separate exercises, or along with a group study of this book.

1. The Forty-Day Experiment

Goal: To encourage participants to expect ministry opportunities from God.

Steps: Ask volunteers to participate in the Forty-Day Experiment. Try to form a group of at least ten people. Ask them to commit themselves to three things:

1. Pray this prayer every day for forty days: "Lord, please send me a hospitality opportunity today."

2. Journal their experiences daily.

3. Be willing to share some of their experiences with the other participants in a worship service at the end of the forty days.

This experiment can become a life-changing experience for all who participate. For many, this prayer will become a daily part of their lives.

2. Use exercises that nurture hospitality

a. *God I Spy.* In this exercise, participants simply look for ways God is at work in their daily lives. Each time a group meets, they are to relate how they spied God the previous week—through creation, relationships, miracles, and hospitality. As they begin to see ordinary life situations with new eyes of faith, they will respond with new actions of faith as well.

b. *Two-Mug Hospitality*. One person begins this exercise by buying two mugs and inviting two strangers over for coffee or tea. "Strangers" can mean acquaintances or people one only knows by name. After this initial meeting, the two invited people take the mugs and commit themselves to inviting at least one other person they don't know very well to share coffee or tea with them. The process continues as each new person is encouraged to share coffee or tea with someone new.

3. Dedication for a new home

If we are serious about our hospitality ministry, then we see our possessions, including our home, as a gift from God to be used in ministry. The following litany can be used whenever any household in the congregation moves to a new residence. The new resident's friends, Sunday school class, small group, or the entire congregation can join him or her at the new house, read the litany, pray over the home, and celebrate together.

Litany for the Dedication of a New Home

Owner(s): Lord, here is our new home, but it only looks like ours. It is really yours.

Friends: Let this home be a place of peace.

Owner(s): It is really yours.

Friends: Let it be a place that welcomes strangers.

Owner(s): It is really yours.

Friends: Let it be a safe haven, for them and for others.

Owner(s): It is really yours.

Friends: Let it be a place that resounds with laughter and good conversation around the table. Let it be a place where tears are freely shed.

Owner(s): It is really yours.

Friends: Let it be a place where masks come off, values are expressed, and the community gathers.

Owner(s): It is really yours.

Friends: Let it be okay for the walls to get bumped, the woodwork scratched, the floor muddy, as your kingdom troops in.

Owner(s): Let beauty reign here, your beauty.
Friends: Be the Host. Let us meet you here.
Owner(s): Be the Host. We ·welcome you here.
Friends: Here is this home, Lord. Here is your home.
All: *Amen.*

4. Become an "urban planner" in your community

The physical space of your community is an important factor in the hospitality of your area. Work with the urban planners in your community, whether there are official planners or not, and talk about making your community more welcoming. Here are some goals to work toward:

a. Create green spaces. Are there public places where people can meet each other and begin to form relationships? The village green has much more of a purpose than its good looks. It serves as a socially appropriate place where strangers can meet. Here is where neighborhoods can establish their identities. Here is where children can play, youth can mingle, and adults can talk.

b. Advocate for the homeless. Some urban planners work to clear their streets of homeless people. It makes good economic sense, they say. We congratulate urban planners for bringing downtown slum areas back to life, but we look the other way when we see how they achieved that goal. Many times, low-income people and the homeless are simply told to move on. Many times, they have no place to go. God calls us, however, to provide shelter for the "least ones." Christians must work with urban planners to do the hard job of finding jobs, homes, and dignity for homeless people. It's fine to renovate the downtown areas, but it can't be done at the expense of people.

c. Encourage your church to become community minded. Our congregations are great settings where the public and private aspects of our lives can blend together. Our church meetinghouses are public places, safe public places. As relationships form, those who felt safe to meet publicly can begin to meet with their new friends in the private arenas of our homes. It's much easier to meet strangers as God calls us to do in a public place. Congregations must work to become places for the larger communities to come and visit us.

5. Work as communities to break down the barriers of racism through hospitality

One organization that works at community issues like race relations through the value of hospitality is Study Circles. In this program, people of different races, ages, and economic levels gather in each other's homes to exchange ideas and grapple with critical public issues. Most importantly, they share their own stories. The six-week session concludes with the group forming an action plan to improve the status of race relations in the community. For more information, please write:

Study Circles Resource Center, PO Box 203, Pomfret, CT 06258, or call 860-928-2616, or e-mail at scrc@neca.com.

6. Focus on hospitality in your times of worship

Use the following litanies to support hospitality themes in your occasions for worship.

a. Who Is My Neighbor?

Leader:	"When an alien resides with you in your land, you shall not oppress the alien. The alien who resides with you shall be to you as a citizen among you.
Congregation:	**"You shall love the alien as yourself, for you were aliens in the land of Egypt:**
Leader:	I am the Lord your God." (Lev. 19:33-34).
Congregation:	**Who is my neighbor? (Luke 10:29-37).**
Leader:	The question of the lawyer echoes in our ears as we consider the deportation of hundreds of undocumented immigrants from our country in the past year. Jesus' response was to tell the story we know as the good Samaritan. In Jesus' world, Samaritans were immigrants of low status.
Congregation:	**Who is my neighbor?**
Leader:	The Mexicans who have been arrested in these raids are clearly not lazy, not on welfare, and not supporting themselves through

criminal activity. It is our immigration policy that defines them as "illegal."

Congregation: **Who is my neighbor?**

Leader: United States immigration policy is racist in the disparity of quotas. Enforcement has been racist, with workers arrested simply on the basis of skin color. We ourselves do not have to act racist to be racist, when our government, acting in our name, does it for us.

All: ***Who is our neighbor?***

Note: This litany was read by the delegates of the Mennonite Church General Assembly in Orlando, Florida, July 1997. It was followed by a recommendation by the delegate body to address the issue.

b. The Cupboard

The following meditative reading would be useful as a gathered congregation strives to work on conversion issues that relate to hospitality (chapter 3).

Please note that this is an extended meditation and may take up to twenty minutes. It is important that the leader anticipate the listeners' need to pause and think.

The meditation will not be suitable for every gathering of people. It was originally intended for a group of very busy church workers who were reflecting on their concerns at a conference.

It does not have a musical interlude, but it may be followed by music leading to a hymn or song. If you are tempted to follow the meditation with a prayer, think twice. Participants may have shared with God something that another person's prayer might belittle or fail to encompass.

Think of the cupboard.

It is in the corner of your house
and you have not opened it for a long time.
Picture it.

The paintwork is old; the handle is dusty.
You stand facing it,

trying to remember what is behind the door, but not quite sure
. . .

is it books from the past,
or old files or old clothes,
or the things left over from childhood,
or glass jars and rolls of wallpaper
kept in a safe place but never needed?

Because you cannot quite remember,
and because there is time,
you stretch out and touch the handle.
You open the door.

The smell of mustiness meets you instantly,
That's the smell you expected . . . but the sight is different.

The shelves are neatly stacked,
stacked with cardboard boxes . . . the size of shoeboxes . . .
And all are in attractive colors—
scarlet and orange
and apple green and turquoise,
lilac and bronze
and deep yellow and silver gray.
Such attractive boxes . . . and each one has a white label . . .
some have writing on them . . . others have not.

You look at the labels
. . . and read the words printed on some of them:

MAJOR DISAPPOINTMENTS . . . says one,
BROKEN PROMISES . . . says another.
LOST LOVES
UNRESOLVED CONFLICTS
NAGGING DOUBTS
BIGGEST FAILURES

There are more yet as you move your eyes along . . .

ANGER
NO ENCOURAGEMENT
NO THANKS
UNANSWERED PRAYERS
SECRET WISHES

Perhaps there are thirty boxes in all . . .
and perhaps twenty or twenty-five have names on white labels.

But some labels are blank.
You see resting on the shelf
a black ink marker and you wonder . . .
You wonder should you?
Then you decide to write some other categories
on the blank labels.

What will you write?
What words will ring bells about who has failed you
or what you fear or what annoys you?
You write . . . what do you write?. . .

PERSONAL HIT LIST
CHIEF REGRET
AWKWARD CUSTOMERS

. . . or what? What do you write?

(Pause)

You stand back and you look again at the boxes,
at the labels you noticed earlier:

MAJOR DISAPPOINTMENTS
BROKEN PROMISES
LOST LOVES
UNRESOLVED CONFLICTS
NAGGING DOUBTS
ANGER

NO ENCOURAGEMENT
NO THANKS
SECRET WISHES.

And the labels which you wrote yourself . . .

(Pause)

You look at them and sense a weird attractiveness in it all.

Maybe these boxes could be of some use . . .
maybe letters could be filed in them . . .
maybe slips of paper . . . names, could be put in them . . .
maybe . . . maybe . . .

You lift one of the boxes, a scarlet one . . .
it's empty and it's light.
You reckon you could perhaps take eight or nine in your arms.
So you choose which ones you'll take.

You look again at the labels facing you
and you choose the ones you want to take.

(Pause)

You pile them on your arms . . . the labels facing you . . .
they come up to your chin . . . and a bit above . . .
you balance the boxes
and with your foot you shut the cupboard.
And you're just thinking
about where to put your new discoveries
when the front doorbell rings.

Who could it be?

You go to the window and look outside . . .
three houses along, nuns are collecting money for charity . . .
but you can't see if it is a nun at your door.

You can't see the door.

The doorbell rings again.

You go to another window . . .
You peer round the boxes and see,
on the other side of the street,
a little girl crossing the road . . . she's running fast . . .
you see her trip . . .
down she goes . . .
and the tears start . . .
and you want to help her . . .
but you're holding these boxes . . .
and there is someone at the door.

You begin to panic . . .
where will you put them?
They're getting heavier now . . .
awkward to carry.
You can't return them to the cupboard,
because you have shut it.
You can't put them in the hall or in the sitting room . . .
What would anyone think if they saw these titles
that so attracted you earlier?

The doorbell rings again . . .
and you feel you have to answer it . . .
it might be important . . .

So, in a sweat, you make your way to the door,
watching your feet in case you stumble.
As you get to it, the bell rings again.
Almost in desperation you say . . . "It's open!"

The handle turns and the door swings towards you.

But who is standing there you can't see . . .
because the boxes are between you and the stranger.

And just as you feel you are going to panic,
a warm, reassuring voice says,
"I've come to take your boxes away."

Then two hands touch yours and relieve you of your burden.
And you see going away from you
the things you were so keen to clutch not so long ago . . .
you watch them move away from you . . .
the attractive boxes . . .
with the curiously attractive titles . . .
    THE DISAPPOINTMENTS,
    THE LETDOWNS,
    THE HIT LIST,
    THE POOR-ME'S,
    THE CHIEF REGRETS YOU HAVE ALMOST COME TO
CHERISH.

(Pause)

You do not see the face of the stranger
who has relieved you of your load . . .
you only see the back.

You stare as the stranger walks down the street
and into the distance
and you would stare longer . . .
but something is pulling at your leg.

You look down . . .
and there on the doorstep is the little girl
with the skinned knee.

You can help her now . . .
Your hands are free.

Note: *This meditative reading was taken from* He Was in the World
*by John Bell. Copyright © 1995 by GIA Publications, Chicago, Illinois.
It is included by permission.*

7. Evaluate your congregation

Periodically, every congregation needs to take a hard look as to how it welcomes strangers. The following questions can serve as a beginning point of that evaluation.

a. How difficult is it to find the bathrooms?
b. Can people who arrive late still find a back pew?
c. Are there greeters at every entrance before the services begin?
d. How welcoming are the greeters? Does their welcome seem genuine or contrived?
e. What connections are made between newcomers and members of the congregation?
f. Is the worship service confusing to newcomers? Are acronyms and insider language used?
g. Are newcomers welcomed during the worship service in a way that doesn't embarrass them yet acknowledges their presence?
h. How intentional and systematic is the congregation in making follow-up contacts with all newcomers?

One way to help your congregation understand the great barriers that most newcomers face is to encourage your members to visit another church. Set aside a weekend and give it a special name, such as Church Visitation Weekend. On this weekend, members are encouraged to visit an area where they are strangers. They are to spend Saturday looking for churches and evaluating the barriers that exist in just finding a church. On Sunday, they attend the church of their choice. Afterward they process and evaluate their experience as newcomers. Finally, the congregation gathers for a debriefing meeting to share observations and to begin evaluating the quality of their hospitality toward newcomers.

Discussion Guide

How to use this discussion guide

This guide is designed to enhance reader understandings of this book. Suggestions are provided for each chapter. This guide will assist leaders and teachers who use this book in teaching-learning settings.

In each chapter the following three movements are designed to take readers and study groups from real life experiences into the Bible and then to make applications for living today.

1. Jump In

In this movement, participants are asked to share from their life experiences as a starting point in the lesson.

2. Dig Deeper

This movement will connect those life experiences to the Scripture text, and then readers will be asked to grapple with the biblical issues as they present themselves.

3. Reflect

In the final movement, with a firm grasp of the biblical message, participants are ready to work on making real life applications, bringing biblical teachings to bear on their own behaviors and attitudes.

Helpful Hints

1. Encourage full participation from everyone, but don't insist upon it. Stress confidentiality and model a nonjudgmental attitude. *Group leaders*, be comfortable with silence. In other words, practice hospitality in the process of facilitating the lesson.

2. Encourage participants to read the corresponding chapter in the book as a resource for the group process. The discussion guides are written to stand alone, but the discussion and the chapter form a strong unit for understanding hospitality.

3. Use your time wisely. Don't let the discussion get bogged down with long answers that take the group off the issue. Facilitate the discussion so that everyone has a chance to speak. Don't allow harsh judging when people speak from their own stories. Begin and end the time together in prayer.

1. The Stranger as Host

Jump In

1. Share stories of disastrous dinner parties. Why did things go so badly? Now share your experience about a meal where you felt welcomed and loved. What were the characteristics of this meal?
2. If you knew that Jesus might stop over at your house tonight, what would you do to get ready?

Dig Deeper

1. Read the passage in Luke 10:38-42. Note how many times that Martha says "me," "my," or "myself." What does this say about her?
2. How do these two sisters differ? What clues about them can you find in this passage?

3. Note the proximity of the parable of the good Samaritan to this story. How are the two stories related? What does the story of Mary and Martha have to do with Luke 10:25-29? How does the parable of the good Samaritan relate to Luke 10:25-29?

4. Why is Mary's choice better? What point is Jesus making here?

Reflect

1. Are you more like Mary or Martha?
2. Are you more likely to be hospitable or merely charitable (hospitable without challenging the status quo)?
3. How do you intentionally nurture within yourself the balance between doing and being?
4. If Jesus were to come to your house and you sat at his feet and listened, what would he say to you?

2. The Stranger Brings Gifts

Jump In

1. Describe a time when a stranger frightened you. Was your fear justified?
2. Are you more likely to fear the possible violence of a stranger or the awkwardness of being around someone you don't know?

Dig Deeper

1. Read 1 Kings 17:1-16. If you had been the widow, how would you have responded?
2. Why was Elijah sent to Sidon? Why was he sent to a widow?
3. Was this woman a believer or did she just feel like she had no other options? Was she aware that the Lord had commanded her to provide food for Elijah?
4. What is the significance of Elijah being fed first?
5. Read the rest of the story: 1 Kings 17:17-24. Why did this tragedy occur after such faithfulness?

Reflect

1. In what situations do you feel like your jar of flour is empty and your jug of oil dry? What will you do about it?
2. What would it mean for you to "hide yourself by the Wadi Cherith"? Who or what have been the ravens in your life?
3. Which character can you relate to the most? Elijah? The widow? The son? Why?
4. When it comes to being a host, how well do you receive gifts? How have you grown spiritually through welcoming a stranger?

3. The Stranger Within

Jump In

1. On a scale of one to ten (one = feel great; ten = feel very uneasy), how do you feel about visiting a nursing home? Having a missionary stay in your home? Becoming friends with a homeless person?
2. If you are uneasy about doing these things, how much of that is due to shyness? How much to the fear of the unknown? How much to your prejudices? How much to a lackluster faith?

Dig Deeper

1. As a group read Acts 16:22-34. Explain that this is a story of hospitality following conversion like Peter's story in Acts 10.
2. List the actions of the jailer before his conversion.
3. How was the earthquake a worst-case scenario for the jailer?
4. What helped to bring about the jailer's conversion? The Holy Spirit? The presence of strangers? A deep look within himself?
5. What are the jailer's actions after conversion?
6. What risks did he take in showing hospitality?

Reflect

1. What kind of earthquake/conversion do you need right now? Courage? Need to hear someone praising God while in

chains? The earthquake of confronting your worst fear? Seeing a miracle? Giving up traditions? Other?

2. For the jailer, conversion led to hospitality. Has that been true for you? How?

4. Better to Receive

Jump In

1. When you were growing up, who were the people you were told not to associate with?
2. If you were Hansel or Gretel, who would be the witch?
3. Which is easier for you—giving or receiving hospitality? Why?

Dig Deeper

1. Read John 4:1-26 together. What is the significance of these sentences?
   "But he had to go through Samaria."
   "It was about noon."
   "Give me a drink."
   "How is it that you, a Jew, ask a drink of me, a Samaritan woman?"
2. Why did Jesus risk his reputation by asking a questionable woman for a drink?
3. What are the deeper meanings of the water? The drinking vessel? Jacob's well?
4. Why was it important for Jesus to be the guest before he became the host?
5. What further hospitality took place after this initial encounter (vv. 39-42)? What did it mean for the Samaritans that Jesus stayed in their homes?

Reflect

1. How have you ministered to someone by receiving his or her hospitality?
2. How have you been ministered to by other's hospitality?
3. What barriers must you overcome to be a better receiver of another's hospitality? Pride? Prejudice? A need to control?

5. Meeting Jesus in the Stranger

Jump In

1. Share experiences of offering hospitality when "nothing happened."
2. Share experiences when you suspected the stranger you welcomed was really an angel.
3. If your class is participating in the Forty-Day Experiment, talk about the down days, if some have experienced them. What role does faith play on these days?

Dig Deeper

1. Read Matthew 25:31-46. List the six characteristics or actions of sheep. Why these actions and not others, such as preaching and evangelism?
2. How do these actions benefit the sheep?
3. How are the sheep and the goats similar? How are they different?

Reflect

1. Is Jesus as judge a comfortable image in your understanding of the Christian faith?
2. What comfort do you receive from knowing that the sheep didn't recognize Jesus?
3. Who are you? A sheep? A goat? A least one?
4. Can one be a sheep and a goat? What do you think about that possibility?
5. Who are the least ones in your community?
6. Which of the six actions are you most comfortable doing? Which of them are you least comfortable doing?

6. Hospitality as Worship

Jump In

1. Share one fond mealtime memory.
2. Which would you rather attend and why?
   Office-party buffet

Sit-down meal
Church potluck
Family picnic
3. What are the unique food rules in your family?

Dig Deeper

1. Read Judges 6:11-24 as a group. As implied in the story, how was food more important to Gideon than to you?
2. What would be lacking from this story if there were no meal?
3. "Go in the strength you have . . ." (NIV). What does this mean for our call to hospitality? (v. 14).

Reflect

1. How can mealtimes become more sacred for you?
    Thinking about starving children?
    Inviting strangers to your table?
    Seeing your meal preparation as a ministry of love?
    Growing a garden and canning the food?
    Looking for God in the people you feed?
2. What is our equivalent to food as wealth? Money? Time? Other things?
3. How is God calling you to share your money or time in more hospitable ways? In more worshipful ways?

7. Hospitality: The Giving and Receiving of Honor

Jump In

1. List the reasons why people are hospitable. Which reasons are better than others?
2. Relate times when you were invited to someone's house but were not really welcomed. What was the clue that made you realize you were not wanted?
3. Have you ever given phony excuses to avoid going to someone's party? Why did you do it?

Dig Deeper

1. Divide the group into three smaller units. Give each group

one of the following Scripture passages and direct each group to answer this question: What does Jesus say about hospitality? Ask each group to create a bumper sticker slogan for their main hospitality message.

Group 1—Luke 14:1-6
Group 2—Luke 14:7-14
Group 3—Luke 14:15-24

2. Discuss these quotes:

"The issue was more complicated than just healing this man. His condition was chronic, not acute. He could come on other days to be healed. The Sabbath was too important to break for such non-emergency healings."

"Jesus was not addressing the appropriate way to get honor; he was exhorting them not to seek honor at all. The Pharisees were throwing parties and receiving hospitality only to enjoy respect in the eyes of their fellow guests. But the way to receive respect, Jesus said, was not to seek it at all."

"Jesus was not talking only about forsaking a cherished way of social stratification. He also was talking about downward mobility. He was talking about bringing unclean people into your house, people who would defile you. Jesus was talking about others laughing at you or scorning you. He was talking about the inconvenience of beggars and blind people at your table. Jesus was talking about seeing everyone as your equal and demonstrating that with your hospitality.

Jesus was talking about turning the world upside down—hospitality as a subversive act."

Reflect

1. How have you experienced God's lavish banquet this past month?
2. What priority does hospitality have in your life compared to tradition? Status?

8. Buying Friends

Jump In

1. Relate a time when your guests really messed up your things. How was it resolved?
2. How did your family of origin view money? As evil? As good? As neutral? As god-like power?

Dig Deeper

1. Read Luke 16:1-13. What is one thing that disturbs you about this passage?
2. What was Jesus saying about dishonesty (v. 10)?
3. What was Jesus saying about shrewdness?
4. According to this passage, how are we to use our Master's money and possessions?
5. How are we to connect people in "debt" with the generous Master?
6. Read Luke 16:19-31. How does the story of Lazarus and the rich man illustrate Luke 16:9?

Reflect

1. How has hospitality helped dethrone the money-god from your life?
2. How has hospitality been the test of idolatry in your life?
3. Is your hospitality motivated more by obligation or by a sense of identity? Are you comfortable with that motivation?
4. Review the seven reasons why money has a god-like power. With which reason do you connect the most? Is it easier to see the positive side of this power or the negative side?

9. Breaking Down Barriers

Jump In

1. Relate a time when a stranger awakened you at 2:00 a.m.
2. Have you ever been hospitable to your enemy? What happened?
3. What strangers make you the most uncomfortable? People of

a certain income level? Persons of a certain ethnic background? People you've never met? Persons you know very well?

Dig Deeper

1. Read Philemon as a group. On a scale of (one = excellent, ten = poor), rank Philemon's hospitality before Onesimus came back.
2. What was at stake for Philemon if he welcomed Onesimus?
3. What part did pride, hurt feelings, and a sense of control play in Philemon's dilemma?
4. What debt did Philemon owe Paul?
5. How did hospitality challenge the status quo in this story? How does hospitality challenge the status quo in your life?
6. What do you think happened? Did Philemon send Onesimus back to Paul, forgive and keep him as a servant, forgive him and set him free, or prosecute?

Reflect

1. Who are the Onesimuses in your life? Who are the Philemons? Who are the Pauls?
2. How has hospitality been a way to break down barriers between you and others?
3. What would you have done if you would have been in Philemon's shoes? Would you have read the letter to the faith community?
4. How closely does your hospitality and your faith community interact? Do you depend on your community to help you make decisions, provide you with resources, help keep you safe, and keep you accountable?

10. Two Sides of the Same Coin

Jump In

1. Relate your hospitality experiences with unbelievers. In general, does your hospitality play itself out differently with unchurched people than it does with believers? In your

hospitality, did your friends meet your Best Friend? How did this happen?

2. How comfortable are you sharing your faith? How comfortable are you in hosting people?

Dig Deeper

1. Read Acts 9:10-28. What important role did Ananias and Barnabas play in Paul's life? In the development of the early church?

2. Read Luke 17:7-10. If plowing the fields and watching the sheep are symbolic evangelism roles, and waiting tables is a symbolic hospitality role, what is this parable saying about evangelism and hospitality?

3. Discuss these quotes.

"In the early church, then, hospitality went hand in hand with evangelism. The two made up the two-sided coin of mission—private and public, house church and synagogue. The host stood equal to the itinerant guest. At least, most of the time."

"The true host doesn't offer refreshment in an empty house. Likewise, spiritual hosting cannot be devoid of our values and beliefs."

Reflect

1. Share how you balance receptivity and confrontation. Use these examples or choose others.

   A smoker comes to stay at your house.

   A woman you befriended makes her living as a stripper. She needs you to drive her to work.

2. Assess your faith community. Does the sense of community tend to attract new people or drive them away? Does your closeness attract people and then drive them away? How easy is it for new people to feel a part of your faith community?

11. Remembering Who We Are

Jump In

1. Share your ethnic background with each other. How many generations do you go back before you have ancestors living on another continent?
2. What place do you consider home?

Dig Deeper

1. Read Hebrews 11:13-16. List five characteristics of our identity as "strangers and foreigners on the earth."
2. Read Numbers 35:6-15. Why did the Lord establish the cities of refuge? What application can we draw from this mandate for our own lives?
3. Read Leviticus 19:34. State two reasons why the aliens were to be treated as citizens. Are those reasons still applicable today?

Reflect

1. When is it right for people to cross a border illegally and when is it wrong? Is it permissible for religious reasons? For economic reasons? For both? Neither? What responsibility do we have to improve the economic and religious situations in their country?
2. Do you claim a stranger identity? In what ways? How would claiming a stranger identity reshape your faith? How would it help you catch a vision? How would it help you make priorities? How would it strengthen your compassion for others?
3. How does your hometown compare to Goshen, Egypt? Goshen, Indiana?

12. Hospitality and the Lord's Supper

Jump In

1. Talk about your best and worst experiences during the Lord's Supper.

2. Did you ever receive communion by yourself? How did that feel?

Dig Deeper

1. Read 1 Corinthians 11:17-33. Discuss this statement.
   "For Paul, hospitality and community were important elements of the Lord's Supper—so important that if hospitality was not practiced and community not nurtured, their gathering with the bread and wine was not the Lord's Supper at all."
2. How was this situation a conflict between rich and poor? How could hospitality break down that barrier?
3. What characteristics of the Lord's Supper help believers understand what it means to be community with each other? What role do these factors play?
   Participation with everyone
   Symbolism of the bread and cup
   Remembering the life and death of Jesus
   Waiting on each other
   The mystery of the body of Christ
4. In what two ways can Jesus be present at the Lord's Supper? What happens when people don't welcome each other as Christ when they gather for communion (1 Cor.10: 3-5)?

Reflect

1. What barriers to community do you see in your present communion service?
2. If you could change one thing about the way you receive the symbols of the Lord's Supper, what would it be?
3. How well does your faith community balance the ritual of the Lord's Supper with the ethical behavior and attitudes that Paul suggests? How well do you balance those things?

13. Strength for the Task

Jump In

1. Relate one experience where you ran out of food at a dinner party.
2. Relate one experience when you had unexpected guests for dinner.
3. How difficult is it for you to live expecting surprises?

Dig Deeper

1. Close your eyes and listen while one person reads Mark 6:30-44. What do you see? What do you hear? What do you smell?
2. Why was the first piece of fish so hard to pass? How does that relate to your own hospitality experiences?
3. How did the disciples see the situation differently after Jesus performed the miracle? How did they view the crowd differently? How did they see time differently? How did they see themselves differently? How did they see God differently?
4. What do the leftovers symbolize in the story? What does it mean to have leftovers in a famine (2 Kings 4:42-44)?

Reflect

1. What do you need to help you see yourself as a feeder of five thousand? Group support? Another miracle from God? Just taking a step in faith? Letting go and letting God?
2. What does it mean to believe in a God of leftovers?
3. Share one time when God took your measly five loaves and two fish and turned them into a huge meal.
4. If you could ask God for one miracle today, what would it be?
5. What surprise are you expecting in the near future?

The Author

Whether in her hobby, skydiving, or other activities, Michele Hershberger whole-heartedly jumps into every project she undertakes. Earlier Michele gave her energies to youth and youth ministry, an age group she loves. She served as youth pastor at Zion Mennonite Church, Hubbard, Oregon, for six years. During that same time, Michele and her husband, Del, were area conference youth ministers for the Pacific Coast Mennonite Conference. Michele was head of the Bible Department of Western Mennonite School, Salem, Oregon, for one year.

Michele's current passion is stewardship. She holds a position as project associate for The Giving Project, a stewardship education program of the Mennonite Churches in North America.

Michele serves the church through speaking and writing. She has given the keynote addresses at various area Mennonite conference youth events and adult renewal services. She was lecturer and playwright at the four recent North American Mennonite youth conventions. Hershberger authored four youth curriculum titles: *True Friends* (about friendship), *The Story of Jesus* (Gospel of Luke), *Stand Firm* (Daniel and Ezra), and *What Gives? Using God's Money. A Christian View of Hospitality: Expecting Surprises* is her most recent work. Michele has also contributed to a variety of church publications.

Michelle holds an A.A. from Hesston (Kansas) College and a B.A. in communications from Goshen (Indiana) College. She is currently working on an M.Div. at the Associated Mennonite Biblical Seminary, Elkhart, Indiana.

Born in Garden City, Missouri, Michele now lives in Goshen, Indiana, with her husband, Del, and three children—Tara, Erin, and J. D. The Hershbergers are members of the Belmont Mennonite Church, Elkhart, Indiana. Michele enjoys piecing quilts, pug puppies, and camping with her family.